Sound Doctrine:

Rightly Dividing the Word of God

By Ann Rowan

Sound Doctrine: Rightly Dividing the Word of God
By Ann Maria Rowan

Unless otherwise noted, the Scripture quotations are from The King James Version of the Bible.

International Standard Book Numbers:
ISBN-10: 1542515742
ISBN-13: 978-1542515740

This book was previously published by Ann M. Rowan,
ISBN 0-8187-0347-4 in 2016.

Printed in the United States of America

ACKNOWLEDGMENTS

I gratefully acknowledge from whence cometh my help... My help comes from the Lord, Who made Heaven and Earth. I thank God who gave me the vision to write this book and helped me see it through to completion. All glory goes to my Lord Jesus Christ, Who loved me in spite of me, gave Himself for me, and washed me from my sin in His Own Blood.

For those who have encouraged, prayed for, and supported me in this endeavor, thank you so much! It has meant more than you'll ever know. May God bless and keep you always!

TABLE OF CONTENTS

Preface...7

No Greater Love..9

A Brand New You...22

A Strong Foundation.....................................35

Repentance From Dead Works.....................37

Faith Toward God..66

The Doctrine of Baptisms.............................77

Laying On Of Hands....................................107

Resurrection From The Dead.......................128

Eternal Judgment...140

The Truth About Hell..................................159

Women In Ministry.....................................171

The Christian And The Church....................185

Biblical Finances...208

Divorce And The Church.............................218

Eternal Security Error..................................232

Catholic Doctrine- Truth Or Consequences...........248

Jesus Only?..259

Jesus Is Jehovah..271

Amazing Facts In The Bible........................289

Origin Of The Bible....................................302

Dominionism: Demonic Deception..............315

Closing..337

Bibliography..338

PREFACE

My hope is that the Biblical truths shared in this book will enlighten and inspire the reader. God's Word is alive… The Bible is a spiritual book that can transform us into the very image of Christ. With that goal in mind, one can never study the Word enough. As the Apostle Paul admonished Timothy: *"Study to show yourself approved unto God, a workman that needs not to be ashamed, rightly dividing the Word of truth."*[1] The purpose of studying Bible doctrine is not to have a wealth of intellectual information, but rather, as the apostle so aptly states, *"The end of the commandment is charity (love) out of a pure heart, and of a good conscience, and of faith unfeigned."*[2] The truth that we glean from God's Word should result in a heart of love for God and others, and a pure lifestyle that reflects our faith.

God's Word also provides spiritual protection against the onslaught of false teaching that is so prevalent today. One must have a firm foundation of Biblical principles established in their heart and mind. Then, one will be able to recognize spiritual error that could subvert the soul. If we hide God's Word in our heart, the light of truth will expose the darkness of error. We then can then walk in the paths of righteousness that God has ordained for us. *"The entrance of Your Word gives light"* and *"Your Word is a lamp unto my feet and a light unto my path."* -Psalm 119

---

[1] II Timothy 2:15
[2] I Timothy 1:5

NO GREATER LOVE

Of all the themes in the Bible, the pre-eminent message is that of God's great love for us. The Bible is the story of the Heavenly Father's love relationship with man, of man's treacherous betrayal, and of the extreme measures to which the Father would go to reinstate that relationship.

God originally created man in His image.[3] Man was the crown of God's creation—a source of joy for the Heavenly Father, and the focus of His love and attention. The Heavenly Father graciously granted mankind free will so that the relationship and fellowship between God and man was based on man's choice, not out of compulsion. The Heavenly Father lavished upon mankind a perfect environment, including total provision, peace, love, and enjoyment. Additionally, He gave mankind authority over the earth.

In an act of total, selfish rebellion, man chose to betray God's trust. Rather than follow God's one command that had been instituted to protect mankind, Adam and Eve decided to listen to satan and disobey God. With that choice, they opened the door for the enemy of God to bring sin, sickness, death, and destruction into the earth, and upon every generation that would follow. In choosing to follow satan, mankind had become a captive slave of the enemy. Man was totally separated from God, and destined to follow his master (satan) to hell for eternal damnation.[4]

God So Loved...

In spite of their willful betrayal, God still loved Adam and Eve. From the Father's heart of infinite love and compassion, He devised a

---

[3] Genesis 1:26
[4] Isaiah 59:2

plan to reverse the death sentence that mankind had brought upon himself. The Law of sin and death required transgressors to die for their sin.[5] In order to pay the penalty for our sin, God was willing give His Only Begotten Son, Jesus, to be the ransom for us. The ultimate demonstration of God's great love for mankind was in giving Jesus to die in our place. Jesus died a torturous death on the Cross to free the souls of humanity from death: *"For God so loved the world that He gave His only begotten Son, that whosoever believes in Him should not perish, but have everlasting life."[6]* God's love is so magnificent. He proved His love for us in that while we were yet sinners, Christ died for us.[7] In spite of the fact that we were God's enemies and were in willful defiance of His Law, God sent Jesus to save us:

> *"But God, who is **rich in mercy, for His great love wherewith He loved us, even when we were dead in sins,** has made us alive together with Christ, (by grace you are saved;) And has raised us up together, and made us sit together in heavenly places in Christ Jesus: **That in the ages to come he might shew the exceeding riches of his grace in his kindness toward us through Christ Jesus.**"[8]*

...That He Gave His Only Begotten Son

In His great love for us, the Father was willing to give His most precious possession--His dearly beloved Son. Psalm 40 tells us when the Father searched for a ransom to pay for man's sin, He determined that animal blood sacrifice was not adequate to pay that enormous debt. Then Jesus spoke up. He volunteered to become the ransom for man's sin by offering His Own Blood.

---

[5] Romans 6:23
[6] John 3:16
[7] Romans 5:8
[8] Ephesians 2:4-6

What motivated Jesus to endure the horrendous suffering of the cross? As He hung on that bloody tree in great anguish of soul and body, He could have called Heaven's angels at any time to rescue Him. What kept Jesus hanging in agony on the cross, suspended between Heaven and earth? It was the "joy" that He looked to obtain; a prize that His suffering would secure.

> *Looking unto Jesus the author and finisher of our faith;* ***who for*** *the joy* ***that was set before Him endured the cross****, despising the shame, and is set down at the right hand of the throne of God."*[9]

Worth Enough To Die For!

What was the "joy" that motivated Jesus to endure the cross? You and me! Knowing that we would be eternally lost without His Blood sacrifice to purchase us, Jesus willingly laid down His life. He considered us that valuable…valuable enough to die for! ***"Unto Him that loved us, and washed us from our sins in His own blood…****to Him be glory and dominion forever…"*[10]

Just For You!

Christ was willing to die for the sins of the whole world. But, we cannot lose focus that He died for us individually. He loves you so much that if you were the only person on earth that needed a Savior, He still would have gone to the Cross! Incredible love! Paul understood this. He said, *"I live by the faith of the Son of God, Who* ***loved me and gave Himself for me.****"*[11] Jesus endured the cross for you! The Eternal God came as a man to suffer punishment for *your* sin!

---

[9] Hebrews 12
[10] Revelation 1:5, 6
[11] Galatians 2:20

Predicted By The Prophets

To better understand the extent of Jesus' love for us, consider Old Testament prophecies of His suffering. They give astonishing insight as to what Jesus actually experienced. It was not just the horrendous, physical torture of the Cross, but unspeakable torment in the spirit realm.

Suffered in the Flesh

Though Jesus was God, He suffered punishment in the flesh as a Man. He felt all the pain as they beat Him with a cat-o'-nine-tails (Roman scourging whip) that left long rows of ripped flesh on His back. He felt as they beat and pummeled His face so that it was beyond recognition:

> *"Many a time have they afflicted me from my youth: yet they have not prevailed against me. The plowers* ***plowed upon my back: they made long their furrows****... As many were astonished at you; his visage was so* ***marred more than any man****, and his form more than the sons of men: So shall he sprinkle many nations"[12]*

He felt His bones being pulled out of joint, and the half inch stakes that were hammered into His hands and feet. David graphically prophesied of the crucifixion, alluding to the Roman soldiers that surrounded Jesus (described as "dogs" since they were frequently homosexuals), and of the demonic hoards ("bulls of Bashan" and "roaring lion") that encompassed Him as He suffered:

> *"Be not far from me; for trouble is near; for there is none to help. Many* ***bulls have compassed me****: strong bulls of Bashan have beset me round. They gaped upon me with their mouths, as a* ***ravening and a roaring lion****.*

---

[12] Psalm 129, Isaiah 52

*I am poured out like water, and **all my bones are out of joint**: my heart is like wax; it is melted in the midst of my bowels. **My strength is dried up** like a potsherd; and my tongue cleaves to my jaws; and Thou hast brought me into the dust of death. **For dogs have compassed me**: the assembly of the wicked have enclosed me: **they pierced my hands and my feet.** I may tell all my bones: they look and stare upon me. They part my garments among them, and cast lots upon my vesture...* "[13]

Forgiveness Through Jesus' Sacrifice

Isaiah prophesied the "suffering Servant's" afflictions hundreds of years before Christ fulfilled it on the Cross. It was God's eternal plan to redeem man back to God through Jesus' sacrifice:

*"...to whom is the **arm of the LORD** revealed? ...**He is despised and rejected of men; a man of sorrows, and acquainted with grief**: and we hid as it were our faces from him; he was despised, and we esteemed him not. Surely **he has borne our griefs, and carried our sorrows**: yet we did esteem him stricken, smitten of God, and afflicted. But **he was wounded for our transgressions, he was bruised for our iniquities: the chastisement of our peace was upon him; and with his stripes we are healed.** All we like sheep have gone astray; we have turned everyone to his own way; and **the LORD has laid on him the iniquity of us all**"[14]*

All of us have gone astray from God's way. We have all sinned and faced eternal damnation in hell. God loved us so much that He

---

[13] Psalm 22
[14] Isaiah 53

allowed Jesus to take the punishment for our sins. We can now be forgiven and reconciled back to God by simply believing what Jesus did for us! He suffered immensely for all of humanity's sins. In God's court of judgment, the punishment for our sin was "Paid In Full" by the Blood of Jesus. We are now justified in God's eyes by faith!

> *"... for **he was cut off out of the land of the living: for the transgression of my people was he stricken**. And he made his grave with the wicked, and with the rich in his death; because he had done no violence, neither was any deceit in his mouth. **Yet it pleased the LORD to bruise him; he has put him to grief: when you shalt MAKE HIS SOUL AN OFFERING FOR SIN**... He shall see of the **travail of his soul, and shall be satisfied: by his knowledge shall my righteous servant justify many; for he shall bear their iniquities.** "*

The pain of the crucifixion was just the beginning of Jesus' suffering. There was much more...

Rejected By God

Even more painful than the cross was the anguish that Jesus experienced by being rejected by His Father. Consider Jesus' cry from the cross as He pleads with God to acknowledge Him:

> *"My God, my God, why have you forsaken me? why are you so far from helping me, and from the words of my roaring? O my God, I cry in the daytime, but you hear not; and in the night season, and am not silent... "*[15]

---

[15] Psalm 22

The Father refused to look upon Jesus as He suffered on the tree. Dark clouds veiled the Father's eyes from seeing Jesus bear our sins in His body. As He carried our sins He literally *became the sin offering for us* on the cross.[16] Because God cannot look upon sin,[17] the Father turned His back on His Son! For the first time in eternity communion was severed between Jesus and His Father. In utter despair and astonishment, Jesus cries out to God, and realizes the Father will no longer hear His prayers.

Rejected By Society

Jesus' heart was also broken by rejection and reproach from those for whom He came to die. He was *"despised of the people."* All that passed by the cross laughed and mocked Jesus saying, *"He trusted in the LORD... let Him deliver Jesus if He **really** delights in him!"* The very thoughts of Jesus' heart were prophesied, telling the great shame, hurt and rejection that He felt:

*"You have known my reproach, and my shame, and my dishonor: mine adversaries are all before you. **Reproach has broken my heart;** and I am full of heaviness: and I looked for some to take pity, but **there was none**; and for comforters, but I found none. They gave me also gall for my meat; and in my thirst they gave me vinegar to drink... they **persecute him** whom you have smitten; and they **talk to the grief** of those whom you have wounded."[18]*

Even drunkards mocked Jesus with their raucous songs as they meandered by His cross:

---

[16] II Corinthians 5:21
[17] Habakkuk 1:13
[18] Psalm 69:21

*"They that sit in the gate speak against me; and **I was the song of the drunkards**... Deliver me out of the mire, and let me not sink: let me be delivered from them that hate me... let not the pit shut her mouth upon me..."[19]*

Jesus died an innocent man on the cross of dishonor and shame. Today if one visits the "Place of the Skull" (the hill of crucifixion outside of Old Jerusalem), it is still a place of disregard and desecration. A bus station on a busy street is at the base of it, with garbage strewn around. When Jesus hung there it was a busy place outside of the city gates where the main thoroughfares met. The Romans crucified their criminals to make them a public spectacle. As they hung there, humiliated and suffering excruciating pain, it served as a deterrent to others for breaking the law. Though Jesus never sinned, He hung there. He did not have to, but chose to.

Rejected By His Community

If a stranger criticizes you, it is unpleasant, but bearable. But, if those you know criticize and taunt you, it hurts to the heart. Jesus was reproached by those of His own community:

*"**I was a reproach among all mine enemies, but especially among my neighbors, and a fear to mine acquaintance:** they that did see me without fled from me. I am forgotten as a dead man out of mind: I am like a broken vessel. For **I have heard the slander of many:** fear was on every side: while they took counsel together against me, they devised to take away my life.[20] **My heart is sore pained within me...**"*

---

[19] Psalm 69:20
[20] Psalm 31:11-13, Psalm 55, Psalm 56

Rejected By Friends

Those with whom Jesus had close fellowship also turned on Him. Having lost communion with the Father made rejection from Jesus' friends even more devastating. *No one* cared for His soul:

> *"My heart pants, my strength fails me: as for the light of mine eyes, it also is gone from me.* **My lovers and my friends stand aloof from my sore; and my kinsmen stand afar off. They also that seek after my life lay snares for me**: *and they that seek my hurt speak mischievous things, and imagine deceits all the day long...Mine enemies speak evil of me,* **When shall he die, and his name perish?"**

> " *...Yes,* <u>**my own familiar friend, in whom I trusted, which did eat of my bread, has lifted up his heel against me.**</u>[21] **As with a sword in my bones, mine enemies reproach me; while they say daily unto me, Where is your God?** *...Because of the voice of the enemy, because of the oppression of the wicked: for they cast iniquity upon me, and* **in wrath they hate me.**"

Rejected By Family

Psalm 69 describes the shame that Jesus felt when even His immediate family rejected Him:

> *I am weary of my crying: my throat is dried: mine eyes fail while I wait for my God.* **They that hate me without a cause are more than the hairs of mine head:**

---

[21] Psalm 38, Psalm 41, Psalm 42

*they that would destroy me, being mine enemies wrongfully, are mighty... Because for your sake **I have borne reproach; shame has covered my face. I am become a stranger unto <u>my brethren, and an alien unto my mother's children</u>**...*

Jesus' half-brothers and half-sisters (children of Joseph and Mary's union after Jesus was born) hated Him.[22] The townspeople assumed that Jesus was Joseph's son, and treated Him as just "the carpenter." He had no honor in His hometown, and certainly not among His family!

Can you imagine being a sibling to Jesus? He was a perfect son. He never sinned. He was fully obedient and always manifested the fruit of the Spirit! It would have been natural for Joseph and Mary to compare the siblings to Him: "Why can't you be more like Jesus?" was likely said more than once in their household. His brothers resented Him. They even tried to put Jesus in harm's way by encouraging Him to go to Jerusalem when they knew the Jews there wanted Him dead![23]

Job also prophesied that Jesus' friends and family would turn against Him and even mock Him:

*"He has put my brethren far from me, and my acquaintance truly are estranged from me. **My kinsfolk have failed, and my familiar friends have forgotten me**...All my close friends abhorred me: and **they whom I loved are turned against me.**[24] And **now am I their song**, yea, **I am their byword**. They abhor me, they flee*

---

[22] Matthew 13:54-56
[23] John 7:3-7
[24] Job 19, 30

*far from me, and spare not to **spit in my face. My friends scorn me...**"*

Why would the Almighty God put up with that kind of abuse from mere creatures?! Why?

The Sorrows Of Hell

Certainly, the physical pain of crucifixion was terrible, but Jesus also suffered spiritually. The Psalmist prophesied that Jesus' soul would go to hell! *"For you will not leave **my soul in hell**; neither will you allow thine **Holy One to see corruption**."* Hell is not an imaginary, mystical mindset, but a literal place of unfathomable torment, pain and suffering. When Jesus gave up the Ghost on the cross, His spirit descended into hell. Psalm 18 describes it: *"The **sorrows of death** compassed me...The **sorrows of hell** compassed me about."* "Sorrows" means pain in Hebrew. Jesus endured the pain of hell for us! Psalm 40 calls hell "a horrible pit":

> *"For My soul is full of troubles: and My life draws **near to the grave**. I am counted with them **that go down into the pit**: I am as a man that has **no strength**: Free among the dead, like the slain that lie in the grave, whom You remember no more: and they are cut off from Your hand. **You have laid Me in the lowest pit**, in **darkness, in the deeps.** <u>**YOUR WRATH LIES HARD UPON ME, and You have afflicted Me with all Your waves.**</u> Selah. You hast put away My acquaintance far from Me; You have made Me an abomination unto them: **I am shut up, and I cannot come forth**...*[25]

---

[25] Psalm 88

When in hell Jesus actually experienced the **wrath** of Almighty God for us… God's fierce, burning wrath (that is reserved for His enemies) was poured out upon Jesus without mercy:

> "…*why do You cast off My soul? why do You hide Your face from Me? I am afflicted and ready to die from My youth up: while **I suffer Your terrors** I am distracted. **Your fierce wrath goes over Me; Your terrors have cut Me off**… Lover and friend You have put far from Me, and my acquaintance into darkness… But **You have cast off and abhorred, You have been wroth with Your Anointed. How long, LORD? will You hide Yourself forever? shall YOUR WRATH BURN FOREVER?** The sorrows of death compassed Me, and the pains of hell gat hold upon Me: I found trouble and sorrow.*[26]

When Jesus carried our sins, He was counted as God's enemy…and incurred God's cruel wrath:

> "*Know now that **God has overthrown Me**, and has compassed Me with **His net…He has fenced up My way that I cannot pass, and He has set darkness in My paths. He has stripped Me of My glory, and taken the crown from My head. He has destroyed Me on every side… He has also kindled His wrath against Me, and He counts Me as one of His enemies…** "I cry to You, and You do not hear Me… **You are become cruel to Me: Your strong hand opposes Me.**"[27] …He has **pulled Me in pieces** and made me desolate… He has bent His bow,*

---

[26] Psalm 88, 89, 116
[27] Job 16, 19

and ... caused the arrows of His quiver to enter into My heart... **Remembering My affliction and My misery, the bitterness and gall. My soul has them still in remembrance, and is humbled in Me...**"[28]

The misery that Jesus experienced was horrific. It is unthinkable that Jesus—Eternal God and second Person of the Godhead-- allowed Himself to take the full brunt of the wrath of God for us in hell! As Jesus now sits exalted and triumphant over death, hell, and the grave, His soul is still *humbled* by the memory of that dreadful terror that He endured! His suffering was so extreme that it totally *paid in full* the punishment due to every sinner: from Adam, to Hitler, to you, and to me.

The Father executed complete judgment of sin by pouring out His burning wrath upon His Beloved Son. Even more incredible is that Jesus was willing to endure the pains of hell for us. He willingly gave Himself to ransom our souls, sealing with His Blood the proof of His love.

---

[28] Lamentations 3

A BRAND NEW YOU!

The gift of eternal life through Jesus is God's ultimate gift of love to all of humanity. You receive brand new spiritual life when you are born into God's family! To have this gift of new life, however, one must personally *accept* and *receive* it. Becoming a true, born-again Christian is not the result of joining a church, or following a certain code of conduct, or giving intellectual assent to some religious dogma. In order for one to become a Christian, one must have a supernatural experience in which one's spirit is regenerated—that is, made alive. You must be changed from within.

Jesus declared: *"Truly I say unto you, unless one is born again they cannot see the Kingdom of Heaven."*[29]   Jesus explained this to a very sincere, religious man named Nicodemus when he questioned how he might obtain eternal life. Nicodemus did not understand how one *could be* "born again." Did Jesus really expect a man to go back into his mother's womb and have another physical birth?? Of course not! Jesus explained to Nicodemus that as we have a natural birth in the flesh to become part of the human family, we must also have a spiritual birth to become part of God's family. We need this spiritual birth from God to receive a new nature. That is because we were all born into this world with a sin nature. No parent has to teach a child to lie, or to disobey. Sinning comes natural to us. Our natural human tendency is to rebel against God and His Laws. We all have chosen to go our own way instead of God's way.[30]

Even "good" people need to be born-again. Though most people believe that they are good people in and of themselves, God looks at the heart. Until one is born-again, the motives of the heart are

---

[29] John 3:3
[30] Psalm 14:2, 3

not pure. The human heart is by nature, self-centered. It is filled with pride, self-will, unforgiveness, fear, and unbelief—sins that are just as wicked as murder or adultery. The Bible declares that *"all have sinned."* The penalty for sin is death and damnation.[31] We were all destined for hell… that is, until Jesus gave Himself as a ransom to pay for our sins with His Blood.

> *"For God so loved the world that He gave His only Begotten Son, that whosoever believes in Him should not perish, but have eternal life. For God did not send His Son into the world to condemn the world; but that the world through Him might be saved."[32]*

Jesus purchased forgiveness of sin for every man, woman and child. Does that mean that everyone is going to heaven? Only if they will **repent and believe** in Jesus, and **receive Him** as the **<u>Lord</u>** of their life: *"As many as **received Him**, to them He gave power to become the sons of God, even to them that believe on His Name… which were born of God (born again)."[33]*

Notice that one must believe and receive **JESUS**. Forgiveness is not through Buddha, Mohammed, Krishna, or the Virgin Mary. Salvation is only through Jesus Christ. One might think it sounds narrow minded, saying that one can only get to God through Jesus. Jesus said, *"I am the way, the truth and the life; no one comes to the Father but by Me."[34]* It is a "narrow way" to eternal life… not everyone who believes that they are going to heaven *are* going to heaven!

---

[31] Romans 3:23; 6:23
[32] John 3:16
[33] John 1:12, 13
[34] John 14:6

The key is, have you been born-again? How? First, repent. Simply put, be willing to *turn away from sin*. Then, confess your sins to God and ask Jesus to be the Lord of your life. *"If you shall **confess with your mouth the Lord Jesus, and believe in your heart that God has raised Him from the dead,** you shall be saved (born-again)."*[35] Eternal life is a gift that you receive by faith. You cannot earn it by doing good works. Your works are not good enough.

> *"For by grace (undeserved favor from God) you*
> *have been saved by faith, and that not of yourselves; it*
> *is the gift of God; not a result of your works, so that no*
> *one can boast."*[36]

God made it so easy. Repent and believe. Believe that God loved you so much that He sent Jesus to die for your sin, and that He rose to life the third day. Then, invite Jesus into your life to rule as your Lord. If you will confess Jesus as Lord of your life, you will be saved.

What happens when you ask Jesus to forgive you of sin and to come into your life? His Blood completely *washes away all of your sin!* *"If we confess our sins He is righteous and just to forgive us our sin and to cleanse us from all unrighteousness."*[37] No matter what sins you have committed in your life, God completely forgives and forgets them! You are totally <u>justified</u> in God's sight--just as if you had never sinned! He sees you as righteous because your heart is cleansed from sin by the powerful Blood of Jesus. To God you are as clean as the driven snow!

---

[35] Romans 10:9, 10
[36] Ephesians 2:8, 9
[37] I John 1:9

"Come now, and let us reason together, says the Lord, though your sins are as scarlet, they will be as white as snow; though they are red like crimson, they will be like wool."[38]

When you are born again, your life begins with a brand new slate. It is as if we were in a prison serving life for crimes we committed. Then the judge steps in, graciously pardons us, and completely expunges our records--even though we were guilty! That is what God did in the courts of Heaven for us! We are forgiven and pardoned of sin! What an amazing gift from God!

In addition to receiving a full pardon of sin when one receives Jesus into their life, one also experiences a spiritual *transformation*. God takes out the hard heart of sin in your spirit and fills your heart with His love.[39] He literally writes His laws in your spirit so that you have new desires and want to do God's will.[40] You become a new, born-again person in Christ Jesus *spiritually*. The old sin nature is replaced with a new spiritual nature that is alive and pleasing to God. *"If any man be in Christ, he is a new creation; old things are passed away, behold, all things have become new."[41]* You are no longer satan's servant. You now belong to God!

You will start to notice changes in your desires. You will want your behavior and thoughts to be pleasing to your Heavenly Father. Things that did not bother your conscience before suddenly are noticeable. That is because your new born-again spirit is sensitive to the sin that you were blinded to before. You actually *want* to avoid sin because you recognize it is a trap from satan to try to destroy you. Does

---

[38] Isaiah 1:18
[39] Romans 5:5
[40] Jeremiah 31:33
[41] II Corinthians 5:17

that mean you are instantly perfect? No. Man is a triune being, comprised of a body, mind (soul), and spirit. Your spirit is born again, but your body and mind have not yet been made new. The Bible says that we need to renew our minds by washing them with the Word of God.[42] The old, negative, self-serving thought patterns need to be reprogrammed (so to speak) with the truth of God's Word in the Holy Bible.

The more you read the Bible and connect with God in prayer, the more change you will see in yourself. As you follow your born-again spirit's desires, your mind and fleshly desires will be transformed for the better. That is called the "sanctification" process. You cooperate with the Holy Spirit's inner leading and instructions. Following the Spirit confirms that you are God's child and that Jesus really is the Lord of your life: *"For as many as are led by the Spirit of God, they are the sons of God."*[43] If you fall into sin, repent and ask for forgiveness. We cannot take His mercy for granted, but God will forgive if we repent of our sin and confess it to Him.[44]

How can you be sure that you *really are* saved? What if some of the initial feelings you may have experienced…love, peace, and joy, wane with time? We are not saved by feelings that we may or may not have experienced when we asked Jesus to be Lord of our lives. We are saved by FAITH. Faith is believing what God says in His Word; and His Word is truth.[45] If you do what He tells you in the Word…repent and believe Jesus died for your sin, was raised to life the third day, and you confess with your mouth the Lord Jesus…you will be saved! Just believe!

---

[42] Ephesians 5:26
[43] Romans 8:14
[44] Proverbs 28:13
[45] John 17:17

"Whoever believes that Jesus is the Christ [God's Son who died for our sin] *is born of God... These things I have written to you who believe in the Name of the Son of God in order that you may KNOW that you have eternal life."[46]*

Remember, we are saved by grace through faith. Have faith in God's Word! God does not lie.[47] Do not listen to satan. He will whisper lies to your mind trying to get you to doubt God.[48] That is because we are in spiritual warfare, and satan is now your mortal enemy! He will try his best to deceive you and try to turn you away from God. The good news is that you have authority over every lying spirit once you are in Christ. You can resist the devil and he will flee in terror from you![49] The way to resist those lies is to declare God's Word with your mouth.

How can you stay spiritually strong as a Christian? There are several ways.

Read The Word!

First, read God's Word! It will literally build your faith! The Bible tells us, *"So then, faith comes by hearing and hearing by the Word of God."[50]* Jesus said, *"If you continue in My Word, then you are My disciples indeed... If anyone loves Me, he will keep My Words."[51]* The Apostle Peter admonishes us, *"like newborn babes earnestly desire the sincere milk of the Word, that you may grow thereby."[52]*

---

[46] I John 4:15, 5:1
[47] Numbers 23:19
[48] II Corinthians 10:4, 5
[49] James 4:7
[50] Romans 10:17
[51] John 8:31, John 14:23
[52] I Peter 2:2

Reading and heeding God's Word is not an option... It is as essential as food and water is for our natural bodies. Just as a newborn baby must constantly feed on milk in order to be healthy and grow, so we must feed on the Word of God. If we neglect the Bible we will become weak and faithless. As Jesus tells us: *"Man shall not live by bread alone, but by every Word that proceeds out of the mouth of God."*[53]

Prayer Protocol

In addition to reading God's Word, we need to pray. Prayer means spending time talking with God. God loves to fellowship with us! He *"delights in the prayers of the upright,"* just as a loving father delights in conversing with his children.[54] There is a proper way to approach God in prayer, just as there is appropriate protocol when one comes into the presence of an earthy king. The Bible tells us, *"Enter His gates with thanksgiving, and come into His courts with praise."* We don't start with our "gimme" list when we talk with God. We first give Him thanks and praise for what He has done and Who He is in our lives. Jesus gave us a model prayer[55]:

The Lord's Prayer

"Our Father, which is in Heaven, hallowed is your name" We need to first acknowledge who God is and worship Him. *"Thy Kingdom come, Thy will be done in earth as it is in Heaven."* Then, pray for God's will and purposes to be done in earth, especially for the salvation of all men everywhere. We are also to pray for those in authority that we may lead a quiet and

---

[53] Matthew 4:4
[54] Proverbs 15:8
[55] Matthew 6:9-15

peaceable life.[56] *"Give us this day our daily bread..."* Ask for the needs that you have in your life. Note that this is not a greedy prayer of "give me this day five people's daily bread," but "our" daily bread. God often gives us much more than we can ask or think as we focus on putting Him first,[57] but our prayers should not be self-centered or greedy. As a wise Heavenly Father, He will give us what we need when we ask Him.

"And forgive us our debts (sins) as we forgive our debtors (those who sin against us)." Forgiveness is an imperative. In order for us to receive forgiveness for *our sins,* we must forgive others. If we will not forgive, we will not get forgiveness. No matter what anyone has done to you, it wasn't as bad as you (by your sin) nailing the Son of God to the Cross and causing Him to taste of death and experience the pains of hell. If you expect God to forgive your sins against Him, you MUST forgive others!

"And lead us not into temptation, but deliver us from evil." Ask for God for guidance, and for deliverance from any evil influence in your life. *"For Thine is the kingdom and the power and the glory forever."* Finally, give God the glory for all that He has done through His power.

Stay Calm And Pray

God's Word tells us to *"pray without ceasing"* and to *"be anxious about nothing."* As God's children, we have the privilege to

---

56 I Timothy 2:1-4
57 Matthew 6:33

cast all our cares upon Him so that HE can care *for us!* When we invite God into our life situations—those things that concern us, we have all of the resources of Heaven working on our behalf. Jesus is interceding for us. As we pray in the spirit, the Holy Ghost prays for us. Therefore, we know that all things will work out for our good.[58]

Don't Forsake Church

Our personal time with God in prayer and in the Word is so important to our spiritual life. But, we also need to fellowship with other believers. You are a member of a corporate *Body,* the Church.[59] From the church we get spiritual encouragement. We are admonished: *"Do not forsake assembling yourselves together as is the habit of some, but encourage one another: and all the more as you see the day approaching."*[60] Church is especially important to strengthen our faith. Christian fellowship can counteract the wicked influences of society that are all around us:

"Do not be bound together with unbelievers, for what partnership has light with darkness... Therefore, do not be partakers with them (sinners); for you were formerly darkness, but now you are light in the Lord; walk as children of light."[61]

Walk Like Jesus

We are to walk as children of light and not to be conformed to the spiritual darkness around us:

"Therefore, having these promises, beloved, let us cleanse ourselves from all defilement of flesh and spirit,

---

[58] I Thessalonians 5:17, Philippians 4:6, Romans 8:27, 28
[59] I Corinthians 12:14-27
[60] Hebrews 10:25
[61] II Corinthians 6:14, Ephesians 5:7, 8

perfecting holiness in the fear of God."[62] *The one who says he abides in Him ought himself to walk in the same manner as Christ walked...Set your affections on things above, not on things that are on the earth.*[63]

Talk About Jesus

Finally, we need to be a witness to others about what Jesus has done for us. Jesus told us to *"Go into all the world and preach the Gospel to every creature."*[64] Jesus does not want anyone to perish in hell. He tells us, *"freely you have received, freely give..."* Give to others the good news of how they can be saved through Jesus.[65] You do not have to be a Bible scholar to share what Jesus has done for you. The woman at the well (John 4) was not a religious woman. She just told everyone about her encounter with Jesus. Then, those in her city believed in Jesus!

Don't Be Ashamed

We should never be ashamed of Jesus. *"Everyone therefore who shall confess Me before men, I will also confess him before My Father Who is in heaven. But whoever shall deny Me before men, I will also deny him before My Father who is in Heaven."*[66] He loved us enough to pay for our sin with own His blood and to die for us. The least that we can do is to live for Him!

Confessing Who You *Really* Are In Him!

Because you are in Christ, you have a new identity. The Word of God tells you who you really are. As you read these truths and speak them out loud, it will renew your mind and produce faith in your heart.

---

[62] II Corinthians 7:1
[63] I John 2:6, Colossians 3
[64] Mark 16:15
[65] Romans 10:9
[66] Matthew 10:32, 33

The following declarations are powerful spiritual weapons. Speak them out loud daily and you will become strong in the Lord:

I am not who you say that I am.
I am not who I think that I am.
I am who God says I am.
<u>Because I am in Christ I am</u>:
- **An imitator of God** (Ephesians 5:1)
- **Redeemed from the enemy** (Psalm 107:2)
- **Crucified with Christ** (Galatians 2:20)
- **Forgiven** (Colossians 1:13, 14)
- **Washed** (I Corinthians 6:11)
- **Saved by grace through faith** (Ephesian 2:8)
- **Justified** (Romans 5:1)
- **Born again** (I Peter 1:24)
- **Sanctified** (I Corinthians 6:11)
- **A new creature** (II Corinthians 5:17)
- **His workmanship** (Ephesians 2:10)
- **A partaker of His divine nature** (II Peter 1:4)
- **Pure** (I Peter 1:22)
- **Holy** (Hebrews 3:1)
- **A saint** (Colossians 1:12)
- **In His Hand** (John 10:28, 29)
- **Redeemed from the curse of the law** (Gal. 3:13)
- **Delivered from the powers of darkness** (Col.1:13)
- **Led by the Spirit of God** (Romans 8:14)
- **Kept safe wherever I go** (Psalm 91:11)
- **Getting all my needs met by Jesus** (Phil. 4:19)
- **Strong in the Lord & His mighty power** (Eph.6:10)
- **Seated with Christ in heavenly places** (Eph. 2:6)
- **Blessed with all spiritual blessings** (Ephesians 1:3)
- **Speaking the truth in love** (Eph. 4:15)

- **Set free from sin** (Romans 8:1-2)
- **Set free from satan's control** (Colossians 1:13)
- **Predestined to be like Jesus** (Ephesians 1:11)
- **Forgiven of all my trespasses** (Colossians 2:13)
- **Washed in the blood of the Lamb** (Revelation 1:5)
- **Given a sound mind** (2 Timothy 1:7)
- **Adopted into God's family** (Romans 8:15)
- **Justified freely by His grace** (Romans 3:24)
- **Kept from falling** (Jude 1:24)
- **Not condemned** (Romans 8:1-2)
- **On my way to heaven** (John 14:6)
- **His sheep** (Psalm 23, John 10:14)
- **A citizen of heaven** (1 Peter 2:11)
- **Protected from the evil one** (1 John 5:18)
- **More than a conqueror** (Romans 8:37)
- **Healed by His stripes** (I Peter 2:24)
- **Walking by faith and not by sight** (II Cor. 5:7)
- **God's child** (John 1:12)
- **God's friend** (James 2:23)
- **God's temple** (I Corinthians 3:16, 6:16)
- **Christ's witness** (Acts 1:8)
- **Christ's ambassador** (2 Corinthians 5:20)
- **God's beloved** (Romans 1:7)
- **God's precious jewel** (Malachi 3:17)

Because I am **in Christ I HAVE**…

- **The mind of Christ** (1 Corinthians 2:16)
- **Peace with God** (Romans 5:1)

I can do all things through Christ Who strengthens me (Philippians 4:13)

Romans 5:5: "*The love of God is shed abroad in my heart.*"

According to 1 Corinthians 13: "*I am patient and kind. I am not envious or jealous. I am not boastful, conceited, or inflated with pride. I do not condemn, criticize, or complain. I am not rude. I do not insist on my own way. I am not self-seeking. I am not touchy or resentful. I forgive freely. I pay no attention to a suffered wrong. I do not rejoice in evil but I rejoice when right and truth prevail. I bear up under anything that comes. I am always ready to believe the best of every person. My hopes are fadeless in every situation. I endure everything without weakening. God's love in me never fails!"*

These truths will greatly enrich your life and strengthen your foundation in Christ!

A STRONG FOUNDATION

Any building that is going to be structurally sound must be built with a strong foundation. Near where I live a marina advertises that soon it will have the strongest boat house in the world, able to withstand hurricane force winds. Though they have been working on the project for over six months, when one walks by one only sees what appears to be an empty lot. That is because the builders are focusing on digging deep to lay the best foundation possible, upon which the great marina walls will be erected. If a foundation is built upon rock, it will withstand storms that the Gulf of Mexico churns out. Jesus taught that our spiritual life must be built on a rock:

> *"Therefore whosoever hears these sayings of mine,* ***and does them****, I will liken him unto a wise man, which built his house upon a rock: And the rain descended, and the floods came, and the winds blew, and beat upon that house; and it fell not: for it was founded upon a rock. And every one that hears these sayings of mine, and does them not, shall be likened unto a foolish man, which built his house upon the sand: And the rain descended, and the floods came, and the winds blew, and beat upon that house; and it fell: and great was the fall of it."[67]*

Jesus did not say that the house fell because the builder did not *know* the Word of God. No… It fell because they heard God's Word but *did not do* what it said. We can deceive ourselves spiritually if we only hear God's Word, but do not do it.[68] True faith always has corresponding actions. When studying the basic Christian foundational

---

[67] Matthew 7:24-27
[68] James 1:22

principles, we must be careful not to just hear and assent to them. We must be willing to put them into practice. If we do not, we will deceive ourselves. The six foundational principles are found in Hebrews:

> *"Therefore leaving the **principles of the doctrine of Christ**, let us go on unto perfection; not laying again the **foundation of <u>repentance from dead works</u>**, and of <u>**faith toward God**</u>, Of the doctrine of <u>**baptisms**</u>, and of <u>**laying on of hands**</u>, and of <u>**resurrection of the dead**</u>, and of <u>**eternal judgment.**</u>"* (Hebrews 6:1, 2)

As you can see by this statement, the apostle tells us these principles are the *foundation* of the Christian life. Incorporating these truths into one's spiritual life is a prerequisite to growing and maturing in Christ. These are not an "all in all" end of Christian learning, but are the foundation upon which one's faith can grow. It is imperative to be grounded in these doctrines in order to go on to spiritual maturity. True spiritual maturity can best be summed up in this: *"And this is eternal life, that they might know You, the only true God, and Jesus Christ whom You have sent."* Knowing God intimately and allowing Christ's life (both character and deeds) to manifest through us should be our goal. To do so, we must be grounded in these principles of the faith.

REPENTANCE FROM DEAD WORKS

The first principle of the Christian faith is repentance from dead works. When Jesus preached, He said, *"**Repent** and believe the Gospel."[69]* Notice it was not just, "Believe the Gospel," but first "*Repent* and believe!" Repentance is necessary before one is truly converted.

Today there are many churches with "easy believe-ism." They teach a cheap Gospel that all one must do is simply believe in Jesus and ask Him into their life. Just believing in Jesus is easy. He was a historical figure so prominent that our calendar dating is based upon His birth. The Bible says that *"even the devils believe* [in God and Jesus] *and tremble."*[70] Devils are not saved simply because they believe. Neither are people. There must be submission of one's heart and will, and true repentance.

Some try to pawn Jesus off as simply a commodity that can benefit one's life-- like a new nutritional supplement they are trying to entice you to take: "Jesus can make your life better, you can be happier, and all your needs will be met." But, they never bother to mention the "sin" factor. Following Jesus is more than having a desire to be "the best me I can be." It is a submission to His Lordship; a willingness to turn away from sin, and to follow Jesus as Master:

> *"He that loves father or mother more than me is*
> *not worthy of me: and he that loves son or daughter*
> *more than me is not worthy of me. And he that takes not*
> *his cross, and follows after me, is not worthy of me. He*

---

[69] Mark 1:15
[70] James 2:19

that finds his life shall lose it: and he that loses his life for my sake shall find it."[71]

Repent and Be Saved

Salvation is free, but it will cost you everything. That is why Jesus tells us to *"count the cost."*[72] Is eternal life worth forsaking all to follow Jesus? If you have true faith in what the Bible says, it most definitely is. There is a wonderful heaven to gain and a real, eternal hell of torment to shun! Guess what? You are not doing God a favor by deciding to follow Jesus. He is not privileged that you chose to show up at church and give Him an hour on Sunday! In deciding to forsake sin and follow Jesus you are wisely doing the only thing that will save you from an eternal hell. God loves you and desperately desires that you make the right decision. But in the end, it is your decision—right or wrong. God has done His part. He has poured out His Spirit upon all flesh and He is wooing mankind to Himself by the Holy Spirit. God has initiated the pursuit. The Bible says, *"the goodness of God leads you to repentance."*[73] He invested His Son's Blood to make the way possible for you to go to heaven.

Are you going to take advantage of God's grace while He is calling you? Will you go through that door that is opened for a limited time and enter into the ark of safety? Now you have the opportunity to escape sin and eternal damnation through receiving Jesus. You may not have tomorrow. The Bible teaches TODAY is the day of salvation. Your very life's breath is in God's hand, and you and I need Him desperately! If you are wise enough to receive eternal life offered to you by the Father, then you have made the right choice. But, if wallowing in sin and temporal pleasures is more important to you than

---

[71] Matthew 10:37-39
[72] Luke 14:28
[73] Romans 2:4, II Timothy 2:25

receiving eternal life, then you are very short-sighted. You need a mind change. You need to repent! To choose sin means you really do not believe what the Bible teaches about heaven and hell. If you did, you would *RUN* to Jesus as fast as you could!

What *IS* Repentance?

Repentance is more than just being sorry. The term in the Greek is "metanoeo," which means "to think differently, reconsider, compunction, reformation, change mind and attitude, reversal." It means to make an "about face!" and go the other direction. It implies not just a turning *from* sin, but a turning *to* God.[74] A change of mind will always result in a change in one's behavior. It is not simply a matter of regretting one's actions, but true repentance entails having "Godly sorrow" for one's sin.[75] That sorrow causes one to turn from sin to God for forgiveness. Repentance is a work of God's Spirit. He reveals to us the evil nature of our sinfulness, and gives us the grace to come to God's throne to receive mercy. God never leaves us in despair when we humbly repent from the heart. He gently restores and forgives us as we come to Him in heart-felt repentance.

In my own spiritual quest to find God I started out with a wrong premise. I was religious, believed in God, and attended church. Because I "believed" I assumed I was right with God. However, I had never truly acknowledged my own sinfulness. I thought that I was a good person (and better than most!) I never really considered myself as being a "sinner" needing forgiveness, and so never truly repented from the heart. I may have said, "I'm sorry God... I told a little lie," but in my heart, I did not consider myself to be a bad person.

---

[74] W.E. Vine, *An Expository Dictionary of New Testament Words*, (Old Tappan, NJ: F. H. Revell Company, 1966), 280
[75] II Corinthians 7:9, 10

One day, however, as I was praying, the Spirit of God convicted me of sin. His presence came in a tangible way into the room where I was. The very essence of God's Holiness was revealed to me. In the light of His presence, the evil of my proud heart was exposed. I realized that I stood filthy and sinful before the Lord and I wanted to flee from His awesome and terrible Presence. I was like Isaiah of old who recognized his own sinfulness when he saw the Lord:[76]

"Woe is me! For I am undone; because I am of unclean lips...for my eyes have seen the King..."

It was then that I had a change of mind and heart. I realized that I wasn't that perfect, good person that I had convinced myself that I was. I was a filthy sinner with attitudes more evil than a murderer in God's sight; and I deserved hell. I repented from the heart and trusted in God's mercy and forgiveness. I no longer considered myself God's gift to the world, but knew that I was a sinner desperately needing a Savior. When I *repented* and believed, then I was born again.

As Jesus tell us, *"They that are whole have no need of the physician, but they that are sick: I came not to call the righteous, but sinners to repentance."*[77] Even if we do not realize it, we are all sinners... sick with the plague of sin. Unless you admit your sick condition, you will not feel the need to repent. If you will acknowledge sin, you can be forgiven. Who needs to repent? Everyone! You and me! God has commanded *"all men everywhere,"* to repent.[78]

Repentance is necessary for salvation. Peter preached *"repent and be converted,"* and Jesus said, *"except you repent, you shall all*

---

[76] Isaiah 6:5
[77] Mark 2:17
[78] Acts 17:30

likewise perish."[79] God is not willing for any to perish, but desires that all will come to repentance.[80]

Regret is not repentance. You may regret that you drove 45 miles per hour in a 25 miles per hour zone when the police pull you over and give you a citation. You may be sorry about the outcome of your actions (a $250.00 speeding ticket), but you may not have truly repented about driving faster than the law allows. If you knew there were no police around and no possibility of getting a ticket, you might speed through there again. You have not really changed your mind and heart regarding your actions. You simply regretted the consequences. If you had truly repented (had a sincere change of heart and mind about your actions), you would not even consider speeding again. There is a difference between true repentance and simply regret.

True Repentance

Judas Iscariot "repented *himself.*"[81] In other words, *he* greatly *regretted* what he had done, but was not brought to true repentance by the Spirit of God. Apparently he had hardened his heart toward God's conviction to the point that he could not be brought to Godly repentance. Instead of turning from his sin of betrayal and turning to God for mercy, he hung himself.

Peter, on the other hand, also sinned grievously against Jesus. He denied Jesus three times in one night, cursing and swearing that he did not know Him. When God's Spirit convicted Peter of his sin, he wept bitterly. He repented from his heart and looked to the mercy of God to forgive and restore him. The next time that Peter had opportunity to stand up for Jesus (on the day of Pentecost), he did so

---

[79] Acts 3:19, Luke 13:3
[80] II Peter 3:9
[81] Matthew 27:3-5

with boldness.[82] His repentance brought a change in his heart and actions.

True repentance will always have corresponding actions. Paul said that his message of the Gospel was to tell Jews and Gentiles that they should *"repent and turn to God, and do works fitting for repentance."*[83] Your actions do not save you, but they indicate that you have sincerely turned from sin to God from the heart.

John the Baptist rebuked the religious Pharisees and Sadducees of his day when he saw their self-righteousness. They refused to admit that they were sinners, and therefore did not submit themselves to John's baptism. That would have been a public acknowledgement that they *needed* repentance. They were too proud for that! John called them a generation of vipers and said, *"Bring forth fruits suitable for repentance, and do not think to say within yourselves, 'we have Abraham for our father'"* [trusting that their religious heritage put them in right standing with God].[84]

Just because you grew up in church or in a Christian family does not mean you have no need to repent. Religious pride is one of the worst sins that there is. It blinds men from the truth and keeps them from salvation. Many cite their religious affiliation when they are asked if they have been born-again. They are not being honest about the condition of their hearts. In Jesus' day the harlots and tax collectors humbly submitted to John's baptism. Jesus said these "sinners" were more justified than the self-righteous Pharisees (who did not think they needed forgiveness of sin). The harlots and tax collectors were willing to admit they did not have it all together. That is what God wants--an

---

[82] Matthew 26:74, 75; Acts 2:36-38
[83] Acts 26:20
[84] Matthew 3:8, 9

honest heart willing to acknowledge the need to change. He is more than willing to forgive those that come unto Him in true repentance.

The Bible says the people were *"baptized, confessing their sins."*[85] They then asked John what corresponding *works* they should do in order to follow God. They publicly admitted their sin, and were then willing to change their behavior and do good. That is true repentance. Humbling one's self before God by confessing one's sin is the first step. Then, one must have corresponding actions, which includes forsaking (leaving) the sin. That shows you are serious about your decision to follow God. As Proverbs 28 tells us, *"those who confess **and** forsake sin shall receive mercy."* It is not a ritualistic confession to God, but a true change in one's lifestyle.

Repentance for Believers

What about Christians? Some teach that once one repents and believes in Jesus for salvation (once they are born-again), they never have to repent or confess sin again. That is certainly not the case. When we are born-again our spirit man is made brand new and we stand clean and justified in God's sight. We have the ability *not* to sin if we walk in the Spirit.[86] But we still have our carnal mind and flesh to contend with. Paul admonishes us in Colossians to *"put off the old man, and put on the new man."* We are to put to death the old man with its lust:

> *"Mortify therefore your members which are upon the earth; fornication, uncleanness, inordinate affection, evil concupiscence, and covetousness, which is idolatry: For which things' sake the wrath of God cometh on the children of disobedience: In the which ye also walked some time, when ye lived in them. But now*

[85] Mark 1:5
[86] Galatians 5:16

43

ye also put off all these; anger, wrath, malice, blasphemy, filthy communication out of your mouth. Lie not one to another, seeing that ye have put off the old man with his deeds; And have put on the new man, which is renewed in knowledge after the image of him that created him:" (Colossians 3:5-9)

At times, however, we may follow the flesh and sin. If so, we need to repent and confess our sin to God. If we honestly endeavor to follow Jesus (the Light), then His Blood cleanses us:

> *"If we say that we have fellowship with Him, and walk in darkness, we lie, and do not the truth: But **if we walk in the light,** as He is in the light, we have fellowship one with another, and **the blood of Jesus Christ His Son cleanses us from all sin.** If we say that we have no sin, we deceive ourselves, and the truth is not in us. If we **confess our sins, He is faithful and just to forgive us our sins, and to cleanse us from all unrighteousness."**[87]*

That means that unrighteousness enters the believer's life when they sin, and they must be cleansed of it. If they are truly trying to follow the Lord, His blood avails. We are not "kicked out of the family of God" for slipping up. The Blood of Jesus cleanses us from ALL unrighteousness! But you must repent and confess it to God to be cleansed. One cannot willfully continue down a path of sin and stay in right standing with God. Don't become comfortable with sin. Paul tells us *"let all who name the Name of Christ depart from iniquity."*[88]

---

[87] I John 1:6-9
[88] II Timothy 2:19

When God shows a believer an area of sin in their life, they need to repent of it immediately. Do not ignore it or make excuses for it... Do not become comfortable with it. For a believer to willfully continue in sin with no repentance is very dangerous. One can actually harden their heart to the Spirit's conviction to where it is impossible to be drawn to repentance. Only through God's goodness we are led to repentance. Do not harden your heart to His Spirit:

> *"For **if we sin willfully after that we have received the knowledge of the truth,** there remains no more sacrifice for sins, but a certain fearful looking for of judgment and fiery indignation, which shall devour the adversaries. He that despised Moses' law died without mercy under two or three witnesses:*
>
> *Of how much sorer punishment, suppose ye, shall he be thought worthy, who has trodden underfoot the Son of God, and has counted the blood of the covenant, **wherewith he was sanctified**, an unholy thing, and has done despite unto the Spirit of grace? For we know him that has said, Vengeance belongs unto me, I will recompense, says the Lord. And again, The Lord shall judge **His people.** It is a fearful thing to fall into the hands of the living God"*[89]

Repent Church!

Christians must repent. It is not a one-time event that occurs at salvation, but a walk of obedient faith. Paul said that he would come weeping if some of the church had sinned but had not repented of their unclean, promiscuous lifestyle.[90] The church needs to judge itself. In

---

[89] Hebrews 10:26-27
[90] II Corinthians 12:21

the book of the Revelation Jesus sternly warns the *churches* (local bodies of believers) to repent:

> *"Nevertheless I have somewhat against you, because you have* <u>*left your first love*</u>*. Remember therefore from where you are fallen, and* **repent,** *and do the first works; or else I will come unto you quickly, and will remove your candlestick out of his place,* **except you repent**... **Repent;** *or else I will come unto you quickly, and will fight against them with the sword of my mouth..."*

This church group started out loving and obeying God, but their faith and love waned. They needed to repent or Jesus will fight against them! Others allowed false teachers into their midst or were lukewarm spiritually. Unless they repent they will be cast into the great tribulation!

> *"you allow that woman Jezebel, which calls herself a prophetess, to teach and to seduce* **my servants** *to commit fornication, and to eat things sacrificed unto idols...Behold, I will cast her into a bed, and them that commit adultery with her into* **great tribulation,** *except* **they repent of their deeds**... *Remember therefore how you hast received and heard, and hold fast, and* **repent.** *If therefore you shalt not watch, I will come on you as a thief, and you shalt not know what hour I will come upon you. So then because you are lukewarm, and neither cold nor hot, I will spew you out of my mouth... As many as I love, I rebuke and chasten: be zealous therefore, and* **repent.**"[91]

---

[91] Revelations 2 and 3

Repentance is not reserved for unregenerate "sinners." Jesus warned the seven *churches* of Asia to repent of evil deeds, doctrines, and attitudes or they will be spewed out of His mouth!

What are the *"dead works"* (works that result in death) from which we must repent? Basically, dead works are works of sin. Romans tells us *"For the wages of sin is death..."* and *"sin...works death."*[92] The only way to be cleansed from dead works is through Jesus' blood[93]:

> *"How much more shall the blood of Christ... purge your conscience **from dead works** to serve the living God? And for this cause he is the mediator of the new testament, that by means of death, for the redemption of the **transgressions**..."*

Transgressions from which we must repent are numerous. Sin is transgressing God's Law. God's Law can be summed up in two basic commandments: *"You shall love the Lord your God with all your heart, and mind, and soul, and love your neighbor as thyself."*[94] If you are not walking in love, you are transgressing God's Law. If you love your neighbor, you will not commit adultery with their spouse... you will not steal from them... you will not murder them. Romans 14 defines another aspect of sin: ***"Whatsoever is not of faith is sin!"*** That includes fear, doubt, and unbelief.

When In Rome *DO NOT* Do As The Romans!

God loves us and wants us free of sin. He tells us in Romans chapter 1 to repent of sexual sin (homosexuality specifically), as well as other forms of rebellion against God's Law:

---

[92] Romans 6:23, 7:13
[93] Hebrews 9:14, 15
[94] Matthew 22:37-40

"men, leaving the natural use of the woman, **burned in their lust one toward another; men with men** *working that which is unseemly, and receiving in themselves that recompense of their error which was meet."[95] And even as they did not like to retain God in their knowledge, God gave them over to a reprobate mind, to do those things which are not convenient;"*

"being filled with all unrighteousness, fornication, wickedness, covetousness, maliciousness; full of envy, murder, debate, deceit, malignity; whisperers, backbiters, haters of God, despiteful, proud, boasters, inventors of evil things, disobedient to parents, without understanding, covenant breakers, without natural affection, implacable, unmerciful: Who knowing the judgment of God, that they which commit such things are **worthy of death***, not only do the same, but have pleasure in them that do them."*

The "obvious" sins of fornication and sexual immorality, murder, and lying are listed. Here we are also warned against the not-so-obvious sins of greed, gossiping, pride, and breaking covenant. They are also classified as sins "worthy of death." We must realize that the "heart" sins of hate, judgmental attitudes, and pride are evil in God's eyes. We must all guard our heart!

In Mark 7:21-23, Jesus tells us of sins that will defile us spiritually:

"That which cometh out of the man, that defiles the man. For from within, out of the heart of men, proceed evil thoughts, adulteries, fornications,

---

[95] Romans 1:

murders, thefts, covetousness, wickedness, deceit, lasciviousness, an evil eye, blasphemy, pride, foolishness: All these evil things come from within, and defile the man."

Wow! "Evil thoughts." What does that encompass? Not just *doing* evil against someone, but having evil thoughts about them. Or entertaining unclean, evil thoughts in your mind and heart. The Bible tells us, *"As a man thinks in his heart, so is he."*[96] What have you been thinking about? We are instructed to "think on things that are true, honest, just, pure… anything worthy of praise…"[97] We are to cast down every vain imagination—every stronghold in our thought life-- that is contrary to God's Word.[98] That is spiritual warfare: your mind is the battlefield. Do not let satan get place in your thought life! You must guard your heart and mind.

See No Evil! Do No Evil!
Then, "adulteries" are listed. The New Covenant has a higher standard than Moses' Law. According to Jesus if one just *looks* on a woman (or man) to lust after them, you have committed adultery already in your heart! One can hardly turn on a T.V. without seeing half-dressed people trying to evoke lust from the viewers. We must guard ourselves from falling into the lust that is so entrenched in our society. Job said, *"I have made a covenant with my <u>eyes</u>; why then should I <u>think upon</u> a maid."* What one sees is what one will think about. Men are especially visual creatures, and so they must carefully guard their eyes from looking on things that will evoke lust.

---

[96] Proverbs 23:7
[97] Philippians 4:8
[98] II Corinthians 10:4-6

Christian women have their responsibility as well. If you are out on the beach wearing a string bikini, how are you not evoking men to lust after you? You are causing men to sin by your seductive attire (or lack thereof). Even in church women often come dressed as if they are going to a night club... tight pants, short skirts, cleavage showing. Godly women are to dress modestly.[99] "Modestly adorned..." It does not say frumpy or sloppy. If you think you cannot "get a man" without showing off your body, then you are selling yourself off very short-- just a piece of flesh--and any dog will go for it. A Godly woman pleases God in her dress and attitude.

Related to adulteries is "fornications." The word in the Greek is "porneia." It means illicit sexual intercourse. This includes any sex outside of the God-ordained marriage of a man and a woman. This includes pre-marital sex. Living together does not constitute marriage. Just because you have a ring doesn't make it legal. Until one is legally bound by the law in a marriage covenant, it is fornication. Paul warns the Corinthians not to even touch a woman (in a sexual manner) or else it will cause one to burn in lust and lead to fornication.[100]

Fornication also includes masturbation, and oral and anal sex. We are warned to "flee fornication" because we are the Temple of the Holy Ghost. The term "porneia" also includes pornography. Internet pornography is a demonic snare that has entrapped many. Just because you do it behind closed doors does not make it okay. These unclean behaviors are sin, and will result in spiritual death. Don't white-wash your behavior. It is sin. And the wages (result) of sin is eternal death and separation from God!

---

[99] I Timothy 2:9
[100] I Corinthians 7:1, 2

What's In The Heart?

The next on the list of defiling sins is "murders." Obviously, physically murdering someone is sin. But Jesus said that just being angry with one's brother without a cause can put you in danger of hell fire.[101] One can also assassinate someone's character by being a false accuser. Hatred in one's heart is the same as murder in God's eyes.

Then there is the murder of unborn babies. The Bible speaks much about the personhood of unborn babies... Prophets are "called from their mother's womb," and leap in their mother's womb.[102] Abortion is murdering a human being. The Old Testament states if a pregnant woman is harmed so that the baby comes forth and dies, the penalty is "a life for a life"[103] (the penalty for murder). Abortion not only kills a baby, but brings trauma and spiritual death to the mother. If you do not want a baby, then do not get pregnant. If you do get pregnant, there are other viable options, including adoption.

"Thefts" is the next defiling sin that Jesus mentions. The term in the Greek is "klepto" (hence the term, "kleptomania"). It means to steal. Obviously, we should not take that which is not ours. But there are different ways that we can steal from others. Are you an employee that does personal business during work hours? Are you texting and talking when you should be working? You are stealing your employer's time. Are you using the copy machine excessively without authorization for your personal things? Are you taking pens and office supplies home? If so, you are stealing from your employer. Do you get government food stamps by lying about your income? (A double sin... deceit and theft!) Just because it is taking from the government,

---

[101] Matthew 5:21-23
[102] Jeremiah 1:5, Galatians 1:15, Luke 1:41
[103] Exodus 21:22-25

it is still theft. Do you take tax benefits that you do not deserve? There are many ways one can steal.

Where Your Treasure Is

Then comes covetousness... In the Greek it means "desiring to have more." I think the most horrendous example of covetousness is that which religious salesmen purport to be "God's prosperity." I get sick of hearing of the Gospel of greed by those who try to manipulate their congregation or audiences by promising them a big return on their "faith seed."

It is true that as we seek first the Kingdom of God that everything we need will be supplied. It is God's will that we prosper and be in health *as our soul prospers.* Deuteronomy 8:18 tells us that when God does bless our finances we are to remember that God gave us the power to get that wealth, and the purpose of it is to establish His covenant. We are to be conduits of God's blessings to others. We are not to hoard everything up for ourselves so we can prove how "spiritual" we are.[104]

Greed peddlers, on the other hand, cause people to focus on money, instructing adherents to "call in prosperity" and "claim the blessings" ... a big car, jet, and homes. They infer that something is spiritually wrong with those who do not obtain great wealth—living in mansions, and having a fleet of Mercedes... Jesus did say something about "storing up treasure in heaven." But, perhaps He was never "properly educated" at the latest prosperity seminars.

The writer of Hebrews said that the righteous prophets were *"destitute, afflicted... and wandered in deserts and in caves."[105]* James

---

[104] I Timothy 6:5
[105] Hebrews 11:37, 38

tells us that God has chosen the poor of this world to be rich in faith.[106] It is not wrong to be prosperous, but it is wrong to be greedy. Colossians 3:5 states that covetousness is idolatry! Prosperity for the right purpose--blessing others—is the right focus.

Abhor That Which Is Evil

Then, there is wickedness... satan is called "that wicked one." Extreme evil and demonic influences are all around us... Look at the evil in society... games, T.V., movies. This whole world lies in wickedness.[107] Everything that opposes God's essence of purity and love and holiness is wicked. We tend to be desensitized to the evil around us... terrorists decapitating innocent people, devil worshippers murdering, aborting babies... it goes on and on. Christians should not sit in front of a TV or movie screen and feed on wickedness—lust, murder, vulgarity.

The next sin that can defile us is deceit. It is defined as "to bait or to snare." It means to trick and trap with lies. satan is called the "father of lies" and is the master of deceit. If we deceive, we are doing the works of satan. God is the God of truth, and Jesus is truth. Are we lying, exaggerating, or misrepresenting the truth in any way? We need to repent of deceit!

To stay undefiled, we must also avoid lasciviousness. Lasciviousness is defined as "excess, lacking moral and sensual restraint, licentiousness." According to II Peter 2:7, it can be likened to the society of Sodom and Gomorrah... unrestrained lust to the point of homosexual men trying to rape angels! The lust with which our society is inundated makes one wonder how much longer before God must allow the fire and brimstone to fall!

---

[106] James 2:5
[107] I John 5:19

What is an "evil eye"? According to Matthew 20:15, an evil eye is the negative, angry feeling you get when someone else gets what you did not. In other words, envy. Are you angry when someone else gets to sing the solo in the choir that you wanted to sing? Are you angry at your co-worker for getting a raise or a better position than you did? Are you envious of the recognition others receive, and you do not? Be careful. You may be acquiring an envious spirit.

We must also guard ourselves against the sin of blasphemy. We usually equate blasphemy to being irreverent to God. That is certainly one definition. But the term includes a broader meaning. Blasphemy literally means "injurious speech" or "speech that injures." It means harsh speaking, to inflict or harm with one's words. It includes slander, evil speaking, and cursing. One can have injurious speech even in how they speak to children: "You're never going to amount to anything!" "You idiot! Can't you do anything right?" Watch your tongue!

Not *ME!!*

The next sin listed in Mark 7 is pride. Pride is a major characteristic of society in the last days.[108] It is a manifestation of lucifer... the beautiful archangel who fell because of the pride of his heart.[109] Pride means to be haughty. The term in the Greek is "huperephanos," meaning to "show ones' self above others, to appear above, preeminent." Wasn't that satan's mindset? "I will exalt myself above the Most High"? It is always used in an evil sense of arrogant, disdain, haughty, an inflated opinion of self, puffed up, false perception, to think more highly than one ought to of one's self.

---

[108] II Timothy 3:2
[109] Obadiah 3

54

Pride is the ultimate in self-deception. It is a deception in perception. If one focuses on one's self and not on God, they will have a perverted, twisted world view. One can deceive himself into thinking he is something, when actually he (compared to God) is nothing.[110]

I Was *JUST* Joking!

The last defiling sin is foolishness. The term in Greek is "aphrosune," which means, "senselessness, want of mental sanity and sobriety, a reckless and inconsiderate habit of mind, lack of common sense, perception of the reality of things natural and spiritual." That is a mouthful! Could some of the "drunk in the Spirit" antics fall into this category? or "Toking on the Holy Ghost"? Staggering around the stage in a pseudo-drunken state with slurred speech and claim it is of God?

When such activity is going on you will note that people are focused on the "show" being exhibited in front of them, laughing at the antics--*not* on worshipping Christ. That nonsense brings reproach to the Kingdom of God. It causes unbelievers to say you are mad, which Paul highly discouraged.[111] The Holy Spirit is not going to transgress God's Word that instructs us to do all things decently and in order.[112] Foolishly laughing at inane, superficial nonsense is not the joy of the Lord nor a fruit of the Spirit. It is simply fleshly laughter with a temporary "feel good." The joy of the Lord is deep, abiding delight in the Presence of the Lord.

Paul instructs us in Ephesians 5:4 that the following should not be engaged in by the saints: *"filthiness, nor foolish talking, nor jesting, which are not convenient* (befitting for Christians)*: but rather giving of thanks. "* I have been convicted at times when I said, or wanted to say,

---

[110] Galatians 6:3
[111] I Corinthians 14:23
[112] I Corinthians 14:40

something that I thought was funny. Why did I want to say it? So that others would think I was funny… to draw attention to me.

What does Paul say we are to do? Instead of trying to be the center of attention and get people to laugh at us, we are to give thanks. That puts the focus on Jesus, where it should be. The world should see us as sincere people with a message of truth. If you are had in reputation for teaching or preaching the Word of the Lord, folly and foolishness can actually tarnish your reputation: *"Dead flies cause the ointment of the apothecary to send forth a stinking savor: so does a little folly him that is in reputation for wisdom and honor."*[113]

This is not to say that God does not have a sense of humor. Certainly He does! Proverbs tells us that a "merry heart does good like a medicine." This is confirmed even by medical science where cancer patients often see improvement by simply engaging in laughter.

Consider the humorous accounts of Elijah jabbing the false prophets (I Kings 18:27). Or, the incredulous "believers" who wouldn't acknowledge Peter's miraculous deliverance from prison and left him outside knocking at the door, even as they prayed for his deliverance.[114] Certainly we can laugh at humorous circumstances, but to engage in excessive, senseless foolishness is not pleasing to God.

Put It Off!

As we grow in the Lord we should put off sinful tendencies and put on Christ's nature: love.

---

[113] Ecclesiastes 10:1
[114] Acts 12:13-16

"Now the works of the flesh are manifest, which are these; adultery, fornication, uncleanness, lasciviousness, idolatry, witchcraft, hatred, variance, emulations, wrath, strife, seditions, heresies, envyings, murders, drunkenness, revellings, and such like: of the which I tell you before, as I have also told you in time past, that **they which do such things shall not inherit the kingdom of God.** *"[115]*

That is pretty plain. If you actively do them--if you continue in a lifestyle where you practice these sins-- **_you shall not inherit the kingdom of God_**. In addition to sins previously mentioned there are uncleanness, idolatry, witchcraft, variance, wrath, heresies and drunkenness.

Uncleanness in the Greek is "akatharsia" (not cleansed). It has the connotation of being "unclean spiritually and morally..." impure both in one's actions and in one's heart.[116] Sensuality and evil doctrine are often tethered together. Many times where there is spiritual error and false teaching, there is also unclean sexual behavior. How many leaders of cults and false religions engage in child molestation, pedophilia, and polygamy? Unclean spirits cause people to engage in unnatural sexual behavior.

No Other God

The next sin is that of idolatry, which (according to Paul) is the sin of the mind against God:

"Because that which may be known of God is manifest in them; for God has showed it unto them. For

---

[115] Galatians 5:19-21
[116] I Thessalonians 2:3

*the **invisible things of Him from the creation of the world are clearly seen,** being understood by the things that are made, even His eternal power and Godhead; so that they are without excuse: Because that, when they knew God, they glorified Him not as God, neither were thankful; but became vain in their imaginations, and their foolish heart was darkened... Who **changed the truth of God into a lie, and worshipped and served the creature more than the Creator,** who is blessed forever. Amen.*"[117]

Choosing to worship creation instead of the Eternal Creator is a willful denial of the truth of God's existence. Creation proves there is a God, but man chooses to deny the obvious. Some prefer to hug a tree instead of honor the One who created it. Another form of idolatry is following after the god of pleasure: *"Neither be you idolaters, as were some of them; as it is written, the people sat down to eat and drink, and rose up to play."*[118] Our society is so hedonistic... living for pleasure and self-indulgence. If it feels good, just do it... Partying and eating and drinking is called idolatry. The god of pleasure is all that many live and die for. How many times does one hear co-workers say: "I can't wait for Friday... I'm going to party hardy!" It is sad that their life is so empty spiritually that it has to be continually anesthetized by alcohol or drugs.

Those who constantly are drinking or drugging are showing that there is something on the inside that they do not want to deal with—emptiness, hurt, rejection, a broken heart. Trying to fill that void with things other than God's love is vain, and it will ultimately lead to death.

---

[117] Romans 1:19-21
[118] I Corinthians 10:7

Idolatry also is associated with the sin of stubbornness, as I Samuel 15:22, 23 tells us:

> *"And Samuel said, Has the LORD as great delight in burnt offerings and sacrifices, as in obeying the voice of the LORD? Behold, to obey is better than sacrifice, and to hearken than the fat of rams. For rebellion is as the sin of witchcraft, and* **stubbornness is as iniquity and IDOLATRY.***"*

Wow… you could be wearing holy church clothes and act sanctimonious, and still be an *idolater* because of your stubborn will! Idolatry is holding your own opinion above God and His Word. Do you fight against any change in the status quo of a church service? Do you stubbornly refuse to reconcile unless someone else apologizes first? You could be an idolater!

Rebellion As The Sin Of Witchcraft

Then, there is *witchcraft*. I Samuel states that *"rebellion is as the sin of witchcraft."* No, it is not cute to let little Johnny tell you "NO!" and throw a tantrum. Rebellion is not of God. To willfully go against God's expressed will and word is rebellion. We often conjure up an image of "witchcraft" as an evil lady stirring her potions in a cauldron. Actually, that is not totally off-track. The term "witchcraft" in the Greek is *pharmakeia*, from which we get the term pharmacy. Drugs (which can include some legal drugs) are associated with witchcraft. Substances that take away one's control of the mind are aspects of "witchcraft."

Witchcraft also encompasses dealing with occult powers and the practice of the magic arts. Tarot cards, horoscopes, Wicca, communicating with the dead, astral-projection, Ouija boards, New

Age (including Yoga meditation), séances… all of these are forms of witchcraft. There is no such thing as "white" (good) witchcraft. Any form of sorcery, spells, illicit drugs, and trying to control others is witchcraft. It is of the devil. Avoid it!

Be Angry But Sin Not

Anger is an emotion that is not sinful in itself. The Bible tells us, *"Be angry and sin not, neither let the sun go down on your wrath."* [119] Jesus was angry when He cleared out the Temple of the greedy money-changers who had made His Father's house a den of thieves. But He never sinned. It is not wrong to be angry with injustice, but to habitually have a hot temper is something else.

The term for "wrath" in the Greek is "thumos" (from which we get the term "thermos.") It means "hot." Wrath means bottled up, "hot anger; agitated outbursts of anger." In other words, you frequently "blow your stack and EXPLODE with anger!" That is the opposite of God's peace and forbearance. Patience means longggg suffering. You do not have a short fuse. The Bible says much about an angry man, and that it is best to avoid that type of person, as their tendencies will rub off on you. We must be careful not to entertain wrath. There are legitimate reasons to be angry, but do not hold onto it or it will consume you. Stop making excuses for your explosive wrath: *"Well, that's just my Irish temper"* or *"I was under stress."*

Divide And Conquer

The next sin that we need to avoid is "variance." This term in the Greek is "dichazo," which means "to divide in two" and "partiality." It has the connotation to "separate, and distinguish." Often times there are little "clique's" in church—the inside group that

---

[119] Ephesians 4:26

no one else can join. I have heard it said that the most segregated place in our country is in the churches every Sunday morning.

In addition to denominational splits in the church, there are racial divisions: Hispanics worship in one place, Korean Christians in another, Afro-Americans in another, and whites in a separate place. That is sad. I have heard of people from the Northeast who try to assimilate into churches in the deep South, but are given the cold shoulder since they are a "Northerner" (not really "one of us"). How long ago was the Mason-Dixon line drawn!?

In Christianity there should not be prejudice. As Paul said, *"In Christ there is neither Jew nor Greek, Barbarian, Scythian, bond nor free, but Christ is all and in all."* (Colossians 3:11) The early Church was very integrated. The leaders in the Antioch church were blacks and Jews.[120] Division in the Body of Christ is a trick of the devil. he knows where there is unity, there is power: *"And they lifted up their voice to God in **one accord**...[they] were of one heart and of one soul. And with **great power** gave the apostles witness of the resurrection of the Lord Jesus."[121]*

Spiritual Heresy

The next two "works of the flesh" are somewhat related. They are seditions and heresies. The term "seditions" in the Greek is "dichostasia," which means "standing apart, dissension, division" (especially in doctrine). Often times those who get into spiritual error have a unique "hobby horse" doctrine to which they adhere. They consider themselves the exclusive bearers of truth and often discount legitimate Christian groups as being inferior or not right with God.

Some churches have the audacity to say that unless one is part of their particular brand of Christianity one cannot be saved. Whether

---

[120] Acts 13:1
[121] Acts 5

it's their formula for water baptism or the day in which they choose to worship, they put emphasis on their particular belief or rite. Usually it is religious works by which they presume to approach God more acceptably. It is a form of error and religious pride to promote a unique doctrine for justification, rather than Jesus' Blood alone.

Heresy is a more extreme type of spiritual error. It is a blatant, willful choice to deny essential Biblical truth from God's Word and instead hold to one's own opinion. It is putting one's own opinion above God's revealed truth. Heresy, according to Vine's Greek dictionary, is:

> "a choosing, choice; then, that which is chosen, and hence, an opinion, especially a self-willed opinion, which is substituted for submission to the power of truth, and leads to division and the formation of sects... such erroneous opinions are frequently the outcome of personal preference or the prospect of advantage; see 2 Pet. 2:1, where "destructive" signifies leading to ruin..."[122]

One may say, "I know the Bible says homosexuality is wrong, but *I think* as long as one highly regards their partner it is okay." Or, "I know Jesus said, 'I am the way, the truth and the life, and no one comes to the Father but by *Me.*' But I think if someone is a good person they can get to God without Jesus." In both cases these statements reflect what someone *wants to believe* in spite of the fact that it is in direct contradiction to the Word of God. *"Let God be true and every man a liar."[123]* Someone who exalts their own opinion above God's Word is in error.

---

[122] Vine, An Expository Dictionary
[123] Romans 3:4

Many times people will have a spiritual experience and never test it according to the Word of God. They act as if their experience supersedes the truth in Scripture! We must reject *anything* that contradicts the Bible: manifestations, doctrines, etc. Heretics deny God's Word. Some heretics today deny that Jesus Christ is God in the flesh. Those who teach this have an anti-Christ spirit:[124]

> *"Beloved, believe not every spirit, but try the spirits whether they are of God: because many false prophets are gone out into the world. Hereby know ye the Spirit of God: Every spirit that confesses that Jesus Christ is come in the flesh is of God: And every spirit that <u>confesses not that Jesus Christ is come in the flesh</u> is not of God: and this is that <u>spirit of antichrist,</u> whereof ye have heard that it should come; and even now already is it in the world."*

We can mark a group or sect as being a cult or in error firstly by checking their doctrine concerning Jesus Christ. If they elevate man to Jesus' supreme place, or demote Jesus to being a mere man or angel (not fully God and man), then red flags should wave. Jehovah Witnesses and Mormons hold to false, deceptive teachings concerning Jesus. Jehovah Witnesses say that Jesus is not the one true God. Mormons teach that Jesus was simply a created being on the level of lucifer who grew spiritually to be God's son. These teachings are heresy. If you share Biblical truth with a heretic twice and they still refuse to listen to God's Word, then we must reject them.[125] They are willfully opposing God's Word. If they come to your door, do not allow that spirit of error into your home.[126] Just pray for them!

---

[124] I John 4:2
[125] Titus 3:10, 11
[126] II John 10

Be Not Drunk With Wine

Then there is drunkenness… When you give your conscious mind over to outside control and influence (including drugs and alcohol) you open yourself up to spiritual defilement. satan takes advantage of those who are not in control of their mind. Drugs and alcohol open people up to demon spirits. When some people drink, they become totally different people—violent and evil. That is because another spirit is in control when they are in a drunken state.

Just as one gives their mind over to "spirit guides" (demons) through New Age meditation and channeling, so does drunkenness open one's spirit to evil influences. Christians are commanded to be sober. The Bible says much about the excessive use of alcohol, and how it deceives people.[127] Christians must avoid making others stumble. You may say that one drink does not make you drunk, so it cannot hurt. But your liberty could adversely harm a weak brother or sister to feel it is okay for them to take one drink, then another, and another.[128] We are told not to be drunk with wine, but to be filled with the Spirit.[129] We must live soberly if we are to be ready for Jesus' coming.[130]

Related to drunkenness is "revelry." Basically, it is partying, which expressed in the Greek is "drunkenness, jovial, riotous drinking party, boisterous, merrymaking…" Sounds like campus life! Remember, *those who do such things shall not inherit the Kingdom of God."[131]* God does not want us ignorant about sin. If you are unrighteous you will not go to heaven:

---

[127] Proverbs 20:1
[128] Romans 14:21
[129] Ephesians 5:18
[130] Titus 2:11, 12; Luke 21:34
[131] Galatians 5:21

"Know you not that the unrighteous shall not inherit the kingdom of God? Be not deceived: neither fornicators, nor idolaters, nor adulterers, nor effeminate [cross dressers, transvestites, transgenderism], *nor abusers of themselves with mankind* [homosexuals], *Nor thieves, nor covetous, nor drunkards, nor revilers, nor extortioners, shall inherit the kingdom of God."[132]*

If one is following the Spirit of God, they will put off the works of the flesh. A born-again person will not *want* to sin because God's law is written in their heart. As they grow in grace and the knowledge of God, they will walk more and more in the light of God's Word. Through repentance they progressively put off the works of darkness. As long Jesus is Lord of their life, and they walk in the light as He is in the light, the Blood of Jesus cleanses from all unrighteousness.[133] If they stumble, they are not cast away. By repentance they are brought back into fellowship with God. However, if one continues willfully *in sin* with no repentance, they are not truly Christ's disciple. Jesus said that His sheep hear His voice and follow Him.[134]

Remember, God loves you and is on your side. Jesus is praying for you. When you are faced with temptation, He promises that He will provide a way of escape for you. If you do sin, don't continue in it. Repent and confess that sin to God. He will cleanse you. Keep the faith!

---

[132] I Corinthians 6:9, 10
[133] I John 1:7
[134] John 10:4

FAITH TOWARD GOD

The next tenet of basic Christianity is "faith toward God." This may seem simplistic and self-explanatory, but we do need to clarify what true "faith" is. And, with the increase of false religions, we also need to understand what the Bible teaches concerning the person of "God."

What *Is* Faith?

What is "faith?" Faith is the "persuasion, credence, conviction (of religious truth or truthfulness of God)-especially reliance on Christ for salvation."[135] Further, "it is the constancy in such profession, assurance, belief...firm persuasion, a conviction based on hearing... It is trustworthy, fidelity, faithful, stability..." Faith is not only an internal, spiritual force of heart-felt belief, but it becomes part of one's character. When one truly believes something, it affects how they live. In other words, faith does not just talk the talk, but walks the walk consistently.

The Bible definition states that *"faith is the substance of things hoped for, the evidence of things not seen."*[136] This definition limits "faith" to belief in things that *we desire* will happen ("things hoped for"). This hope is not wishful thinking. It is assurance that what we hope for will happen because the source of our hope is God's Word. He doesn't lie. His Word is truth!

A loving parent may promise their child a special treat. Assuming the parent has kept their word to the child in the past, that child will have an eager expectation to receive what was promised. That is the same with our Heavenly Father. He is trustworthy. The

---

[135] Vine, An Expository Dictionary, 71
[136] Hebrews 11:1

promises in His Word are the basis for our expectant belief. You do not have to first see the promise to believe that God will give you what He promised. You know He will because God keeps His Word.

Our faith comes from hearing God's promise and believing He will fulfill it: *"So then, faith comes by hearing, and hearing by the Word of God."[137]* To help your faith, God wrote us a love letter (the Bible) in which He gives us many examples of how He kept His word to others who trusted Him. As you read the Holy Bible, a spiritual force of faith will come into your heart.

Abraham's Faith

When you became a believer in Christ, you were given the gift of faith. A measure of God's faith is already in your heart![138] Faith grows by exercising it, even as exercising your muscles cause them to grow. How can you exercise your faith? By putting into action what you believe. As James tells us, "faith without works is dead." Abraham was considered a man of great faith because he obediently stepped out and did whatever God told him to do—even if he didn't agree or understand it. God promised that He would give Abraham and his descendants the promise land. In obedience, Abraham left all that he had in Mesopotamia to sojourn in the land of promise.

Had Abraham never taken a step to travel to the promise land, he never would have inherited it. Abraham did step out in faith, not knowing where he was going. The Bible tells us that Abraham's bold faith in God's promise pleased God. Because of his trust, Abraham was called the friend of God! Though Abraham was not perfect, his faith brought him into right standing with God: *"Abraham believed*

---

[137] Romans 10:17
[138] Romans 12:3

God, and it was counted to him for righteousness."[139] As we trust God's promise for salvation through Jesus we also are counted righteous with God!

Why Is Faith Important?

Why is faith so important to God? Because faith in God shows that you trust His character... that you consider Him trust-worthy. Had Abraham sent a delegation out to explore the land westward to see if there really was a land of milk and honey for him to inherit *before* stepping out to sojourn there, it would have been highly insulting to God. When we do not believe the promise that God has given us, it is like saying, "God, you are a liar. You do not keep Your Word and You do not have the power to back up Your promises." But, when we believe and confess God's promise as true in our lives, it pleases God and gives Him glory.

The Bible tells us, *"Without faith it is impossible to please God, for he who comes to God must believe that He is, and that He is the rewarder of them that diligently seek Him."*[140] *And whatsoever is not of faith is sin."*[141] If you really believe that God will reward you if you diligently seek Him, you will diligently seek Him (and you won't be disappointed!) If you really believe there is a heaven to gain and a hell to shun, you will not only make sure that you are right with God, but you will do everything in your power to persuade those you love to be saved as well. Your faith will cause you to live right.

How Does Faith Work?

---

[139] Romans 4:3
[140] Hebrews 11:6
[141] Romans 14:23

Faith is a powerful commodity! According to Jesus, just a tiny grain of faith has enough power to move a mountain![142] How is this faith activated? Once one has heard God's promise, faith is received in one's heart. That faith is then released by speaking out that Word that is in our heart:

> [143] "*That if you shall confess with your mouth the Lord Jesus, and shall believe in your heart that God has raised him from the dead, you shalt be saved. For with the heart man believes unto righteousness; and with the mouth confession is made unto salvation.*"

We see that when one speaks the truth out in faith, it brings the promise (in this case, salvation). In order to activate your faith, you must first hear God's promise from His Word. Then, receive the Word in your heart. When you speak the Word out, you affirm your belief with your actions.

Conditions for Faith

Faith comes by hearing God's Word, but there are other conditions necessary for faith to operate effectively in our lives. As it tells us in Galatians 5:6, "*faith works by love.*" I recall a testimony in which a mother who really did not have much faith in God or about divine healing, was faced with a life or death situation. Her son was dying from a blood infection in the hospital. The doctors could do no more. Out of desperation and love for her child she was willing to step out in faith and believe for a miracle. She boldly stepped out and prayed in front of doctors and nurses, asking God to heal her son. Guess what? God did not disappoint her. He raised her son off his

---

[142] Mark 11:22-24
[143] Romans 10:9, 10

death bed. Even the medical team declared it to be a miracle! It was her faith motivated by her love for her son that caused the miracle.

Notice the passage in Mark 11:22-25. Here Jesus tells His disciples if they have just a tiny grain of faith they can move mountains. Immediately following that declaration Jesus reminds them to *forgive* when they stand praying if they have a grievance against anyone. In this way, the Heavenly Father can forgive them as well. If we regard iniquity in our hearts, God will not hear our prayers. So love and forgiveness is a condition for our faith to work effectively.

Only Believe!

Sometimes we do not see answers to our prayers because we are not willing to completely rely on God's promise for the answer. We have other options. We may think, "Why should I ask God to heal me when I can take two Tylenol's and the pain will leave eventually?" Some missionaries notice that they have great success seeing miracles overseas in the third-world countries because the people are so desperate and have no other choice. It's either believe God or die!

In fact, scripture teaches that belief is a choice. We have to actively refuse to fear and doubt, and choose to believe. The ruler of a synagogue, Jairus, had a very sick daughter. He petitioned Jesus to come and heal her. When messengers informed Jairus that his daughter had already died, Jesus gave him this Word: *"Do not be afraid; only believe."*[144]

Jesus was the only hope he had to see his daughter alive again. In spite of the fact that religious leaders often opposed Jesus' ministry, Jairus was willing to go against social pressure and invite Jesus to his

---

[144] Mark 5:36

home. It was his only hope. He had to reject fear, and ONLY believe. His daughter was raised from the dead.

Another desperate woman was mentioned in the same chapter. She had spent all her money on doctors but only grew worse. She was willing to take a step of faith in her weakened condition and push through the crowd to touch Jesus. She made a determined choice to trust God for her healing. In her heart she said, "If I just touch the hem of Jesus' garment I will be healed." She recognized who Jesus was (the Anointed Messiah with healing in His wings[145]) and reached out in faith for healing. She was willing to trust God because the doctors could not help her. As a result, God's power flowed through Jesus and healed her. Jesus said it was *her faith* that made her whole.

True Faith

When you believe God's Word concerning a promise He has given (healing for example), you will have actions accompanying that faith. In the second chapter of Mark we see where men brought their paralyzed friend to Jesus for healing. They could not get into the crowded house where Jesus was, so they climbed up on the roof to let their friend down through a hole in the ceiling. The man was healed because of their *active* faith. True faith has corresponding actions.

True faith will not only manifest in your actions, but also in your words. From the abundance of the heart the mouth speaks. As II Corinthians 4:13 says, *"We having the same spirit of faith, believe and therefore speak."* As you read and meditate on God's Word, it will fill your heart with faith. When God's Word fills your heart and you are faced with a crisis or a dangerous situation your response will be *"There shall no evil happen to the just"* or *"God is an ever present help in time of trouble"* instead of the natural reaction of despair or fear.

---

[145]Malachi 4:2

God said it. Believe it!

True faith believes God's promise solely on the fact that God has said it. Jesus commended a Gentile military man for understanding the concept of the power in God's Word:

> *"And when Jesus was entered into Capernaum, there came unto him a centurion, beseeching him, and saying, Lord, my servant lies at home sick of the palsy, grievously tormented. And Jesus says unto him, I will come and heal him.*

> *"The centurion answered and said, Lord, I am not worthy that you should come under my roof:* ***but speak the word only, and my servant shall be healed.*** *For I am a man under authority, having soldiers under me: and I say to this man, Go, and he goes; and to another, Come, and he comes; and to my servant, Do this, and he doeth it.*

> *"When Jesus heard it, he marveled, and said to them that followed, truly I say unto you, I have not found so great faith, no, not in Israel...And Jesus said unto the centurion, go your way; and* ***as you hast believed, so be it done unto you.*** *And his servant was healed in the selfsame hour."[146]*

The Roman Centurion told Jesus to *"speak the Word only."* He believed in the power and authority of Jesus' spoken Word alone to effect the healing that was needed. His trust in Jesus' Word resulted in the healing he desired. We can also trust Jesus' Word implicitly. If

---

[146] Matthew 8

Jesus is the Lord of your life, then *"all of the promises of God in Him are 'yes' and 'amen'"* to you![147] You are blessed if you will take God at His Word and believe it without needing to see a sign.[148]

Patience!

True faith will endure the time of testing. Hebrews 6:12 tell us that *"through faith and **patience** that we inherit the promises."* Abraham was given the promise that his seed would inherit Canaan land many years before his heir was ever born. Abraham was fully persuaded that God would keep His word, so he gave glory to God as he waited. Finally, at one hundred years old Abraham received the promised seed, Isaac. Had Abraham given up at ninety-nine, he would not have received the promise. Do not give up. God's promise will be fulfilled.

"God is not a man that He should lie, neither the son of man that He should repent. Has He spoken it, and shall He not do it? Has He said it, and will he not bring it to pass?"[149]

Trust His Word! True faith waits expectantly till the answer manifests. Faith is being assured that you will receive the promise because you trust God's fidelity and His ability to perform His Word.

God is...

What does the Bible tell us about God? According to Genesis 1, He is the Creator of Heaven and Earth. He is the almighty, eternal, omnipotent Ruler of the universe. God is love.[150] God is *"patient, kind, longsuffering, is not envious, is not proud, is not rude or self-seeking,*

---

[147] II Corinthians 1:20
[148] John 20:29
[149] Numbers 23, Romans 4
[150] I John 4:8

73

is not easily provoked, thinks no evil; does not rejoice in iniquity, but rejoices in the truth; bears all things, believes all things, hopes all things, endures all things. Love never fails. "[151]

God is a Spirit and He is Light.[152] God is holy.[153] God is good.[154] God is faithful[155]… There are too many wonderful attributes of our God to name. But there are certain attributes that we must know and acknowledge to stay within the realm of the Spirit of Truth. Those who stray from what the Bible teaches about God get into spiritual error that can shipwreck their souls.

Almighty God is one. *"Hear oh Israel, the Lord our God is one Lord…"*[156] Though there is only one God, He is expressed in three persons, called the Trinity: *"For there are three that bear record in heaven, the Father, the Word, and the Holy Ghost: and **these three are one**…"* (I John 5:7) This union of the Personage of God is also called the "Godhead" in Colossians 2:9:

*"For in him [Christ] dwells all the fullness of the **Godhead** bodily."*

Many places in scripture this triune nature of God is manifested, including at creation where the plural term "Elohim" is used as God declares *"let US make man in OUR image…after the image of God created He male and female."*[157] At Jesus' baptism the Godhead were all present: Jesus manifested as the man, the Voice from Heaven was the Father, and the Spirit took the form of a dove.[158] In the Great

---

[151] I Corinthians 13:4-8
[152] John 4:24, I John 1:5
[153] I Peter 1:16
[154] Psalm 118:1
[155] I Corinthians 1:9
[156] Deuteronomy 6:4
[157] Genesis 1:26, 27
[158] Matthew 3:16, 17

Commission we are told to baptize in "the name of the Father, the Son and the Holy Ghost."[159]

A very important aspect is the DIETY of Christ. Jesus is call the Word of God made flesh:

> *"In the beginning was the Word, and the Word was with God, and the* **Word was God.** *The same was in the beginning with God. All things were made by him; and without him was not anything made that was made. In him was life; and the life was the light of men... And the Word was made flesh, and dwelt among us, (and we beheld his glory, the glory as of the only begotten of the Father,) full of grace and truth...No man has seen God at any time; the only begotten Son, which is in the bosom of the Father, he has declared him."*[160]

Jesus is God in the flesh. He is the Word made flesh. Jesus is the only way to the Father: *"I am the way, the truth, and the life; no one comes to the Father but my Me."* (John 14:6)

One must acknowledge Jesus as God in the flesh. False teachers say Jesus is only spirit, but that is error. He rose bodily from the dead on the third day and ascended up to the Father in that glorified Body. The angels declared that He will return the very same way that He left.[161]

The Bible teaches Jesus came in the flesh (He was "born") and His Divinity ("the Mighty God"). Isaiah prophesied of this eternal mystery of God taking on human flesh:

---

[159] Matthew 28:19
[160] John 1
[161] Acts 1:11

*"For unto us a **child is born**, unto us a son is given: and the government shall be upon his shoulder: and his name shall be called Wonderful, Counselor, **The mighty God**, The everlasting Father, The Prince of Peace. Of the increase of his government and peace there shall be no end, upon the throne of David, and upon his kingdom, to order it, and to establish it with judgment and with justice from henceforth even forever."*[162]

Jesus is the Messiah, God in the Flesh. God is one, but He is expressed as three distinct Persons of the Godhead: Father, Son, and Holy Spirit. God is *"the blessed and only Potentate, the King of kings, and Lord of lords; Who only has immortality, dwelling in the light which no man can approach unto; whom no man has seen, nor can see: to whom be honor and power everlasting."*[163] *"No man has seen God at any time; the only begotten Son, which is in the bosom of the Father, he has declared him."*[164] Jesus has declared to us who God the Father is: God is light, love and truth.

Faith toward God comes by meditating on His Word and prayer. By these we know Him better and develop a trust relationship. Faith toward God is faith in His character (which is love) and His Word (which is truth) and in His ability to perform His Word (which is omnipotent.)

---

[162] Isaiah 9
[163] I Timothy 6:15, 16
[164] John 1:18

BAPTISMS

Note that the third foundational teaching of Christianity is plural: *"Therefore leaving the principles of the doctrine of Christ, let us go onto perfection; not laying again the foundation of...the doctrine of **baptisms**."* That is because there are *four* baptisms. They are the baptism into the Body of Christ, water baptism, baptism of suffering, and the baptism in the Holy Spirit.

Baptized *Into* Christ

The first baptism that a Christian will experience is that of being *baptized* into the Body of Christ. This is also known as salvation. This is a spiritual occurrence when one receives Jesus as Lord of one's life. The Holy Spirit washes us (baptizes by fully immersing us) in the Blood of Jesus to cleanse our spirit. This allows us to be regenerated and become part of the Body of Christ. *"For **by one Spirit** are we all **baptized into one Body**."*[165] As Titus 3:5 tells us:

> *"Not by works of righteousness which we have done, but according to His mercy He saved us, by the **washing** of regeneration, and renewing of the Holy Ghost."*

Notice here that it is the *Holy Spirit* Who baptizes us into the Body of Christ. This is the baptism that Paul is referring to when he wrote of "one baptism" in Ephesians 4:

> *"There is one body, and one Spirit, even as you are called in one hope of your calling; One Lord, one*

---

[165] I Corinthians 12:13, I Corinthians 6:11

*faith, **one baptism**, One God and Father of all, who is above all, and through all, and in you all."*

Paul reminds Christians that they were "washed" from their former sins: *"For you are washed... by the Spirit of our God."*[166] He cites the children of Israel being baptized in the Red Sea as a type of salvation and deliverance from sin-- the Red Sea being a symbol of Jesus' Blood. Being baptized *by the Spirit of God* into Christ is a spiritual experience. When we are born-again, the Spirit washes us in the Blood of Jesus so that we can become a member of the Body of Christ.

Water Baptism

After one becomes part of the Body of Christ by being washed in the Blood of Christ, one should then be ***water baptized.*** Water baptism is an act in which you are submerged under water. *"Baptism"* means "to make whelmed, to cover with water, submerge; fully wet...washing, dip." This is an act that is done as a symbolic expression and public confession of what Jesus has done for you spiritually. Paul describes the significance of going down under the water as *"being buried with Him,"* and coming up out of the water as being *"raised with Him into new life"*:

> *"Know you not, that so many of us as were baptized into Jesus Christ were baptized into his death? Therefore, we are **buried with him by baptism** into death: that like as Christ was raised up from the dead by the glory of the Father, even so we also should walk in newness of life. For if we have been planted together **in the likeness of his death**, we shall be also in the likeness of his resurrection"*[167]

---

[166] I Corinthians 10:1, 2
[167] Romans 6:5

Notice that one is not "sprinkled" with water, but baptized (immersed) in water. It is symbolic of being buried, so one is taken under the surface of the water. Believers are instructed to be water baptized after they are saved. Water baptism is not one's salvation. However, by obeying Jesus' command to be water baptized, it shows submission to His Lordship in one's life.

Jesus Was Water Baptized

Even Jesus submitted to water baptism, and His obedience was pleasing to the Father:

> "Then came Jesus from Galilee to Jordan unto John, to be baptized of him. But John forbad him, saying, I have need to be baptized of you, and do you come to me? And Jesus answering said unto him, Permit it to be so now: for thus it becomes us to fulfil all righteousness. Then he permitted Him.
>
> **And Jesus, when he was baptized, went up straightway out of the water:** and, lo, the heavens were opened unto him, and he saw the Spirit of God descending like a dove, and lighting upon Him: And lo a voice from heaven, saying, This is **my beloved Son, in whom I am well pleased.**"[168]

Jesus is our example. If He who had no sin was baptized, certainly we should humble ourselves and be baptized. Those who refuse to be water baptized are not submitted to Jesus' Lordship.

Believer's Baptism

---

[168] Matthew 3:13-17

Believers are instructed to be water baptized, and to preach and baptize new believers as well:

> *"Go you therefore, and teach all nations,* ***baptizing them in the name of the Father, and of the Son, and of the Holy Ghost****: Teaching them to observe all things whatsoever I have commanded you: and, lo, I am with you always, even unto the end of the world. Amen."*[169]
>
> *"And he said unto them, Go ye into all the world, and preach the gospel to every creature.* ***He that*** <u>***believes***</u> ***and is baptized shall be saved****; but he that* <u>***believes not***</u> *shall be damned."*[170]

Notice the determination for salvation or damnation is whether or not one *believes,* **not** whether or not one is baptized. Baptism does not save; but a true disciple will follow that ordinance once they are saved. As one preacher put it: "He that **believes not** shall be damned-*baptized or not.*" If one does not have the opportunity to be baptized before they die, they will still go to heaven.

Just do it!

The following example demonstrates that one should be eager to be baptized after salvation:

> *"behold, a man of Ethiopia...was returning, and sitting in his chariot read Esaias the prophet... And Philip...said, Do you understand what you are reading? ...Then Philip opened his mouth, and began at the same scripture, and preached unto him Jesus. And as they*

---

[169] Matthew 28:19
[170] Mark 16:16

*went on their way, they came unto a certain water: and the eunuch said, **See, here is water; what doth hinder me to be baptized?***

*And Philip said, **If you believe with all thine heart, you may**. And he answered and said, I believe that Jesus Christ is the Son of God. And he commanded the chariot to stand still: and they went **down both into the water**, both Philip and the eunuch; and he baptized him… and the Eunuch went his way rejoicing… "[171]*

As Philip said, *"If you believe with all your heart"* you may be water baptized. The Ethiopian Eunuch received the message of salvation through Messiah Jesus and wanted to be baptized as soon as possible.

On the Day of Pentecost Peter preached Jesus to the Jewish pilgrims, and those that gladly received the message were water baptized that very day. [172] We see immediate water baptism is a pattern of the early church. Members of Cornelius' household were saved and water baptized immediately. Lydia and her household were immediately baptized after believing. The Philippian jailer and his household were immediately baptized--in the middle of the night![173]

What Is The Purpose?

What is the purpose of being water baptized following salvation? First, it is obedience to Christ's command. It is a public acknowledgement that one has decided to follow Jesus. Water baptism is also an outward testimony of one's new life in Christ. Through it,

---

[171] Acts 8:35-38
[172] Acts 2:41
[173] Acts 10; 16

we demonstrate symbolically that we are dead to our old life of sin, and are risen to new life in Christ. Water baptism produces a good conscience toward God for the believer. Apostle Peter explains this:

> *"The like figure whereunto even **baptism** does also now save us, (not the putting away of the filth of the flesh, but the answer of **a good conscience toward God,**) by the resurrection of Jesus Christ…"*[174]

The result of a new believer submitting to public water baptism was them obtaining a good conscious. They pleased God by their faith by actively confessing Christ. It is so important that immediate baptism of new believers was normal New Testament practice.

Some try to make an issue of the words that are spoken when one is water baptized. They say you must be *"baptized in the name of Jesus Christ for the remission of sin"* (quoting Peter in Acts 2.) Others say that Jesus commanded us to be baptized in the name of the Father, the Son, and the Holy Ghost (quoting Jesus in Matthew 28).

Both are correct. The reason Peter specified the name of "Jesus" was that the Jews believed in "the Son" (i.e., the Messiah), but not all acknowledged that *Jesus* was the Son. Water baptism does not save you. It is a symbolic act that one does *after they are saved*. So the phraseology is not so important. You can be baptized in the Name of Jesus Christ, in the Name of the Father, Son and Holy Ghost, in the Name of Yeshua… as long as one acknowledges what Jesus did for them when He rose from the dead.

Baptism of Suffering

---

[174] I Peter 3:21

Another baptism that is not commonly taught is the *baptism of sufferings*. Jesus talked about having to undergo a "baptism" as He approached the time of the passion and the Cross:

> *"And James and John, the sons of Zebedee, came unto him, saying...Grant unto us that we may sit, one on your right hand, and the other on your left hand, in your glory. But Jesus said unto them, You do not know what you ask: can you drink of **the cup** that I drink of? and be **baptized with the baptism that I am baptized with?** And they said unto him, We can. And Jesus said unto them, You shall indeed drink of the **cup that I drink of; and with the baptism that I am baptized** withal shall you be baptized: But to sit on my right hand and on my left hand is not mine to give."[175]*

> *"And [Jesus] said unto them, My soul is exceeding sorrowful unto death: tarry you here, and watch. And he went forward a little, and fell on the ground, and prayed that, if it were possible, the hour might pass from him. And he said, Abba, Father, all things are possible unto you; take away **this cup** from me: nevertheless, not what I will, but what you wilt."*

The "cup" and "baptism" that Jesus alluded to was the horrendous suffering He was about to experience. As Jesus declared, both James and John suffered for the Name of Jesus. James was beheaded for Christ, and John was banished to the Isle of Patmos' prison for his testimony of Jesus. They partook of the cup of suffering and were baptized with the baptism of suffering. As Paul testified, we will

---

[175] Mark 10:38, 39; Mark 14:36

experience trials, rejection--and some, even death--as followers of Christ:

> "Wherein **I suffer trouble**, as an evil doer, even unto bonds; but the word of God is not bound. Therefore, I endure all things for the elect's sakes, that they may also obtain the salvation which is in Christ Jesus with eternal glory. It is a faithful saying: For if we be dead with him, we shall also live with him: **If we suffer**, we shall also reign with him: if we deny him, he also will deny us "[176]

Baptism in the Holy Spirit

The final baptism is the baptism in the Holy Spirit. It is essential for every believer. Through the baptism in the Spirit, the gift of power to be Christ's witnesses is received. Though it is available to every believer, it is not automatically received at salvation. This baptism is a subsequent spiritual experience that one can receive after they have been born-again. Many confuse the baptism in the Holy Spirit with water baptism or with being baptized into the Body of Christ (salvation). This promise is different. This baptism is when *Jesus* baptizes believers:

> "John answered, saying unto them all, 'I indeed baptize you with water; but One mightier than I comes, the latchet of Whose shoes I am not worthy to unloose; **He shall baptize you with the Holy Ghost** and with fire.'" (Luke 3:16)

Notice that *Jesus* is the Baptizer with the Holy Spirit. Here **Jesus** submerses believers *in the Holy Spirit* and power is given. This is different from the baptism into the Body of Christ where the **Holy**

---

[176] II Timothy 2:12

Spirit submerses believers *in the Blood of Jesus and salvation is given.* In this subsequent experience Holy Spirit dunamis (dynamite) power is received to witness for Jesus.

Don't Leave Home Without It!

Jesus promised the Baptism in the Spirit to His disciples while He was still on the earth, but the Spirit was not poured out upon them until the day of Pentecost (a week Jesus had ascended to Heaven). This gift of the Holy Spirit was considered so important that Jesus told them not to even leave Jerusalem until they received it. Here are Jesus' instructions to them:

> *"And, behold, I send **the promise of My Father** upon you: but you wait in the city of Jerusalem until you be endued with power from on high."* (Luke 24:49)
> *"And, being assembled together with them, commanded them that they **should not depart** from Jerusalem but '**wait for the promise of the Father**, which,' said He, 'you have heard of Me. For John truly baptized with water; but you shall be **baptized with the Holy Ghost** not many days hence... But **you shall receive POWER**, after that the Holy Ghost is come upon you: and you shall be **witnesses unto Me** both in Jerusalem, and in all Judea, and in Samaria, and unto the uttermost part of the earth.'"* (Acts 1:4,5,8)

The Day of Pentecost

After receiving commandment to wait for the Holy Spirit outpouring in Jerusalem, one hundred and twenty disciples faithfully gathered to pray and wait for the gift. This small number is a sad commentary on the fickleness and unfaithfulness of human nature.

During the forty-day period after the resurrection, Jesus was on earth appearing in bodily form to His disciples. He wanted them to have undeniable proof that He really was raised from the dead, so He appeared to many. During that time a crowd of over five hundred disciples witnessed Jesus appearance AT ONE TIME! They all saw Him in His glorified, resurrected body![177]

So, one would think they would listen when the glorified, eternal God-man gave commandment for them to wait for the Spirit. Less than 25% obeyed. (Pastors, don't be discouraged when your flock doesn't come for mid-week services. Jesus didn't have much better turn-out for His Pentecost revival service!) Those who did obey Jesus waited for the promised Holy Spirit. Here is what transpired that day:

> *"And when the day of Pentecost was fully come, they were all with one accord in one place. And suddenly there came a sound from heaven as of a rushing mighty wind, and it filled all the house where they were sitting. And there appeared unto them cloven tongues like as of fire, and it sat upon each of them. And they were all **<u>filled with the Holy Ghost</u>, and began to speak with other <u>tongues, as the Spirit gave them utterance</u>.* "

> *"And there were dwelling at Jerusalem Jews, devout men, out of every nation under heaven. Now when this was **noised abroad**, the multitude came together, and were confounded, because that every man **heard them speak in his own language**. And they were all amazed and marveled, saying one to another,*

---

[177] I Corinthians 15:6

*Behold, are not all **these which speak Galileans?** And how hear we every man in our own tongue, wherein we were born? Parthians, and Medes, and Elamites... we do hear them speak **in our tongues** the wonderful works of God. And they were all **amazed,** and were in doubt, saying one to another, What does this mean? Others mocking said, These men are full of new wine."*[178]

When the Spirit was poured out upon the disciples, they all spoke in other tongues (unknown to themselves). This phenomenon was predicted by the Prophet Isaiah: *"For with stammering lips and another tongue will he speak to this people. To whom he said, This is the rest wherewith you may cause the weary to rest..."*[179] Speaking in unknown tongues is a spiritual refreshing from God. Being filled with the Holy Spirit with the accompanying gift of speaking in other tongues is the Biblical evidence of receiving the power that Jesus promised.

The Gift of Tongues

This gift of the "baptism in the Holy Ghost" for power is also called being *"filled with the Holy Ghost."* As one is filled to overflowing with the Spirit, speaking in other tongues will manifest. Notice that *they* (the disciples) began speaking as the *"Spirit gave them utterance."* They did the speaking, but the Spirit of God determined what language (utterance) came forth.

The tongues that manifested through the one hundred and twenty disciples when the Spirit of God fell on them were not known to them. These were unlearned Galileans that started to give praise to God in many foreign languages. The foreign Jews who came for the Feast in Jerusalem understood their native languages being spoken, and

---

[178] Acts 2
[179] Isaiah 28:11, 12

recognized something supernatural was happening. According to I Corinthians 13:1, when one speaks in an unknown tongue, it could be a language of men or of angels. The Spirit of God allows believers to speak in a language unknown to themselves. The following are references to supernatural "tongues" by which believers are enabled to speak after they have been "baptized" with the Holy Spirit:

> *"And these signs* [supernatural manifestations of God's power] *shall follow them that believe; In My name shall they cast out devils;* **they shall speak with new tongues...** *"*[180]

Notice that these signs follow "*them that believe.*" Speaking in tongues is for "*believers*", not just for the elite, super spiritual apostles. (Even the carnal Corinthians spoke in tongues!)[181]

> *"And* **they were all** *filled with the Holy Ghost, and began to speak with other tongues, as the Spirit gave them utterance...Therefore being by the right hand of God exalted, and having received of the Father* **the promise of the Holy Ghost**, *He has shed forth this, which you now see and* **hear** [the tongues] *...Then Peter said unto them, 'Repent, and be* [water] *baptized every one of you in the Name of Jesus Christ for the remission of sins, and you shall receive the* **gift of the Holy Ghost**. *For the promise is unto you, and to your children and to all that are afar off, even as many as the Lord our God shall call. "*[182]

---

[180] Mark 16:17
[181] I Corinthians 3:3, 14:23
[182] Acts 2:4, 33, 38, 39

At this initial outpouring, all the believers spoke with tongues. Peter promised the crowd who gathered together to hear it, that the same gift of the Holy Spirit was available to them and future generations. The Holy Spirit baptism was evidenced by the tongues that they could "hear." This baptism is available to all believers. Peter was astonished that God gave it even to the Gentiles.

> *"While Peter yet spoke these words, the **Holy Ghost fell** on all them which heard the word. And they of the circumcision which believed were astonished, as many as came with Peter, because that on the Gentiles also was poured out the **gift of the Holy Ghost: <u>for they heard them speak with tongues</u>**, and magnify God. Then answered Peter, Can any man forbid water, that these should not be baptized, which have **received the Holy Ghost** as well as we? And he commanded them to be baptized in the Name of the Lord."[183]*

Notice in this passage that the **reason** the Jews knew that the Gentiles had received the baptism in the Holy Ghost was because "*they heard them speak with tongues,*" (just as they had when they initially were filled with the Holy Spirit.) When Peter heard them speak in tongues, he recognized that these Gentiles had "*purified their hearts*" by faith in Christ Jesus and had actually been saved.[184] He said, "*God, which knows the hearts, bare them witness, giving them the Holy Ghost, even as He did unto us* [the Jews]." Until then, Peter did not even realize that Gentiles could be saved! Their conversion was confirmed by the fact that they received the gift of the Holy Ghost (the experience only available after one is saved). Peter said, "can any man forbid

---

[183] Acts 10:44-48
[184] Acts 15:8,9

water?" In other words, since these Gentiles are saved, they should be water baptized.

A Gift Received After Salvation

This following example verifies that the Holy Ghost baptism is a gift subsequent to salvation:

> *"Paul having passed through the upper coast come to Ephesus; and finding certain disciples, he said unto them, '**Have you received the Holy Ghost <u>since you believed</u>?**' And they said unto him, 'We have not so much as heard whether there be any Holy Ghost.' And he said unto them, 'Unto what then were you baptized?' And they said, 'Unto John's baptism.' Then said Paul, 'John verily baptized with the baptism of repentance, saying unto the people, that they should believe on Him which should come after him, that is, on Christ Jesus.' When they heard this, **they were baptized in the Name of the Lord Jesus. And when Paul had laid his hands upon them, the Holy Ghost came on them; and they spoke with tongues, and prophesied.**"*[185]

Notice that when Paul approached these disciples, he assumed that they were already believers in the Lord Jesus. He assumed they were <u>believers,</u> but *did not* automatically assume that they had already received the gift of the Holy Spirit: *"Have you received the Holy Spirit since you believed?"* For that to be Paul's first question to these disciples shows that Paul considered the baptism in the Holy Ghost to be of paramount importance in a believer's life.

---

[185] Acts 19:1-6

When the disciples responded that they had never heard of the "Holy Ghost," Paul realized these disciples had not even undergone basic water baptism ("in the Name of the Father, the Son, and the Holy Ghost"). Had they had that standard water baptism, they would have heard of the "Holy Ghost." Realizing their ignorance of the basic Christian water baptism, Paul back-tracked to find out their spiritual experience had been only to participate in John's baptism of repentance. Paul then explained to them that John had simply been a forerunner of the Messiah, and that they should believe on the One that came after John, Christ Jesus. Upon them receiving Christ as their Lord and Savior, Paul water baptized them in the Name of the Lord Jesus (instead of John's baptism). THEN, Paul proceeded to lay his hands upon them so that the gift of the Holy Spirit's power could be imparted, and they spoke with tongues, and prophesied.

This is a clear example of three baptisms in a believer's life: First, upon believing in Christ, one is baptized *by* the Holy Spirit <u>into the Body of Christ</u> (i.e., salvation). Then, they were water baptized as an outward testimony of their conversion. Finally, they received the baptism in the Holy Spirit when Paul laid his hands on them. Clearly, the baptism in the Holy Spirit is a separate gift received subsequent to salvation. That gift of power is essential to every believer to be Christ's witness. That is why Paul's first question to the disciples was, "Have you received the Holy Ghost since you believed?" This is another example in which *all* of the believers prayed for *spoke in unknown tongues* when they received the filling of the Holy Ghost.

Separate From Salvation

Other scriptures clearly demonstrate that the baptism in the Holy Spirit is separate from salvation, and is not *automatically* received at salvation. The following are examples in which significant time elapsed between salvation and believers receiving the gift of the Holy Ghost:

> *"But when they believed Philip preaching the things concerning the kingdom of God, and the Name of Jesus Christ, they were* [water] *baptized, both men and women...Now when the apostles which were at Jerusalem heard that Samaria had received the Word of God, they sent unto them Peter and John: who, when they were come down, prayed for them, **that they might receive the Holy Ghost**: (for as yet He was fallen upon none of them: only they were baptized in the Name of the Lord Jesus.) Then laid they their hands on them, and they received the Holy Ghost."*[186]

We see first that the Samaritans believed and were saved, and were immediately water baptized. The apostles made a special trip some days later to pray for them. The term "fallen upon" is used when the baptism in the Spirit's power is poured out. We know that at salvation, (when one receives Jesus as Lord), that His Spirit indwells the believer, as Romans 8:9 tells us: *"Now if any man have not the Spirit of Christ, he is none of His."* However, believers do not necessarily receive the POWER of the Spirit when they are saved. The power is a subsequent gift. Notice also that the apostles in Jerusalem believed the baptism in the Holy Ghost to be so vital to new believers, that they made a special trip to pray for them to receive the Holy Ghost. This was several days after the Samaritans received Christ. When the apostles arrived and laid hands on them, they received the Holy Ghost. Was this their salvation experience? No. This was a subsequent experience in which the believers received the power of the Holy Ghost.

---

[186] Acts 8:12-17

Paul's Salvation and Baptism

Another example that demonstrates that the baptism in the Holy Spirit is a separate and subsequent experience to salvation is described in Paul's conversion experience in Acts 9:1-18:

> *And as he journeyed, he came near Damascus: and suddenly, there shined round about him a light from heaven: And he fell to the earth, and heard a voice saying unto him, Saul, Saul, why do you persecute me? And he said, Who are you,* **Lord***? And the Lord said, I am Jesus whom you persecute: it is hard for you to kick against the pricks. And he trembling and astonished said, Lord, what will you have me to do? And the Lord said unto him, Arise, and go into the city, and it shall be told you what you must do…"*

> *"And Saul arose from the earth; and when his eyes were opened, he saw no man: but they led him by the hand, and brought him into Damascus. And **he was three days without sight**, and neither did eat nor drink… And Ananias went his way, and entered into the house; and putting his hands on him said,* **Brother Saul,** *the Lord, even Jesus, that appeared to you in the way as you came, has sent me, that* **you might receive your sight, and** **<u>be filled with the Holy Ghost</u>***. And immediately there fell from his eyes as it had been scales: and he received sight forthwith, and arose, and was baptized…And immediately he preached Christ in the synagogues, that he is the Son of God."*

When did Saul (Paul) get saved? On the road to Damascus. It was there that he realized that Jesus was raised from the dead, and he confessed Him as "Lord." (Those are the two prerequisites to being saved.[187]) Saul waited three days in the house until Ananias came to pray for him to receive his sight *and be "filled with the Holy Ghost."* Although the manifestation of speaking in tongues is not specifically described, we know that Paul received tongues, and used them frequently in his ministry: *"I thank my God, I speak with tongues more than you all."*[188]

A Gift For All

The baptism in the Holy Spirit with the evidence of speaking in tongues is an experience that is available to every believer. On the day of Pentecost, Peter explained unknown tongues is a ***"PROMISE is unto you, and to your children, and to all that are afar off, even as many as the Lord our God shall call."*** So, firstly, *all* 120 disciples in the upper room were filled with the Holy Ghost and spoke in tongues. Then Peter promised that all three thousand converts who believed his preaching could also have *"This which you now see and HEAR* [the tongues.]" And not only to those converts was the promise of the Spirit given, but to "your children, and *all* that are afar off... as many as the Lord our God shall call." If one is "called" of God to salvation, the baptism in the Holy Ghost with the evidence of speaking in other tongues is for you.

Baptism In The Spirit Power

The purpose of the baptism in the Holy Spirit is to preach the Gospel of Christ with God's power. Jesus promised, *"You shall receive power after that the Holy Ghost is come upon you: and you shall be witnesses unto Me."*[189] Without God's gift of power, there will not be

---

187 Romans 10:9, 10
188 I Corinthians 14:18
189 Acts 1:8

the supernatural signs accompanying the preaching of the Gospel. Christians are not to be seeking signs in order to believe God's Word. Rather, they are to be demonstrating God's signs to get the attention of unbelievers. When unbelievers see God's power in manifestation, they are much more likely to turn from satan's kingdom to God's. These are the signs that should accompany the preaching of the Word of God:

> *"And He said unto them, 'Go you into all the world, and preach the gospel to every creature. He that believes and is baptized shall be saved; but he that believes not shall be damned. And these signs shall follow them that believe: In **My Name shall they cast out devils**; they shall **speak with new tongues**; they shall **take up serpents**; and if they **drink any deadly thing**, it shall not hurt them; they shall **lay hands on the sick, and they shall recover.**' So then after the Lord had spoken unto them, He was received up into heaven, and sat on the right hand of God. And they went forth and preached everywhere, the Lord working with them, and confirming the Word with signs following. Amen."*
> (Mark 16:15-20)

Jesus wants supernatural signs to accompany the preaching of the Gospel. In fact, He expects even greater manifestations of God's Spirit in believers than He had in His Own ministry! These signs will bring glory to the Father and the Son as they are done in Jesus' name.

> *"Truly, truly, I say unto you, he that believes on Me, **the works that I do shall he do also; and greater works than these shall he do; because I go unto My Father.** And whatsoever you shall ask in My Name, that*

will I do, that the Father may be glorified in the Son."
(John 14:12,13)

After one is baptized in the Holy Spirit, there are nine supernatural gifts of the Spirit (in addition to the praying and speaking in tongues) by which a believer can be endowed:

> *"But the manifestation of the Spirit is given to every man to profit withal. For to one is given **by the Spirit** the **word of wisdom**; to another the **word of knowledge** by the same Spirit; To another **faith** by the same Spirit; to another the **gifts of healing** by the same Spirit; To another the working of **miracles**; to another **prophecy**; to another **discerning of spirits**; to another **various kinds of tongues**; to another the **interpretation of tongues**: But all these work that one and the selfsame Spirit, dividing to every man severally as he will."*

The "word of wisdom" is supernatural understanding of futuristic things that will happen and the wisdom of God on how to do act upon that information. For example, Agabus was told of a future famine, and the church was then instructed to make provisions for it in advance.[190]

The "word of knowledge" is a bit of information given about an existing situation (that you do not know naturally). In one case, Peter was shown that Ananias and his wife were lying about the amount of their offering for the church: *"But Peter said, Ananias, **why has satan filled thine heart to lie to the Holy Ghost, and to keep back part of the price of the land?** ... you hast not lied unto men, but unto God."*

---

[190] Acts 11:28

Ananias died on the spot.[191] The word of knowledge need not be so dramatic. It could be a thought about an ailment someone has that you were not aware of. It is knowledge supernaturally given by God. In the case of a sickness being revealed, you can know that it is God's will for you to pray for that person's healing since God revealed it to you.

Faith is the next gift. It is having supernatural faith to believe for a miracle. Perhaps you will be given faith to cause a storm to cease, or a fig tree to dry up at the roots, as did Jesus.[192]

The next is gifts of healing. Though all believers can lay hands on the sick in Jesus' name and expect the sick to get well, there are specialized "gifts of healing" whereby many healings are frequently manifested. Sometimes one type of healing is more frequent than others.

Miracles can be instantaneous healings, as well as raising the dead and casting out devils. Jesus multiplied bread and fishes. Miracles are supernatural signs of God's mighty power and compassion to meet the need of His people. True miracles are not frivolous side-shows of signs.

The gift of prophecy is a supernatural unction to speak forth the Word of the Lord to encourage, edify, and comfort God's people. This is the basic gift of prophecy. One in the office of a prophet (such as Agabus) can be given futuristic revelations as well. Prophecy should always be *tested.* If a "prophet" prophesies something and it doesn't happen, they are liars. Everything spiritual that is said or done must be tested and agree with the Word of God. No one can say "Jesus is Lord"

---

[191] Acts 5
[192] Mark 4, Mark 11

but by the Holy Ghost. Those who say Jesus is accursed is not of God.[193]

The next gift is "discerning of spirits." This is recognizing what spirit is manifesting (Holy Spirit, man's spirit, demon spirit, angelic spirit.) Peter discerned a wrong spirit in Simon, a new believer who wanted to buy the power of the Holy Ghost. Peter said, "You are in the gall of bitterness... your spirit is not right within you." Even believers can have wrong spirits.[194]

Apostle Paul gave guidelines on how to differentiate between God's Spirit and a false spirit: *"...no man speaking by the Spirit of God calls Jesus accursed: and no man can say that Jesus is Lord but by the Holy Ghost."* The Spirit of God will confess Jesus is Lord, and that He is God in the flesh. God's Spirit always exalts Jesus and never contradicts the Holy Bible! The spirit of error exalts people, experiences, or religious institutions instead. God's Spirit will manifest love, joy, peace, patience, kindness, goodness, meekness, faith, and self-control. (I Corinthians 12:3)

Then is "divers kinds of tongues." These are various supernatural languages by which a believer can speak out a message in tongues in the congregation. This is not just a believer receiving the gift of tongues by which he can pray to and worship God. This is a supernatural **message from God** to the church. This gift of divers tongues must be interpreted in Church. The gift of *interpretation of tongues* is used with the gift of tongues to let the Body of Christ know what the message from God is to the church in a language that they can understand.

---

[193] I Corinthians 12:3
[194] Acts 8

All of the gifts are still valid for the church today. The book of Acts should be our handbook for effective Christian living and service. The early church "turned the world upside down" by manifesting God's power with signs and wonders. In Acts three thousand were saved after witnessing supernatural tongues and hearing the Gospel. A lame man was healed in Jesus' name and five thousand were saved as a result.[195] Because of the many signs and wonders being done multitudes (even entire cities) were brought to Christ.[196]

Paul tells us that preaching the Gospel should have power signs following: *"And my speech and my preaching was not with enticing words of man's wisdom, but in demonstration of the Spirit and of power; that your faith should not stand in the wisdom of men, but in the power of God."[197]* The power that one receives through being baptized in the Holy Spirit is what makes one an effective witness for Christ.

Be Filled (Always) With The Spirit

When one is baptized in the Spirit they are filled with the Holy Spirit to overflowing. However, it is necessary for the believer to stay filled with the Spirit. Being refilled with the Spirit should be an ongoing event in the believer's life. Living in this world can drain us spiritually, so we need constant refreshing by the Spirit. The very disciples who were initially filled with the Holy Spirit in Acts 2:1-4, were again filled by the Holy Ghost in Acts 4:29-31. By abiding in Christ through reading the Word, worship, and prayer, we can maintain the state of being "filled" with the Spirit. This will result in enabling us to speak the Word of God with boldness. We are admonished in Ephesians 5:18, 19 to stay filled with the Spirit:

---

[195] Acts 3
[196] Acts 5, 6, 8, 28
[197] I Corinthians 2:4

*"and be not drunk with wine, wherein is excess;
but **be filled** with the Spirit; speaking to yourselves in
psalms and hymns and **spiritual songs**, singing and
making melody in your heart to the Lord."*

The admonition "be filled" means to maintain a continual state of
overflowing with the Spirit. This is done by worship (singing Psalms
and hymns and spiritual songs.) "Spiritual songs" is also called
"singing in the Spirit." It is defined in I Corinthians 14:14,15:

*"For if I pray in an **<u>unknown tongue, my spirit
prays</u>**, but my understanding is unfruitful. What should
I do then? I will **pray with the spirit**, and I will pray with
the understanding also; I will **<u>sing with the spirit</u>, and I
will sing with the understanding also."***

As defined by God's Word, **praying in tongues is praying "in
the spirit;" singing in tongues is singing in the spirit.** So spiritual
prayers or spiritual songs are to be understood as those done in an
<u>unknown tongue</u> (as opposed to those in which one understands the
language). The Word of God teaches us to do *both* in order to stay filled
with the Holy Ghost. In fact, Jesus says that God covets such worship
from His children:

*"But the hour cometh, and now is, when the true
worshipers shall worship the Father in spirit and in
truth: for the Father seeks such to worship Him. God is
a Spirit: and they that worship Him must **worship Him
in spirit** and in truth."* (John 4:23, 24)

*"Let the word of Christ dwell in you richly in all
wisdom; teaching and admonishing one another in*

*psalm and hymns and **spiritual songs,** singing with grace in your hearts to the Lord."* (Colossians 3:16)

Praying In The Spirit

In addition to singing in the spirit, we are instructed to *pray in the spirit* [tongues].[198] Jude 20 and 21 expounds on the benefits of praying in the spirit: *"But you, beloved, building up yourselves on your most **holy faith, <u>praying in the Holy Ghost,</u> keep yourselves in the love of God..."* Praying in tongues builds your faith and keeps you in God's love.

Praying in the spirit is a powerful weapon in our spiritual warfare arsenal. Ephesians 6:11-18 details the armor of God that believers must utilize in order to stand against the wiles of the enemy. It concludes with this element of the armor: *"...and having done ALL, to stand.... Praying always with all prayer and supplication **IN THE SPIRIT**..."* In spiritual warfare, one cannot use natural weapons. Praying in the spirit is a powerful, supernatural weapon because Holy Spirit prayers cannot be intercepted by the devil. It brings the enemy's devices to naught.

Romans 8:26-28 states that the Holy Spirit intercedes for us when we do not have the knowledge to pray for situations as we ought to:

> *"Likewise the Spirit also helps our infirmities: for we know not what we should pray for as we ought: but **the Spirit itself makes intercession for us** with groanings which cannot be uttered. And he that searches the hearts knows what is the mind of the Spirit, because **he makes intercession for the saints according***

---

[198] I Corinthians 14:14, 15

to the will of God. And we know that all things work together for good to them that love God, to them who are the called according to his purpose."

Yielding to the Holy Spirit so that He can pray through us (in supernatural unknown tongues) allows Him to pray God's perfect will in our lives. As a result of this supernatural intercession of the Spirit through us, God can make everything work out for us according to His purpose. Being filled with the Holy Spirit allows for the Perfect Teacher and Comforter to abide within in a greater measure. (John 14:26) As we are filled with and submit to the Holy Spirit, He can then lead and guide us into all truth. A benefit of staying filled with the Spirit is the refreshing one receives from Him on a continual basis. The Apostle Paul acknowledged the benefits of praying in the Holy Ghost and stated: "I thank my God I speak in tongues more than you all." (I Corinthians 14:18)

Common Questions Regarding Holy Spirit Baptism

These are common questions regarding the Holy Spirit baptism:

1.) **Why is tongues the sign of initially being filled with the Spirit?** God sovereignly ordained it as such, as the previous scriptures indicate. It could have to do with the fact that our tongue is considered to be the most "unruly" member of the body. (See James 3:1-10.) When we are willing to submit that most unruly member of the body to the Holy Spirit, and allow Him to form the "utterances" according to His will [rather than our own intellect and understanding], then we have fully submitted to Him. As every member of our being is yielded to the Holy Ghost, we are truly filled, or "baptized" in the Spirit.

2.) **Didn't tongues pass away with the 1st Century Church?**
Have prophecy and knowledge of God passed away yet? No.
Tongues will not be necessary when we are in heaven and *"see
Him face to face"* and *"know, even as we are known."* (I Cor.
13:8-12; I John 3:2) But, until then, tongues are a very
beneficial way in which to worship God and with which to
intercede. (See John 4:23, 24; Ephesians 5:19, 6:18; Romans
8:26-28.) The fact that some have not received this gift does
not mean it is no longer available to the Church. Tongues did
not pass away with the 1st Century Church, but continues to
be available to *"you, your children, and to all that are afar off,
even **as many as the Lord our God shall call**."* (Acts 2:39)

3.) **Isn't tongues only given to some in the Church?** (citing I
Corinthians 12:8-10) The GIFT of tongues (one of the nine
supernatural manifestations of the Holy Spirit) is a special gift
given only to *some* in the Church. This gift is manifested only
as the Spirit wills in a corporate Church setting and must be
accompanied with an interpretation of tongues, to be used
properly. Whereas the tongues received in the baptism in the
Spirit is to praise and worship and pray <u>to God</u> with, the gift of
divers tongues is a special <u>message *from God*</u> <u>to the Church</u>.
Where the gift of tongues operates only *"as the Spirit wills"*,
one's personal prayer language tongues can be used at will in
prayer and worship. (See I Corinthians 14:14, 15.) Though the
gift of divers tongues is given only to "some" in the Church,
the Baptism in the Spirit tongues is available "to as many as
the Lord our God shall call." On Pentecost, all spoke in
tongues as an evidence they were filled (Acts 2:4). Likewise,
all in Cornelius' house spoke in tongues when baptized with
the Holy Spirit. (Acts 10:44-46) Again, the Ephesians all
spoke in tongues when they were filled with the Spirit. (Acts

19:5-7) This is the unknown tongue by which we can sing and pray in the Spirit. The nine supernatural gifts of the Holy Spirit are available to the believer once he has been baptized in the Holy Spirit. The gift(s) assigned to the believer by the Holy Spirit may be the gift of divers tongues, or may be any of the other eight gifts, or any combination thereof. (I Corinthians 12:8-10)

4.) Didn't Paul teach against speaking in tongues in Church?
Not at all. He said, "Forbid not to speak with tongues…"
What Paul did correct was the misuse of tongues in a public service. The entire emphasis in I Corinthians 14 was to correct imbalances that caused confusion in the Church. Paul stressed that the purpose of the gifts of the Spirit is to edify and build up each other in the Body of Christ (i.e., "the Church" -I Corinthians 14:33, 14:12). The overly zealous Corinthians had gone to extremes with speaking in unknown tongues, and did so almost to the exclusion of any other facet of worship. It was so extreme that those unlearned, or unbelievers who came into the Church would consider them to be mad (vs. 23), not understanding anything that was being spoken in the service. Paul had to admonish them to incorporate into the Church service BOTH praying in tongues and praying with the understanding; singing in tongues and singing with the understanding (vss. 14, 15). He then also encouraged the implementation of other aspects of worship, including psalms, teachings, revelation, and interpretation of tongues (vss. 23-26).

Paul knew the power of praying much in the Holy Ghost, and said that he did so more than even the very zealous

Corinthians (vs.18). However, he was trying to emphasize that in Church we should not just be trying to build ourselves up, but we should want to edify and encourage others (vss. 5, 17). He stated that if he had to choose between encouraging himself in tongues, or edifying others in Church, he would prefer to speak in a language others understood in order to edify them (vs. 19).

But, he was not saying one should exclude tongues, and he was in no way demeaning them. In fact, he encouraged the use of tongues (both the prayer and worship language and the gift of a message in tongues) in the Church: *"I would that you all spoke with tongues, but rather that you prophesied: for greater* [for the purpose of edifying the Church] *is he that prophesies than he that speaks with tongues* [the gift of divers tongues], *except he interprets* [in which case it is equal to prophecy] *that the Church may receive edifying."* (I Corinthians 14:5) *What should I do then? I will **pray with the spirit*** [in tongues] *AND I will pray with the understanding also; I will **sing with the spirit**, AND I will sing with the understanding also. Else, when you shalt bless with the spirit* [exclusively], *how shall he that occupies the room of the unlearned say "Amen" at your giving of thanks, seeing he understands not what you say? For you truly give thanks well* [in tongues], *but the other is not edified. I thank my God I speak with tongues more than you all.* (I Corinthians 14:15-18) *What should we do then, brethren? **When you come together (gathered in church)**, let everyone have a psalm, doctrine, **A TONGUE**... Wherefore, brethren, covet to prophesy, and **forbid not to speak with tongues**."*[199]

---

[199] I Corinthians 14:26, 39

All of this encouragement for the use of tongues is in the context of "when you come together, brethren," (when the believers gathered for Church). Obviously, tongues are not only for private use, but also have a place when the corporate Body comes together to worship.

How To Receive The Baptism In The Holy Spirit

How does one receive the baptism in the Holy Ghost? First of all, there must be a desire to receive it. Matthew 5:6 states that if one *"hungers and thirsts after righteousness, they shall be filled."* (Matt.5:6) God promised the Holy Ghost *"to them that obey Him."* (Acts 5:32) We cannot merit any of God's gifts by our own righteousness. We receive the Spirit *"by the hearing of faith,"* (Galatians 3:2.) It is a gift (unearned blessing) received by faith, just like salvation. If one is aware of an area of disobedience, repentance and confession to God is in order: *"If we confess our sins, He is righteous and just to forgive us our sins and to cleanse us from all unrighteousness."* (I John 1:9) We then can approach the throne of grace boldly and make our petitions known unto God. Then, it is simply a matter of asking the Father.

Luke 11:9-13 states *"If you then, being evil, know how to give good gifts unto your children, **how much more shall your heavenly Father give the Holy Spirit to them that ask him.**"* We need to ask the Father in faith, knowing it is His will for us to be filled with His Spirit: *"Be not drunk with wine, wherein is excess, but **be filled with the spirit.**"* (Ephesians 5:18) Jesus said, *"What things so ever you desire when you pray, believe you receive them, and you shall have them."* (Mark 11:24) You may want other Spirit-filled believers to pray with you, as they did in Acts 9:17, 8:17, and 19:6. God tells us in Psalm 81:10 *"I am the Lord your God ...Open your mouth wide and I will fill it."* Ask the Father and receive that Good Gift He has promised!

LAYING ON OF HANDS

One of the most overlooked principles of the Word of God is "The Laying On of Hands." This fourth foundational teaching of the Christian faith is often relegated to being simply a symbolic, liturgical ritual with little bearing on one's spiritual life. However, the Bible teaches there is great significance in the laying on of hands. Four major purposes for this principle are: To impart blessings; to transfer authority; for the baptism in the Holy Spirit; and for healing. By acquainting ourselves with these purposes of the laying on of hands we can have a scriptural basis for receiving the benefits of it, and an understanding of how to avoid its possible misuse.

The first purpose for the laying on of hands it to impart a blessing. The Jewish culture places great importance on the act of imparting a blessing. If one visits Israel today, it is not uncommon to see Bar Mitzvah celebrations taking place on the streets of Jerusalem. A solemn part of the ceremony is when the father and mother lay their hands upon the young man's head and speak over him a blessing as the shofar is blown.

With good reason they consider the laying on of hands as very significant. Throughout Hebrew scripture are many examples of blessings imparted, that have affected the Jews for thousands of years. The goodness enjoyed by Jewish people today can arguably be attributed to the Abrahamic covenant blessing that was transferred by laying on of hands. It was an irrevocable blessing from Abraham to Isaac, and Isaac to Jacob.

Bless *Me!*

In the following account in Genesis 27 we see that Isaac wants to transfer the blessing of Abraham to his offspring. It was traditional for the firstborn to get the prominent blessing. His sons Esau and Jacob were twins, but Esau was born moments before Jacob, and therefore was the heir apparent of the better blessing. Esau, however, had little regard for the birthright blessing and had sold it to Jacob some years before for a bowl of soup! Therefore, when Isaac wanted to give his favorite son, Esau, the blessing, Jacob felt justified in deceiving his father into blessing him instead. With the assistance of his mother, Rebekah, Jacob impersonated his brother, Esau:

> *"And it came to pass, that when Isaac was old, and his eyes were dim, so that he could not see, he called Esau his eldest son, and said unto him, My son: ... Behold now, I am old, I know not the day of my death: Now therefore take...thy quiver and thy bow, and go out to the field, and take me some venison; And make me savory meat, such as I love, and bring it to me, that I may eat; that my soul may bless thee before I die."*

Jacob came to Isaac dressed in Esau's clothes, with animal skins on his arms to simulate Esau's hairy arms. The deception worked. Isaac believed Jacob was his firstborn, and gave him the blessing that he intended for Esau:

> *"And [Jacob] came unto his father, and said, My father: and he said, Here am I; who art thou, my son? And Jacob said unto his father, I am Esau thy firstborn... and [Isaac] smelled the smell of his raiment, and blessed him, and said, 'See, the smell of my son is as the smell of a field which the LORD hath blessed: Therefore, God give thee of the dew of heaven, and the fatness of the earth, and plenty of corn and wine: Let people serve thee, and nations bow down to thee: be*

*lord over thy brethren, and let thy mother's sons bow
down to thee: cursed be every one that curses you, and
blessed be he that blesses you.'"*

After Jacob left Isaac's presence with the blessing, Esau came to Isaac (not knowing that his father had just transmitted the firstborn blessing to Jacob). When Isaac realized that he had laid his hands on the wrong son (mistakenly blessing Jacob instead of Esau), he could not take it back. The blessing had already been transferred through laying on of hands. It was irrevocable even though Jacob received it by deceit. Isaac apologized, but had to give Esau a lesser blessing:

*"I have blessed Jacob... yes, and he shall be
blessed. And when Esau heard the words of his father,
he cried with a great and exceeding bitter cry, and said
unto his father, Bless me, even me also, O my father.
And Isaac said, Your brother came with subtlety, and
hath taken away thy blessing."[200]*

The amazing thing about this incident is that, because Jacob personally had Isaac's hands laid on him, the blessing was imparted to him forever—even though he was not the intended recipient! There is another story very similar in which Jacob (many years later) transferred his blessing to two of his grandchildren. He placed his right hand upon the grandson for whom he wanted to bestow the greater blessing, and his left hand on the one to receive a lesser blessing.[201] Not only is the blessing transferred by laying on of hands, but the right hand can bestow a better blessing!

---

[200] Genesis 27
[201] Genesis 48

Jesus Loves The Little Children

Jesus also laid His hands on people in order that they might receive His blessings:

> *"Then were there brought unto him little children, that he should put his hands on them, and pray: and the disciples rebuked them. But Jesus said, Allow the little children, and forbid them not, to come unto me: for of such is the kingdom of heaven.* ***And he laid his hands on them****, and departed thence."*[202]

Jesus wanted the children to be brought to Him so that He could personally lay His hands on them to bless them. Amazing... The God of the universe reaching out to little children in love to bless them! This was not a symbolic ritual, but an actual transfer of blessings through Jesus' hands! Blessings can transfer by the laying on of hands when we gather in Jesus' name.[203]

Authority And Gifts

Another purpose for the laying on of hands is to transfer spiritual authority and gifts. This occurs when one is ordained for a position or calling by elders or the presbyters. The act of laying hands on the one being ordained for service is how God ordained for the spiritual gifts and authority to transfer. An example of this was when Moses approached the time of his death, God instructed him to transfer authority and wisdom to lead God's people to his successor, Joshua:

> *"And the LORD said unto Moses, Take to yourself Joshua the son of Nun, a man in whom is the spirit, and **lay thine hand upon him;** And set him before*

---

[202] Matthew 19:13-15
[203] Matthew 18:20

Eleazar the priest, and before all the congregation; and give him a charge in their sight. And thou shalt put some of thine honor upon him, that all the congregation of the children of Israel may be obedient... And Moses did as the LORD commanded him: and he took Joshua... And he laid his hands upon him, and gave him a charge, as the LORD commanded by the hand of Moses. "[204]

After Moses obeyed God and laid his hands upon Joshua, he received authority and wisdom: *"And **Joshua the son of Nun was full of the spirit of wisdom; FOR Moses had laid his hands upon him**: and the children of Israel hearkened unto him, and did as the LORD commanded Moses."*[205] Had Moses not laid hands on Joshua, God's wisdom would not have transferred.

Ordain Church Leaders

Those serving in church leadership, including deacons, should have hands laid upon them by the elders before being set in office. The function of deacons was to distribute provisions and food to needy church members. Though their primary function was logistical help (versus spiritual service in the church), the office still required the spiritual blessing of the elders:

"And in those days, when the number of the disciples was multiplied, there arose a murmuring of the Grecians against the Hebrews, because their widows were neglected in the daily ministration. Then the twelve called the multitude of the disciples unto them, and said, It is not reason that we should leave the word

---

[204] Numbers 27:23
[205] Deuteronomy 34:9

of God, and serve tables. Wherefore, brethren, look ye out among you seven men of honest report, full of the Holy Ghost and wisdom, whom we may appoint over this business. But we will give ourselves continually to prayer, and to the ministry of the word."[206]

A couple of points here about the ministry of deacons. Their purpose was to free pastors and leaders to seek God... not to be entangled with the affairs of day to day business. It was not so that they could get more time in at the golf course. Pastors who have to do all the hands-on work at a church are being robbed of precious time they need to seek God on behalf of the people. The church should "step up to the plate" and volunteer help--even without a paycheck.

Notice also that the deacons were not chosen because they donated the most to the church, or because they were a founding member. They were chosen because they were filled with the Holy Ghost and wisdom. In dealing with "church" people it takes supernatural wisdom!

*"And the saying pleased the whole multitude: and they chose Stephen, a man full of faith and of the Holy Ghost, and Philip, and Prochorus, and Nicanor, and Timon, and Parmenas, and Nicolas a proselyte of Antioch: Whom they set before the apostles: and **when they had prayed, they laid their hands on them.** And the word of God increased; and **the number of the disciples multiplied in Jerusalem greatly;** and a great company of the priests were obedient to the faith. And Stephen, full of faith and power, did great wonders and miracles among the people."*

---

[206] Acts 6

Because deacons effectively did their work, church increased greatly. Notice after the laying on of hands that Stephen started having "great wonders and miracles" like the apostles. One often partakes of the spiritual gifts of another when hands for anointing for service are laid upon them.

Lay Hands To Send Out For Ministry

"Now there were in the church that was at Antioch certain prophets and teachers... the Holy Ghost said, Separate me Barnabas and Saul for the work whereunto I have called them. And when they had fasted and prayed, and laid their hands on them, they sent them away."[207]

One important point here is that before the laying on of hands, these men already knew they had a mission from God. You do not need a prophecy to tell you your calling. God will have already put it in your heart. The prophecy simply confirms it. Another point is that though they were called, they waited for the God-ordained leadership to lay hands on them and to send them out.

Timothy's Gifts And Callings

Timothy was the Apostle Paul's spiritual son. He mentored Timothy and was part of the presbytery (i.e., group of elders) by which Timothy was ordained. Paul said Timothy had a gift in him *"which was given thee by prophecy, with the laying on of the hands of the presbytery."*[208]

Paul admonished Timothy to *"stir up the gift of God, which is in thee*

---

[207] Acts 13:3
[208] I Timothy 44

**by the putting on of my hands.** _"[209]_ Spiritual gifts can be transferred by the laying on of hands. Because spiritual transfer through the laying on of hands is real, Paul warns Timothy to lay hands suddenly on no one. In other words, do not give your spiritual blessing to anyone unless they are proven in character. There are too many people with "gifts" and no fruit. You do not want to lend approval to those whom God has not approved by laying hands on them prematurely. Those ordained to ministry should have a proven track record of Godly living and scriptural soundness.[210]

Touch Not!

Conversely, one should not be hasty to have just *anyone* lay hands on them. They could be involved in sexual sin or perversion, and you do not want to inadvertently receive a *bad* spirit from someone you do not know. Test all things; hold to that which is good. Today some irreverently incorporate "prayer tunnels" into their services. They have two lines of people between which the rest of the congregation passes through. Hands are indiscriminately laid on those who go through the prayer tunnel, and spiritual "impartations" are received. Impartations indeed! Impartations of a Kundalini spirit (demonic Hindu god), lust spirit, or whatever spirit those people may have who are allowed to lay hands on others.

The Baptism In The Spirit

Though there are instances in the New Testament where the Spirit of God was sovereignly poured out without using a human instrument, there are a number of examples where the laying on of hands is specifically used in order to impart the Baptism in the Holy Spirit:

---

[209] II Timothy 1:6
[210] I Timothy 3:10

*"Now when the apostles which were at Jerusalem heard that Samaria had received the word of God, they sent unto them Peter and John: Who, when they were come down, prayed for them, that they might receive the Holy Ghost: (For as yet he was fallen upon none of them: only they were baptized in the name of the Lord Jesus.) Then **laid they their hands on them, and they received the Holy Ghost**...when Simon saw that **through laying on of the apostles' hands the Holy Ghost was given**...* "[211]

Paul the Apostle received the Baptism in the Spirit's infilling in this manner as well:

*"And Ananias went his way, and entered into the house; and **putting his hands on him** said, Brother Saul, the Lord, even Jesus, that appeared unto you in the way as you came, hash sent me, **that you might receive thy sight, and be filled with the Holy Ghost.** "*

Jesus could have filled Paul on the Road to Damascus with the Holy Spirit when He sovereignly revealed Himself to Paul. Why did He mandate that Paul wait until a believer in Christ laid hands on him? Perhaps He wanted the Christians to know that Paul truly been converted (as witnessed by one of the believers who formerly was afraid of Paul). But it could also be that the Lord wanted Paul to know that he was not independent of the rest of the Body of Christ. Even though Paul had a mighty revelation of Jesus at salvation and in the subsequent years following in which Jesus mentored him, he still was only one part of the Body of Christ. Regardless of how high a calling

---

[211] Acts 8:15-17

one may have from the Lord, they must recognize that they are not a spiritual island. We need to submit to other members of the Body to partake and benefit from their gifts.

Another example of believers receiving the Baptism in the Spirit were the new disciples in Ephesus: *"**when Paul had laid his hands upon them, the Holy Ghost came on them**; and they spoke with tongues, and prophesied."*[212] So there is definite scriptural precedence for elders laying hands on believers to receive the Baptism in the Holy Spirit.

Healing Hands

Jesus ministry was marked with compassion as He personally reached out to others with healing hands. In fact, one of His titles is called "The Arm of the Lord" who brings salvation and deliverance. Many saw that healing was transferred through the laying on of His hands and so they often would request that Jesus personally come to where the sick were to touch and pray:

*"there came one of the rulers of the synagogue, Jairus by name; and when he saw Him, he fell at His feet, And besought Him greatly, saying, My little daughter lies at the point of death: I pray that you will **come and lay your hands on her, that she may be healed;** and she shall live...Then certain said, Your daughter is dead: why do you trouble the Master any further? As soon as Jesus heard the word that was spoken, He said to the ruler of the synagogue, Be not afraid, only believe...And **He took the damsel by the hand,** and said unto her, Damsel, I say to you, arise.*

---

[212] Acts 19:6

And straightway the damsel arose, and walked; for she was of the age of twelve years. And they were astonished with a great astonishment."[213]

Many were amazed at the power Jesus had when He laid hands on the sick: "*...many hearing Him were astonished, saying, From where has this man these things? and what wisdom is this which is given unto Him, that even such **mighty works are wrought by his hands**?*" "*Now when the sun was setting, all they that had any sick with divers diseases brought them unto Him; and **He laid his hands on every one of them, and healed them**.*"[214]

Sometimes Jesus laid hands on the sick more than once to effect a full healing, such as was the case with the blind man:

"*...and they bring a blind man unto Jesus, and besought Him to touch him. And He took the blind man by the hand, and led him out of the town; and when He had spit on his eyes, and **put His hands upon him**, He asked him if he saw ought. And he looked up, and said, I see men as trees, walking. After that He **put His hands again upon his eyes**, and made him look up: and he was restored, and saw every man clearly.*"[215]

Here we note that Jesus prayed twice for an affliction to leave, both times laying hands on the recipient of the miracle. That is a good pattern for obtaining healing. It did not mean that Jesus did not have adequate faith the first time He prayed. If a partial healing manifests when one is prayed for, it is not wrong to lay hands and pray again until the healing fully manifests.

---

[213] Mark 5:23
[214] Mark 6:2-5, Luke 4:40
[215] Mark 8:22-25

Healing In The Church

God prescribed a method of healing for believers in a local church in the epistle of James. It includes an act of obedient faith of the believer ("call for the elders"), and for elders to pray:

> *"Is any sick among you? let him call for the elders of the church; and let them pray over him, **anointing him with oil** in the name of the Lord: And the prayer of faith shall save the sick, and the Lord shall raise him up; and if he has committed sins, they shall be forgiven him. Confess your faults one to another, and pray one for another, that ye may be healed. The effectual fervent prayer of a righteous man avails much.* "[216]

We see here that it is the prayer of faith that heals the sick, however God prescribed by the Apostle James that the elders were to be called to anoint the sick with oil in the Name of the Lord. First, we must recognize what name has the power. That is the Name of Jesus! As Peter said in Acts 3, *"by His name [Jesus], and faith in His name, was this man made whole."* Faith in Jesus' name, the Name above every name, saves, heals and delivers. But it is noteworthy that the physical touch by the elders anointing the sick with oil is also involved. Perhaps it is necessary because when one is sick their faith is often weak, and the tangible prayer support of the elders is required. Whatever the rationale, it is one way God ordained for the sick to be healed in church.

Apostles' Hands

The early church spread the Gospel by preaching the Word with signs following, including healings. That is still the mandate of the

---

[216] James 5:14-16

church today. The book of Acts gives many examples of believers laying hands on the sick for healing. Acts 5:12 states that *"**by the hands** of the apostles were many signs and wonders wrought among the people..."* And Acts 14 says, *"Long time therefore abode they speaking boldly in the Lord, which gave testimony unto the word of his grace, and granted signs and wonders to be done **by their hands.*** In Acts 19 and 28 *"**by the hands** of the Apostle Paul"* many miracles were wrought, including healing a family member of the island's most prominent man.

Healing By The Church

The ministry of healing by the laying on of hands is not limited to just the Apostles and elders of the church. All believers in Jesus are also commissioned to *"lay hands on the sick"*:

> *"And He said unto them, Go ye into all the world, and preach the gospel to every creature... And these signs shall follow them that believe; **In My name... they shall lay hands on the sick, and they shall recover...** And they went forth, and preached everywhere, the Lord working with them, and confirming the word with signs following."*[217]

Healing through the laying on of hands in Jesus' name is a sign that should follow all believers as they preach the Gospel. It is one way in which God confirms the Word that is preached. What is inferred here is that when one preaches the Gospel, it should include the fact that Jesus still heals... that He is *"the same yesterday, today, and forever."* Healing is one of the benefits that Jesus purchased with His redemption on the Cross. Obviously, our soul's salvation is paramount,

---

[217] Mark 16:15-20

but as Psalm 103 tells us, we should not forget that He also heals *all* our diseases: *"forget not all His benefits; Who forgives all your iniquities, Who heals all your diseases..."* When preaching the Gospel (the "Good News") we need to include the fact that Jesus purchased healing as well as forgiveness of sin. God then confirms His Word with attesting healing signs. Perhaps God ordained healing to be administered through the laying on of hands in Jesus' name was to ensure that the recipient acknowledges who is the Healer: *"I am the Lord that heals you."*

Healing Part Of The Covenant

Healing is an integral part of the New Covenant. The term "salvation" that we normally associate with the forgiveness of sin for the soul is a term that encompasses a very broad scope of "salvation." In the Greek it means "deliverance, preservation, salvation, safety, and health."[218] When Jesus took thirty-nine stripes on His back *before* the Cross, it was specifically to purchase our healing: "Who His own self bore our sins in His own body on the tree, that we being dead unto sin should live unto righteousness, *by Whose stripes we were healed."[219]* His Blood has redeemed us and purchased our salvation, and the stripes on His back were to purchase our healing. Jesus' salvation is complete redemption: body, mind, and spirit.

When one becomes part of the Body of Christ through faith in Jesus, they are heirs of all of God's blessings: *"For all of the promises of God in Him [in Jesus] are 'yes' and 'amen' unto the glory of God by us."[220]* The New Testament abounds with examples of God's willingness to heal and Jesus' admonition for us to receive healing *"according to your faith..."* That healing is God's will is not in

---

[218] Vine, An Expository Dictionary, 316
[219] II Peter 2:24
[220] II Corinthians 2:20

dispute, for the Apostle John (writing by the inspiration of the Holy Spirit) said: *"Beloved above all things I would that you prosper and **be in health**, even as your soul prospers."* The contingency is that our soul should prosper. Assuming that is the case, we can know that it is God's will for us to be healed. When we pray, we can pray in faith believing as we meditate on God's promises to heal us. The following are some of His promises for us:

HEALING SCRIPTURES:

- Deuteronomy 7:15 *"And the LORD will **take away from you all sickness**, and will put none of the evil diseases of Egypt, which you know, upon you…"* All means all.

- Psalm 91:10: *"There shall no evil befall you, neither shall **any plague** come nigh your dwelling. For He shall give His angels charge over you, to keep you in all your ways."* We see that plagues (including diseases) are considered "evil." We know that our Heavenly Father is the giver of every good and perfect gift.[221] Sickness is not of God.

- Psalm 103:1-3: *"Bless the LORD, O my soul: and all that is within me, bless his holy name. Bless the LORD, O my soul, and forget not all his benefits: Who forgives all thine iniquities; **who heals all your diseases**."* God heals *all* our diseases. That is pretty comprehensive health coverage. And thank God, the premium has been PAID IN FULL!

- Proverbs 4:20-22: *"My son, attend to My words; incline thine ear unto my sayings. Let them not depart from thine eyes; keep them in the midst of thine heart. For they are life unto*

---

[221] James 1:17

*those that find them, and **health to all their flesh**.* " Reading and meditating on God's Word cleanses our spirit, but also brings physical health to us. Often the two go hand-in-hand. Jesus said to the crippled man after healing him, *"You are made whole; sin no more lest a worse thing come upon you."*[222] We can receive healing, but are subject to getting even more sick if we open ourselves to the sin of fear, unbelief, bitterness, or a lascivious lifestyle. Unforgiveness is a deadly weapon the enemy uses against saint and sinner alike. As it tells us in Hebrews 12:15, a root of bitterness can spring up and defile many. We must be on guard against the sins of the heart!

- Isaiah 53:4 *"Surely he has borne our **griefs** (**diseases**), and carried our **sorrows** (**pains**): yet we did esteem him stricken, smitten of God, and afflicted. But he was wounded for our transgressions, he was bruised for our iniquities: the chastisement of our peace was upon him; and **with his stripes we are healed**.* " Such a magnificent price the King of Kings paid for our redemption! He was physically wounded to pay for our sins AND to purchase our healing. Let us not doubt His goodness and willingness to extend healing to us today. Today is the day of salvation,[223] which includes healing!

- Jeremiah 30:17 *"For I will restore **health** unto you, and I will heal you of your **wounds**, said the LORD…"* Here God declares clearly that He will restore our health. What a promise! And it is ours if we are in Christ Jesus! Healing, however, is not only for *physical* wounds, but also for those emotional and mental wounds that have been inflicted upon

---

[222] John 5:14
[223] II Corinthians 6:2

our souls. Often times physical ailments are a direct result of having emotional wounds, or soul wounds. Stress in our mind and heart can cause a broad array of physical and mental issues… migraines, heart disease, high blood pressure. The root of the sickness may be an emotional wound. Those harsh words that may have been spoken by an angry adult when you were just a child imbed in the heart. Emotional wounds do not heal up like the scraped knee from the playground. It takes the soothing healing of the Balm of Gilead to be applied to the heart to remedy those wounds. That balm is the realization of God's great love for us. It alone can heal the wounds that have been inflicted in our hearts. He promises us in Psalm 147:3 *"He heals the brokenhearted and binds up their wounds."*

- Malachi 4:2 *"But unto you that fear my name shall the Sun of righteousness arise with **healing** in His wings; and you shall go forth, and grow up as calves of the stall."* If we fear God and depart from evil, then Jesus (our righteousness) arises to heal us.

- I Peter 2:24: *"Who His own self bore our sins in His own body on the tree, that we, being dead to sins, should live unto righteousness: by whose stripes you **were healed**."* Here Peter quotes Isaiah 53:5, and only changes the tense from *"are healed"* to *"were healed."* It is a finished work! We do not have to ask God to provide healing for us, any more than we need to ask Jesus to provide forgiveness of sins for us. The work was completed on Calvary almost 2,000 years ago. *"By His stripes we were healed."* The healing has been purchased. We just need to receive it. Just as one appropriates forgiveness of sin through Jesus' atoning sacrifice (which is

123

by faith), so you appropriate healing. When you ask the Father heal you, do as Jesus instructed: "When you pray, believe you receive and you shall have it." Pray and believe it first. Then the manifestation of healing will come.

- III John 1:2 *"Beloved, **I wish above all things** that you may prosper and **be in health**, even as your soul prospers."* Here is God's expressed will. He desires that you may be in health. No good thing will God withhold from them that walk uprightly. Believe it! John tells us that healing is God's will for you. Therefore, you can ask God in faith for your healing. As John tells us, when you know God's will, you can ask in confidence.

> *"And this is the confidence that we have in Him, that if we ask any thing according to HIS WILL, He hears us; and if we know that He hears us, whatsoever we ask, we know that we have the petitions that we desire of Him."*[224]

- Exodus 15:26 *"If you wilt diligently hearken to the voice of the LORD your God, and wilt do that which is right in his sight, and wilt give ear to his commandments, and keep all his statutes, I will put none of these diseases upon you, which I have brought upon the Egyptians: for **I am the LORD that heals you.**"* Here we see that not only is it God's will to heal us, but healing is the Name of our God! It is His essence to bring light and life to His people. Again, we see here that there are contingencies of obedience for healing. Faith and

---

[224] I John 5:14

obedience are interconnected. You cannot have one without the other.

- Exodus 23:25-26 *"And you shall serve the LORD your God, and he shall bless your bread, and your water; and **I will take sickness away from the midst of you.**"* Here we see that the blessing upon what we eat and drink is related to sickness leaving our bodies. God can bless what we eat, but we should not abuse our bodies. If we eat twice as much as our body requires and we become obese, we cannot blame God for heart problems and poor circulation and all the other issues related to obesity. With all of the chemical and artificial GMO foods we may inadvertently ingest, it definitely pays to pray over one's food and drink, asking for God's blessing. God will take sickness out of the midst of us!

- Psalm 105:37 *"He brought them forth also with silver and gold: and **there was not one feeble person** among their tribes."* Here we see God's blessing on His people (even the elderly) brings health and vitality. Feebleness and weakness is not God's will. Health is.

- Matthew 8:1-3 *"When he was come down from the mountain, great multitudes followed him. And, behold, there came a leper and worshipped him, saying, Lord, **if you will,** you can make me clean. And Jesus put forth his hand, and touched him, saying, **I will; be clean.** And immediately his leprosy was cleansed."* This scripture answers once and for all that it IS God's will to heal us. A leper approached Jesus and asked for healing. Jesus did not say, "Have you been faithful at the synagogue" or "Did you recite the Shema this morning?" He simply said, *"I will."* Healing is God's will for anyone who humbly falls upon the mercy of God that He extends to us: forgiveness of sin and healing of the body.

- Jesus instructed disciples to bless houses they entered: *"when Jesus was come into Peter's house, he saw his wife's mother laid, and sick of a fever. And **he touched her hand, and the fever left her**: and she arose, and ministered unto them. When the even was come, they brought unto him many that were possessed with devils: and **he cast out the spirits with his word, and healed all that were sick:** That it might be fulfilled which was spoken by Esaias the prophet, saying, Himself took our infirmities, and bare our sicknesses."*[225] Jesus is a non-discriminating Healer. He healed ALL the sick brought to Him. He is the same today! *"Jesus Christ, the same yesterday, today, and forever."*[226]

- Matthew 15:30 *"Then great multitudes came to Him, having with them the lame, blind, mute, maimed, and many others; and they laid them down at Jesus' feet, and **He healed them."*** We notice that Jesus did not have a questionnaire for each healing candidate to fill out to get their mailing address. He didn't ask if they were Baptist, Pentecostal, or Lutheran. He didn't request that a "seed faith" gift be sown to reap a harvest of healing. He healed them out of His great power and compassion. He still desires all to be healed.

---

[225] Matthew 8:14-17
[226] Hebrews 13:8

- Psalm 30:2 *"Lord My God, **I cried out to you and you healed me."** Call on the Lord for healing. He is touched with the feeling of our infirmities. Cry out and He will hear you!

- Psalm 107:20 *"He sent forth **His Word and healed them."** The Word of God has power. Jesus is the Word made flesh and He heals us. His spoken Word recorded in the Holy Bible also has power. If we meditate upon it, it brings health to our flesh![227] Hearing the Word will bring faith,[228] and it is through faith and *patience* that we inherit the promises. Healing is in God's timing. It be progressive rather than instant, but God does promise us healing as part of the believer's covenant.

Healings, blessings, Baptism in the Spirit, and ordination giftings are some of the benefits we can receive through the laying on of hands. It is a means ordained by God for blessings to transfer.

---

[227] Proverbs 4:20-22
[228] Romans 10:17

RESURRECTION FROM THE DEAD

The resurrection from the dead is an extremely important tenet of the faith, and one that the adversary tries to misrepresent and twist. That is because one must believe in the *bodily* resurrection of Jesus Christ in order to be saved: *"If you will confess with your mouth the Lord Jesus and believe in your heart that **God has raised Him from the dead**, you shall be saved."*[229] Without Jesus gaining power over death, hell, and the grave there would be no hope for anyone to obtain eternal life. Belief in Jesus' bodily resurrection is essential. His resurrection is only the first resurrection of the "just" (a category also called the "first resurrection"). There is also the category of the "unjust" resurrection at the end of the age (also called the "last resurrection.")

Bodily Resurrection

The term "resurrection" in the Greek is "ANASTASIS, which denotes a raising up, or rising up—to cause to stand."[230] This implies a bodily, physical rising from the dead. Some liberal theologians have espoused that Jesus' resurrection was only *spiritual*—that He was not physically raised from the dead. Scripture totally refutes that demonic heresy in John 2:19-22:

> *"Jesus answered and said unto them, Destroy this **temple**, and in three days **I will raise it up**. Then said the Jews, Forty and six years was this temple in building, and wilt thou rear it up in three days? But he spoke of the **<u>temple of his body</u>**. When therefore **he was risen from the dead**, his disciples remembered that he*

---

[229] Romans 10:9, 10
[230] Vines, An Expository Dictionary, Vol. 2, p. 290

had said this unto them; and they believed the scripture, and the word which Jesus had said."

Jesus spoke of the Temple of His *body* that would be raised on the third day. It was not a spiritual resurrection, but a physical, bodily resurrection. He is risen from the dead, INDEED!

Risen Indeed!

*"And the angel answered and said unto the women, Fear not ye: for I know that ye seek Jesus, which was crucified. He is not here: for **He is risen**, as He said. Come, see the place where **the Lord lay**. And go quickly, and tell His disciples that **He is risen from the dead**; and, behold, He goes before you into Galilee; there shall ye see Him: lo, I have told you."*[231]

The angel said that the place where Jesus' body lay was no longer occupied because "He is risen." It was Jesus' *body* that occupied the tomb that was no longer there but was resurrected!

The Gospel of Luke has this account that also confirms Jesus' bodily resurrection:

*"And they found the stone rolled away from the sepulcher. And they entered in, and found not the **body of the Lord Jesus**. And it came to pass, as they were much perplexed thereabout, behold, two men stood by them in shining garments: And as they were afraid, and bowed down their faces to the earth, they said unto them, Why seek ye the living among the dead? **He is not here, but is risen**: remember how he spoke unto you when he was yet in Galilee, Saying, The Son of man must*

---

[231] Matthew 28:5-8

be delivered into the hands of sinful men, and be crucified, and the third day rise again."[232]

Proof Positive

Then Luke gives this account of Jesus' appearance that confirms His bodily resurrection as well:

> *"And as they thus spoke, Jesus himself stood in the midst of them, and said unto them, Peace be unto you. But they were terrified and affrighted, and supposed that they had seen a spirit. And he said unto them, Why are ye troubled? and why do thoughts arise in your hearts?* **Behold my hands and my feet, that it is I myself: handle me, and see; for <u>a spirit hath not flesh and bones</u>, as ye see me have.**
>
> *And when he had thus spoken, he shewed them his hands and his feet. And while they yet believed not for joy, and wondered, he said unto them, Have ye here any meat? And they gave him a piece of a* **broiled fish, and of a honeycomb. And he took it, and did eat before them."**

With Luke's astute perspective as a physician, he declares this account as proof that Jesus was raised from the dead bodily. Jesus encouraged them to touch Him and even ate in their presence. Thomas had his famous doubts removed about Jesus' resurrection when Jesus personally challenged him to touch Him: *"Jesus said to Thomas, reach hither thy finger, and behold my hands; and reach hither thy hand, and thrust it into my side: and be not faithless, but believing."[233]* Jesus

---

[232] Luke 24:5-7
[233] John 20:25-27

appeared to over five hundred disciples at one time after He was raised from the dead over a period of about forty days. He appeared in His glorified, physical body. When it was time for Him to ascend up to heaven, He did so in His visible, glorified **Body**:

> *"Jesus showed himself alive after His passion by many infallible proofs, being seen of them forty days... And when He had spoken these things, **while they beheld**, He was taken up; and a cloud received Him out of their sight. And while they looked steadfastly toward heaven as He went up, behold, two men stood by them in white apparel; Which also said, You men of Galilee, why stand ye gazing up into heaven? **this same Jesus**, which is taken up from you into heaven, shall so come in like manner as ye have seen Him go into heaven."*[234]

False Teachers Deny Jesus In The Flesh

Why is it important to note that Jesus left in His glorified, visible Body and that the angels declared He would return in the same way? Because there are false teachers that say that Jesus was only *temporarily* in the flesh... that He is "no longer a man, but only spirit." This is anti-Christ heresy. One such "teacher," Rick Joyner, has published and republished this lie, in spite of being confronted about the error in his book, <u>There Were Two Trees In the Garden</u>, page 59. This is what Apostle John wrote concerning the anti-Christ error that denies Jesus in the flesh:

> *"Beloved, believe not every spirit, but try the spirits whether they are of God: because many false prophets are gone out into the world. Hereby know ye the Spirit of God: Every spirit that confesses that Jesus Christ is*

---

[234] Acts 1:11

*come in the flesh is of God: And **every spirit that confesses not that Jesus Christ is come in the flesh is not of God: and this is that spirit of antichrist**, whereof ye have heard that it should come; and even now already is it in the world.* "[235]

The Man Christ Jesus

There are too many false prophets who have gotten away with insidiously infiltrating the church with false doctrine. Sadly, some are best-selling "Christian" authors. We must test ALL things! The Word of God clearly *teaches against* the heresy that Jesus is only spirit, not God in the flesh:

- *"He seeing this before spoke of the resurrection of Christ, that his soul was not left in hell, **neither his flesh did see corruption. This Jesus hath God raised up,** whereof we all are witnesses. "* (Acts 2:31, 32)
- *"There is one God, and one mediator between God and men, the **Man Christ Jesus**..." "**God was manifest in the flesh,** justified in the Spirit...**received up into glory**"* (I Timothy 2:5, 3:16)
- *"[Jesus] God **raised up** the third day, and shewed him openly; Not to all the people, but unto witnesses chosen before of God, even to us, who did **eat and drink with him after he rose from the dead.** "* (Acts 10:40, 41)
- *"That which was from the beginning, which we have **heard,** which we have **seen with our eyes,** which **we have looked upon, and our hands have handled, of the Word of life**... truly our fellowship is with the Father, and with his **Son Jesus Christ.** "* (I John 1:1-3)

---

[235] I John 4:1-3

It is imperative to teach that Jesus is raised from the dead bodily, and He will return in the flesh. Romans 4:22-25 tells us that Abraham was counted as righteous with God because he believed that God was able to raise his son Isaac from the dead. Likewise, we will have righteousness imputed to us if we believe that God raised His Son, from the dead. By this we are justified from sin. Apostle Paul implores the church to recognize that Jesus was raised from the dead, *else they are still in their sin!*[236] There is no salvation without Jesus' bodily resurrection.

The Blessed Hope

Jesus' resurrection gives believers the Blessed Hope that, as Jesus was raised from the dead, even so they will partake of a resurrection. That resurrection, called by many the "Rapture" of believers, is an imminent event. It can take place at any time. In fact, Jesus said to always be looking for and expecting it. Here is what will happen on that day of the believers' resurrection:

> *"For the **Lord Himself shall descend from heaven** with a shout, with the voice of the archangel, and with the trump of God: and **the dead in Christ shall rise first**: **Then we which are alive and remain shall be CAUGHT UP together with them in the clouds, to meet the Lord in the air: and** so shall we ever be with the Lord."*[237]

The Greek word here for "caught up" is "HARPAZO," meaning "to snatch or catch away," "force suddenly exercised, to seize."[238] Paul

---

[236] I Corinthians 15:35-54
[237] I Thessalonians 4:14-18
[238] Vines, An Expository Dictionary, Vol. 1, p. 174

explained that our mortal bodies will need to be changed into immortal bodies (like Jesus' glorified body[239]) so we will be able to inherit God's Kingdom:

*"Behold, I shew you a mystery; We shall not all sleep, but we shall all be changed, In a moment, in the twinkling of an eye, at the last trump: for the trumpet shall sound, and the **dead shall be raised incorruptible, and we shall be changed. For this corruptible must put on incorruption, and this mortal must put on immortality...**Death is swallowed up in victory. O death, where is thy sting? O grave, where is thy victory?"*[240]

Going Up Yonder To Be With My Lord

Jesus wanted to comfort His disciples by letting them know that He was coming back for them:

"Let not your heart be troubled: ye believe in God, believe also in me. In my Father's house are many mansions: if it were not so, I would have told you. I go to prepare a place for you. And if I go and prepare a place for you, I will come again, and receive you unto myself; that where I am, there ye may be also."[241]

A very graphic description of the believer's resurrection is prophesied in Isaiah 26:19-21:

*"**Thy dead men shall live,** together with **my dead body shall they arise.** Awake and sing, ye that dwell in*

---

[239] Philippians 3:21
[240] I Corinthians 15:51-55
[241] John 14:1-3

*dust: for thy dew is as the dew of herbs, **and the earth shall cast out the dead.** Come, **my people,** enter thou into thy chambers, and shut thy doors about thee: hide thyself as it were for a little moment, until the **indignation** be over past. For, behold, the LORD cometh out of his place to punish the inhabitants of the earth for their iniquity..."*

For What Purpose??

Here the purpose of the Rapture is outlined: God raises the dead believers and beckons His people to enter into their heavenly "chambers" while He punishes those on earth for their sin. *God's people will not have to experience the time of God's wrath that is coming to the earth during the seven-year tribulation.* That is why the Rapture (resurrection of believers) is called the "Blessed Hope." Regardless of what you are going through right now, you can look forward to Jesus' soon coming (no man knows the day or hour.) He will secure you into your heavenly mansion *before* the judgments as described in the book of the Revelation 6-19 are poured out.

Order Of The Resurrection Of The Just

Believers will be resurrected before seven-year time of tribulation (when God's judgments are poured out on earth). This "pre-tribulation rapture" is clearly taught in scripture. The next resurrection will occur in the middle of the tribulation. It occurs when two witnesses (Enoch and Elijah) are killed by the anti-Christ. Three and a half days later they are resurrected and raptured up to heaven in the sight of the whole world![242] Then, the 144,000 sealed Jewish evangelists are raptured up to heaven. They are seen before God's throne, having "been redeemed from the earth."[243] At the end of the seven years, those

---

[242] Revelation 11
[243] Revelation 12 & 14:3

who receive Jesus during that terrible time of wrath (and are able to endure to the end without denying Jesus) will be raised from the dead when Jesus returns to destroy the anti-Christ forces and to reign on earth.[244]

Escapism???

II Timothy 2:16-19 warns us against those who teach against the resurrection (rapture) of the church. Apostle Paul considered it spiritual cancer and iniquity in those who taught error concerning the resurrection. There are "preachers" who blatantly deny the scriptural teaching of the Rapture, and cynically consider it to be man-made "escape theology" to which only "carnal" Christians ascribe.

Apparently the Apostle Paul and Jesus Christ were "carnal Christians," for they taught that the true church *will* **escape** God's wrath. In context of the Rapture and the subsequent "day of the Lord" (time of God's wrath during the seven-year tribulation) Paul states: ***"For God has not appointed us to wrath, but to obtain deliverance by our Lord Jesus Christ, who died for us, that, whether we wake or sleep*** [at the rapture]***, we should live together with him."***[245]

Jesus is also guilty of teaching "escape" theology in Luke 21:28-36:

> *"And take heed to yourselves, lest at any time your hearts be overcharged with surfeiting, and drunkenness, and cares of this life, and so that day [Day of the Lord's wrath] come upon you unawares. For as a snare shall it come on all them that dwell on the face of the whole earth.* ***Watch ye therefore, and pray always, that ye may be accounted worthy to ESCAPE***

---

[244] Revelation 20:4, 5
[245] I Thessalonians 5:9

all these things that shall come to pass, and to stand
before the Son of man."

Perhaps someone should airlift a copy of The Harvest[246] to Heaven so that Jesus can be better informed that He is propagating a "ruse" by teaching that if Christians "watch and pray" they will *escape all* of the coming wrath through His "redemption" at the Rapture. Or maybe Jesus can attend the next Morning Star Ministries' prophecy seminar to become "enlightened."

WHEN IS THE RAPTURE?

No man knows the exact "day and hour", but when you see all of the signs we currently see today—social degradation, increase of natural disasters, political and economic unrest--you can *"know it's near, even at the door."*[247] The writer of Hebrews tells us that we can actually "see the day approaching,"[248] but still we cannot put an exact date or time perimeter on Jesus' coming. We *do know,* however, that we are in the generation that will see the Lord's return. Jesus gave us the definitive sign of the fig tree parable:

> *"Now learn a **parable of the fig tree**; When his branch is yet tender, and puts **forth leaves,** ye know that summer is nigh: So likewise ye, when ye shall see all these things, know that it is near, even at the doors. Verily I say unto you, **This generation shall not pass, till all these things be fulfilled.** Heaven and earth shall pass away, but my words shall not pass away. But of that day and hour knows no man, no, not the angels of heaven, but my Father only...* "[249]

---

[246] Rick Joyner, THE HARVEST 1989 /1990 revised booklet on pg.121
[247] Matthew 24, Luke 21
[248] Hebrews 10:25
[249] Matthew 24:32-36

The #1 sign that we are in the last generation is the fig tree, symbolic of the nation of Israel. We see this fig tree analogy for Israel in a number of places in the Old Testament:

> **Hosea 9:10**: *"I found **Israel** like grapes in the wilderness; I saw your fathers as the **first ripe in the fig tree** at her first time..."*

> **Joel 1:7-2:1**: *"He hath laid my vine waste, and barked **my fig tree**...Blow ye the trumpet in **Zion**, and sound an alarm in my holy mountain..."*

> **Jeremiah 24:5**: *"The LORD shewed me, and, behold, two baskets of **figs** were set before the temple of the LORD. Then said the LORD unto me, What do you see, Jeremiah? And I said, **Figs**; the good figs, very good. Thus says the LORD, the **God of Israel**; Like these **good figs**, so will I acknowledge **them that are carried away captive of Judah (i.e., Jewish people) ..."***

> **Ezekiel 36:8**: *"O mountains of **Israel**, ye shall **shoot forth your branches**, and **yield your fruit to my people of Israel**; for they are at hand to come.*

When Israel was reestablished in their own land on May 14, 1948 (after not existing since 606 B.C.) it was the sign that the last generation had begun. Ezekiel prophesied the exact date in which Israel would again become a sovereign nation over 2500 years before.[250] The Psalmist David, three thousand years ago, also prophesied that the generation that sees Israel ("Zion") established and

---

[250] Ezekiel 4

built up, would see the Lord's appearance![251] The fact that the very youngest of the adult generation alive at Israel's birth is already 93 years old (as of 2021), we don't have long to wait. Jesus' coming for the saints at the Rapture is drawing near...even imminent. It is definitely time for the Church to "look up!"[252]

It is also time for the Church to fulfill the great commission to share God's Word with the world. There is little time before their eternal judgment will be sealed one way or the other!

---

[251] Psalm 102:16
[252] Luke 21:28

ETERNAL JUDGMENT

Many live their lives with short-term perspective... What school should I attend? What house should I purchase? Those things are well and good, but in light of the obvious signs of the times indicating Jesus' soon coming, a more far-reaching perspective is in order. What are you doing to affect your eternity? Or your family's eternity? What we do in this limited window of time that we call "life" will determine our *eternal* destiny--either positively or negatively.

There are eternal judgments and rewards that we will receive based on what we have done in the flesh on this earth. Are you living for yourself and your own pleasures? Or, has eternity factored into your daily activities and your relationship with God? As the writer in Hebrews tells us: *"It is appointed for man once to die, and after that, the judgment."*

Jesus The Man

Jesus is God in the flesh. He came as a man to the earth in order to pay for the sin of mankind with His Precious Blood. Philippians 2 tells us that He humbled Himself by being made in the likeness of men. He temporarily set aside His Divine Omniscience, Omnipotence, and Omnipresence to become the "suffering servant." The Gospels tell us that during Jesus' earthly ministry He had human limitations upon Him. In His travels, He questioned the crowd, *"Who touched Me?"*[253] and He became *"weary with travel."* He experienced temptation by the devil, who tried to get Him to sin through the lust of the eyes, the lust of the flesh, and the pride of life.[254] Thankfully, Jesus did not fall for the temptations, but was our perfect example:

---

[253] Matthew 5:30, John 4:6
[254] Matthew 4:1-11

"For verily He took not on Him the nature of angels; but He took on Him the seed of Abraham. Wherefore in all things it behooved Him to be made like unto His brethren, that He might be a merciful and faithful high priest in things pertaining to God, to make reconciliation for the sins of the people. For in that He Himself hath suffered being tempted, He is able to succor them that are tempted."[255]

Jesus The Advocate

Jesus is compassionately seated at the Right Hand of the Majesty on High, *"ever living to make intercession for us."*[256] Because He suffered in the flesh, knows what it feels like to be rejected, spurned, and maltreated. He is *"touched with the feeling of our infirmities, but was in all points tempted like as we are, yet without sin."*[257]

Now Jesus is our Advocate… our Heavenly Attorney, before God's Holy Throne. When satan, the accuser of the brethren, brings charges against God's people for their short comings, Jesus points to the Blood, by which we are justified. As long we are *"walking in the light as He is in the light, the Blood of Jesus cleanses us from all unrighteousness."*

In other words, if Jesus is truly "Lord" of your life, then a misstep by you does not kick you out of God's family. When God's Spirit shows you an area from which you need to repent, simply confess it and begin again to walk right. We have received the "gift of righteousness" (Jesus' perfect, sinless record is counted to us) as long as we are following Jesus as Lord. Those are the "legal" ramifications

---

[255] Hebrews 2:16-18
[256] Hebrews 7:25
[257] Hebrews 4:15

while Jesus acts as our Advocate. However, there is coming a time when He will no longer act as our Attorney, but our Judge.

Jesus Our Judge

For those who know the Lord (those who have been born-again and follow Him as Lord), Jesus will judge us for our good works. For those who have not received Jesus as Lord, they will have to stand before God based on their own merits. God does not grade on the curve. One is either completely righteous (because of the Blood of Jesus) or they are unrighteous (if they try to merit Heaven by their own works). They will fall short of God's standard of perfect holiness.[258]

> *"For as the Father raises up the dead, and makes them alive; even so the Son makes alive whom he will. For the Father judges no man, but has **committed all judgment unto the Son**... Truly, truly, I say unto you, He that **hears my word**, and **believes** on him that sent me, **has everlasting life, and shall not come into condemnation**; but is passed from death unto life."*

> *"...The hour is coming, and now is, when the **dead** shall hear the voice of the Son of God: and they that hear shall live. For as the Father hath life in himself; so hath he given to the Son to have life in himself; And hath **given him authority to execute judgment** also, because he is the **Son of man**... for the hour is coming, in the which **all that are in the graves shall hear his voice, And shall come forth; they that have done good, unto the resurrection of life**; and they*

---

[258] Romans 3:23

*that have **done evil, unto the resurrection of damnation.** "[259]*

Jesus has been appointed the Judge of the living and the dead. He has the power to call all out of their graves and summon them before the Heavenly court. As Paul admonishes the church, knowing that our court date is approaching we *"labor, that, whether present or absent, we may be accepted of him. For **we must all appear before the judgment seat of Christ**; that every one may receive the things done in his body, according to that he hath done, whether it be good or bad."[260]*

Paul further says that he persuades men because he knows the *"terror of the Lord."* Yes, God is love. But He is also a God of judgment. There will come a day that those who have spurned the mercy of God (Who freely offered His Son as a ransom for our sin), will have a million regrets as they are judged by God and must face God's terror and wrath in hell.

Two Judgments: Righteous and Unrighteous

Jesus is ordained to judge the living and the dead.[261] The two categories that will be judged are the righteous and the unrighteous. Only those who have been born again and have their names written in the Lamb's Book of Life are considered righteous.[262] According to Paul, Jesus will judge the living and dead saints at **His appearing** (that is the Rapture of the believers) and **His Kingdom** (after the seven-year tribulation when His 1000-year Kingdom reign begins.)[263]

---

[259] John 5:21-29
[260] II Corinthians 5:10
[261] Acts 10:42, I Peter 4:5
[262] Revelation 21:24-27
[263] II Timothy 4:1

The righteous will be part of the "First Resurrection."[264] Then, after the Millennial Kingdom (Jesus' 1000-year reign on earth) is the "Last Resurrection." The dead and any living people who have not yet had their final judgment will stand before the Great White Throne:

Great White Throne

"And I saw the dead, small and great, stand before God; and the books were opened: and another book was opened, which is the **book of life***: and the dead were judged out of those things which were written in the books, according to their works. And the sea gave up the dead which were in it; and death and hell delivered up the dead which were in them: and they were judged every man according to their works. And death and hell were cast into the lake of fire. This is the second death. And* **whosoever was not found written in the book of life was cast into the lake of fire.** *"[265]*

Sheep And Goats

Only if you are written in the Book of Life (have your sin covered by Jesus' Blood) will you go to heaven. As *Jesus* declared in John 3, *"You must be born-again to enter the Kingdom of Heaven."* He that does not believe will perish and be condemned to hell.[266]

Some reference Matthew 25 (the "sheep" and "goat" judgment) and believe that if they do enough good works they will enter into heaven. That is not accurate. That judgment is based on whether you are a *sheep* (born-again) or a *goat* (gone your own way, trying to make Heaven on your own merits). If you are following Jesus as your

---

[264] Revelation 20:5
[265] Revelation 20:11-15
[266] John 3:3

Shepherd—as a sheep, then every good thing that you do (give to poor, visit sick, etc.) will be added to your credit for a reward. If you are a goat, then Jesus will say to you, *"Depart from me, into everlasting fire..."* Instead of being rewarded for any good thing you do while on earth, you will be judged based on any good thing **that you did not do**:

"When the Son of man shall come in his glory, and all the holy angels with him, then shall he sit upon the throne of his glory [Millennial Kingdom]; And before him shall be gathered all nations: and he shall separate them one from another, as a shepherd divides his sheep from the goats: And he shall set the **sheep on his right hand***, but the* **goats on the left***. Then shall the King say unto them on his* **right hand***, Come, ye blessed of my Father, inherit the kingdom prepared for you from the foundation of the world:*

For I was hungry, and ye gave me meat: I was thirsty, and ye gave me drink: I was a stranger, and ye took me in: Naked, and ye clothed me: I was sick, and ye visited me: I was in prison, and ye came unto me. Then shall the righteous answer him, saying, Lord, when saw we thee hungry, and fed thee? or thirsty, and gave thee drink? When saw we thee a stranger, and took thee in? or naked, and clothed thee? Or when saw we thee sick, or in prison, and came unto thee? And the King shall answer and say unto them, Verily I say unto you, **Inasmuch as ye have done it unto one of the least of these my brethren, ye have done it unto me.** [Any good done gets rewarded.]*

Then shall he say also unto them on the **left hand** *[goats],* **Depart from me, ye cursed, into everlasting** *fire, prepared for the devil and his angels:* *For I was hungry, and ye gave me no meat: I was thirsty, and ye gave me no drink: I was a stranger, and ye took me not in: naked, and ye clothed me not: sick, and in prison, and ye visited me not. Then shall they also answer him, saying, Lord, when saw we thee hungry, or athirst, or a stranger, or naked, or sick, or in prison, and did not minister unto thee? Then shall he answer them, saying, Verily I say unto you,* **Inasmuch as ye did it not to one of the least of these, ye did it not to me.** *And these shall go away into everlasting punishment: but the righteous into life eternal."*

Inheritance In Christ

We see here that the righteous inherit the Kingdom of God, but the unrighteous will be cast into eternal punishment and fire based on them not having a true relationship with Jesus. Scripture tells us that the eternal rewards for the righteous are far beyond our comprehension in wonder and glory: *"Eye has not seen, ear has not heard, neither has entered into the heart of man what God has prepared for them that love Him."*[267] It will exceed our greatest expectations! The greatest reward, of course, is the fact that we receive eternal life in heaven…in the very presence of God. In the presence of the Lord is the fullness of joy. And God is love. Being enveloped in God's love, joy and peace for eternity is in itself amazing. But there are additional rewards for the righteous.

There are *crowns* and *thrones* with which the righteous can be rewarded.[268] This means that we will be reigning with Jesus in Heaven. No matter the lot one has on this earth (perhaps a poor, persecuted saint in Pakistan…), Heaven will more than make up for the temporary pain

---

[267] I Corinthians 2:9
[268] Revelation 3:11, 21

and suffering that one endures on this earth for Christ! God is waiting to lavish His kindness and love upon His children for all eternity!

> *"But God, who is rich in mercy, for his great love wherewith he loved us, Even when we were dead in sins, hath quickened us together with Christ, (by grace ye are saved;) And hath raised us up together, and made us sit together in heavenly places in Christ Jesus: That* ***in the ages to come he might shew the exceeding riches of his grace in his kindness toward us through Christ Jesus.*** *"[269]*

We actually will inherit everything that God has, as we are called *"heirs of God, and joint heirs with Jesus."[270]* Revelation 21:7 tells us that we will *"inherit all things."* Amazing!

There will be levels of rewards for the righteous based on what is done for Christ. The rewards are not necessarily based on the *magnitude* of the work one does... (the biggest church in town or the greatest television evangelistic outreach). Man looks on the outward, but God looks at the heart. It is the *motive and attitude* of the heart that will determine if one receives reward for the work that they do for Christ.

Be Faithful

One basis for receiving reward is for **faithfulness**. Perhaps you faithfully drive that Sunday School bus picking up little children every week for church. You may not receive many accolades in this life, but God sees that as a monumental work. Jesus said much about the importance of faithfulness:

---

[269] Ephesians 2:4-7
[270] Romans 8:17

*"For the kingdom of heaven is as a man...who called his own servants, and delivered unto them his goods. And unto one he gave five talents, to another two, and to another one; to every man **according to his several ability**... After a long time, the lord of those servants cometh, and reckoned with them...*

*Thou delivered to me five talents: behold, I have gained beside them five talents more. His lord said unto him, Well done, thou **good and faithful servant**: thou hast been faithful over a few things, I will make thee ruler over many things: enter thou into the joy of thy lord. He also that had received two talents came and said... I have gained two other talents beside them. His lord said unto him, Well done, **good and faithful servant**; thou hast been faithful over a few things, I will make thee ruler over many things: enter thou into the joy of thy lord.*

*Then he which had received the one talent came and said... I was afraid, and went and hid thy talent in the earth: lo, there thou hast that is thine. His lord answered and said unto him, Thou **wicked and slothful servant**...cast ye the unprofitable servant into outer darkness: there shall be weeping and gnashing of teeth.*[271]

We see that God expects us to use what He gave us to increase the Kingdom. You may not be the preacher, but that does not exempt you from doing God's work. Can you pass out tracts, or visit the sick in the

---

[271]Matthew 25:14-30

hospital? Or call someone and give them an encouraging word? There is a danger for those who are not given as much in the way of spiritual "talents" to think that they do not have to do anything for God—just show up at church on Sunday. As we see, God takes great offence with slothful servants who do not bother to invest what they do have into the Kingdom. God will reward faithfulness, but He will condemn lack of faithfulness.

Be Ready

We see that one's mindset can determine whether or not they will be faithful to God in their Christian responsibilities. Jesus continually admonishes us to "be ready" and watch, expecting His imminent coming:

> "**Watch** therefore: for ye know not what hour your Lord doth come... Therefore, be ye also ready: for in such an hour as ye think not the Son of man cometh. Who then is a **faithful and wise servant**, whom his lord hath made ruler over his household, to give them meat in due season? Blessed is that servant, whom his lord when he cometh shall find so doing. Verily I say unto you, That he shall make him ruler over all his goods.

> But and if that **evil servant shall say in his heart, My lord delays his coming;** And shall begin to smite his fellow servants, and to eat and drink with the drunken; The lord of that servant shall come in a day when he looks not for him, and in an hour that he is not aware of, And shall cut him asunder, and appoint him his portion with the hypocrites: there shall be weeping and gnashing of teeth."[272]

---

[272] Matthew 24:42-51

We see that the lack of believing in the Master's imminent coming causes the servant to cast off restraints and indulge the flesh. There is intrinsic *evil* in one's heart in *wanting* to believe the Lord is delaying His return. You do not want to believe His coming is imminent because there are things in your life that are not right...sins that you want to pursue for which you do not want to stand in judgment.

If you really believed that Jesus was coming tonight would you be holding on to that grudge against your husband or wife? Or would you consider the BIG game more important that taking time to read God's Word or talk to Him in prayer? If you *knew* Jesus was coming tonight, you would first make sure that your own heart was right with Him. Then, you would want to be sure that everyone you love was in right relationship with Him. You would be calling and texting family and friends, encouraging them to be ready. He *could* come tonight.

Work For Rewards

Faithfulness is an important basis for receiving rewards in heaven. Good works and deeds are also a basis for reward:

- *"For the Son of man shall come in the glory of his Father with his angels; and then **he shall reward every man according to his works**."* (Matthew 16:27) We are not saved by works, but we are rewarded eternally for our works.

- *"Be ye holy; for I am holy. And if ye call on the Father, **who without respect of persons judges <u>according to every man's work</u>**, pass the time of your sojourning here in fear: forasmuch as ye know that ye were not redeemed with corruptible things...but with Precious Blood of Christ"* (I Peter 1:16-19) Your works will be judged by God.

- *"Behold, I come quickly: **blessed is he that <u>keeps the sayings</u>** of the prophecy of this book."* (Revelation 22:7) There is a blessing for reading Revelations and obeying the admonitions in it.

- *"Servants [employees], be obedient to them that are your masters according to the flesh, with fear and trembling, in singleness of your heart, as unto Christ; Not with eye service [only when the boss is watching], as man-pleasers; but as the servants of Christ, doing the will of God from the heart;* **With good will doing service, as to the Lord, and not to men: Knowing that <u>whatsoever good thing any man does</u>, the same shall he receive of the Lord, whether he be bond or free."** (Ephesians 6:6-8) This is a powerful promise. If you are a janitor and do what you do for the Lord (the best job you can), you will be rewarded for it—whatsoever you do!

- *"And **whatsoever ye do, do it heartily, as to the Lord**, and not unto men; Knowing that of the Lord ye shall receive the reward of the inheritance: for ye serve the Lord Christ."* (Colossians 3:23, 24) Do your work with all your heart… schoolwork, occupational work, housework… "whatsoever you do," and you will be rewarded.

As Paul tells us in I Corinthians 15:58: *"Therefore, my beloved brethren, be ye steadfast, unmovable, **always abounding in the work of the Lord,** forasmuch as ye know that **your labor is not in vain in the Lord."*** This admonition was in the context of the Lord's imminent coming.

Suffering For Christ's Sake

Suffering for Christ's sake is another basis for one receiving rewards from God:

> *"Blessed are ye, when men shall hate you, and when they shall separate you from their company, and shall reproach you, and cast out your name as evil, for the Son of man's sake. **Rejoice** ye in that day, and **leap for joy**: for, behold, **your reward is great in heaven**: for in the like manner did their fathers unto the prophets."*[273]

Our natural response to being persecuted and rejected and maligned (albeit for Christ's sake) is not to "rejoice" or to "leap for joy." However, if you only knew how great your reward was in heaven, you *would* leap for joy and rejoice! We really need an eternal perspective of life. *As* Paul tells us, *"If we **suffer**, we shall also **reign with him**..."*[274] And that *"the sufferings of this present time are not worthy to be compared with the **glory** which shall be **revealed in us**."*[275] Paul referred to all of the persecution that he endured (beatings, stonings, imprisonment, and ultimately martyrdom) as "light afflictions" (compared to the eternal glory we will receive):

> *"For our light affliction, which is but for a moment, works for us a far more exceeding and eternal weight of glory..."*[276]

Financial Giving, Eternal Earnings

Money is not the root of all evil, but the *love of* money is the root of all evil. It is easy to let finances become a priority in our lives.

---

[273] Luke 6:22, 23
[274] II Timothy 2:12
[275] Romans 8:18
[276] II Corinthians 4:17

But, if we will seek first the Kingdom of God, as Jesus tells us, all the things we need will be added to us. He tells us in Luke 12: *"Sell that ye have, and give alms; provide yourselves bags which wax not old, **a treasure in the heavens that fails not**, where no thief approaches, neither moth corrupts...* Paul admonishes the rich to give:

> *"Charge them that are rich in this world, that they be not high-minded, nor trust in uncertain riches, but in the living God, who giveth us richly all things to enjoy; That they **do good**, that they be **rich in good works**, **ready to distribute**, willing to communicate; Laying up in store for themselves a good foundation against the time to come, that they may lay hold on eternal life."* (I Timothy 6:17-19)

Those who have money should always be ready and willing to do the good works of supporting the Kingdom and helping others. Be open to the Spirit's leading, and be liberal with your giving. By doing so, you will lay up eternal rewards in Heaven for yourself.

Motives Determine Rewards

What is in the heart—that which motivates you—will determine whether or not you receive a reward for the work that you do. Are you doing what you do to please men? Or God? Jesus tells us that if you do good deeds to get men's approval, then you will only be rewarded on earth with their adulation and approval. But if you do what you do with an attitude of love to please God (not to show off to people), you will be rewarded eternally in heaven:

> *"**Take heed that ye do not your alms before men, to be seen of them**: otherwise <u>ye have no reward of your Father which is in heaven</u>. Therefore, when you*

give thine alms, do not sound a trumpet before you, as the hypocrites do in the synagogues and in the streets, that they may have glory of men. Truly I say unto you, **They have their reward.** *But when you give alms, let not thy left hand know what thy right hand does: That your alms may be* <u>**in secret: and thy Father which sees in secret himself shall reward you openly.**</u> *"*

"And when you pray, you shall not be as the hypocrites are: for they love to pray standing in the synagogues and in the corners of the streets, **that they may be seen of men.** *Truly I say unto you, They have their reward. But you, when you pray, enter into thy closet, and when thou hast shut thy door, pray to thy Father which is in secret; and thy Father which sees in secret shall reward thee openly."* (Matthew 6:1-6)

As Paul tells us in I Corinthians 3, *"Therefore judge nothing before the time, until the Lord come, who both will* **bring to light the hidden things** *of darkness, and will make manifest the* **counsels of the hearts***: and then shall every man have praise of God."* The hidden motives you may have for "doing good" will determine whether or not you are rewarded. Are you giving in the offering because you want to show the pastor that you are one of his "faithful sheep," or because God directed you to do so? Are you doing good to try to manipulate others, or make people feel indebted to you? It is only a "good deed" if the motives of the heart are pure.

Love Is The Greatest

Love should be the overriding reason for doing anything that we do for God:

"Though I speak with the tongues of men and of angles, and have not charity, I am become as sounding brass, or a tinkling cymbal. And though I have the gift of prophecy, and understand all mysteries, and all knowledge; and though I have all faith, so that I could remove mountains, and have not charity, I am nothing. And though I bestow all my goods to feed the poor, and though I give my body to be burned, and **have not charity, it profits me nothing.** *"[277]*

Love must motivate what we do for God. Otherwise, there is no profit...no reward for us. Additionally, the willingness to fulfill the call or duty at hand is a factor in being rewarded. As Paul states, *"If I do these things willingly, I have a reward..."[278]*

One scripture that refers to the motives for doing God's work as a basis for reward is in I Corinthians 3:8-15. Here, it refers to rewards either being granted or "burned up," based on the quality of one's work. Was your labor done for the Lord in secret, with a pure heart of love? Or did you look for applause of man for your work? Motives will determine if there is a reward.

Tested By Fire

Paul warns the believers that their works will be tested by God's fire of purity and holiness:

"Now he that plants [spiritual seed of the Word] *and he that waters are one: and every man shall receive his own* **reward according to his own labor.** *For we are laborers together with God: ye are God's husbandry, ye*

---

[277] I Corinthians 13:1-3
[278] I Corinthians 9:17, 18

are God's building. According to the grace of God which is given unto me, as a wise master builder, I have laid the foundation, and another builds thereon. But let every man take heed how he builds thereupon. For other foundation can no man lay than that is laid, which is Jesus Christ.

Now if any man build upon this foundation gold, silver, precious stones, wood, hay, stubble; Every man's **work** *shall be made manifest: for the day shall declare it, because it shall be revealed by fire; and the fire shall try* **every man's work of what sort it is**. [the quality—if it was done for God's glory]. **If any man's work abide** *which he hath built thereupon,* **he shall receive a reward**. *If any man's* **work shall be burned**, *he shall* **suffer loss: but he himself shall be saved**; *yet so as by fire.*"

If, after God's fire burns off the dross (the works done with impure motives of vain glory or to please man), and there remain works that were done with a pure heart, you will receive a reward.

Prepare To Meet Your God

How can we prepare ourselves knowing that we must stand before God and give account of our lives? How should we order our lives? Walking in love is a necessity. I John 4:16, 17 says *"God is love; and* **he that dwells in love dwells in God**, *and God in him. Herein is our love made perfect, that* **we may have boldness in the day of judgment**.*"* Walking in the Spirit with the virtues of faith, knowledge, temperance, patience, godliness, brotherly kindness and love will not only keep you from falling spiritually, but will give you an "abundant entrance" into the Kingdom of God.[279] If you love Christ's appearing, you will receive a crown!

> *"Henceforth there is laid up for me a **crown of righteousness**, which the Lord, the righteous judge, shall give me at that day: and not to me only, but unto all them also that **love his appearing**."*[280]

Peters tells us in light of eternal judgment, we should be people of holy conversation and godliness, without spot and blameless.[281]   It will be worth it all when we see Jesus! Any trial, test, or hardship that you may have endured for Christ will pale in light of the glorious inheritance of the Kingdom of God!

The Unrighteous

The unrighteous (those who do not know the Lord) need do nothing to prepare for their eternal destiny in hell. They can continue to live day-to-day in willful oblivion of the eternal. But that will not spare them from the judgments they will face. It will be horrendous for the lost:

- *"The Son of man shall send forth his angels, and they shall gather out of his kingdom all things that offend, and them which do iniquity; And shall cast them into a **furnace of fire**: there shall be **wailing and gnashing of teeth**.*

- *"And if thy hand offend thee, cut it off: it is better for thee to enter into life maimed, than having two hands to go into hell, into the **fire that never shall be quenched**: Where their **worm***

---

[279] II Peter 1:5-11
[280] II Timothy 4:8
[281] II Peter 3:14

*dies not, and the fire is not quenched. And if thy foot offend thee, cut it off: it is better for thee to enter halt into life, than having two feet to be cast into hell, **into the fire that never shall be quenched: Where their worm dies not, and the fire is not quenched.** And if thine eye offend thee, pluck it out: it is better for thee to enter into the kingdom of God with one eye, than having two eyes to be cast into hell fire: **Where their worm dies not, and the fire is not quenched.** "* Jesus is trying to reinforce the eternal nature of hell by repeatedly stressing the suffering will never end—burning fire and eternal corruption.

- The Apostle John relays what the eternal end of the unrighteous will be: *"But the fearful, and unbelieving, and the abominable, and murderers, and whoremongers, and sorcerers, and idolaters, and all liars, shall have their part in the **lake which burns with fire and brimstone: which is the second death.**"*

Those who knew God's will but did not do it will be judged with a more severe judgment than those in ignorance.[282] There are levels of hell. Religious hypocrites, especially the greedy, will go to a place reserved for them… a place of "blackness of darkness forever."[283] You do not want to be on the wrong side when facing God in judgment:

"It is a fearful thing to fall into the hands of the living God."[284] Heaven is real, and hell is real. Both are eternal. It's your choice.

---

[282] Luke 12:47, 48
[283] Jude 12, 13
[284] Hebrews 10:31

THE TRUTH ABOUT HELL

Many people today either deny the existence of hell, or do not think that anyone will really have to go there. The truth is, there is a hell, and *"MANY there be that go therein."*[285] This, however, was never God's intent. He created hell for the fallen angels and lucifer, not for man. If man goes there it is because he has rejected God's plan and purpose, and instead has followed the devil's lie.

God has given us a free will; He cannot --and will not-- force anyone to follow Him. He does not want anyone to perish, but desires that all would repent and be saved. But, He does not force His will on anyone. If they reject God's plan of happiness and eternal joy in heaven, He has to allow them to go their own way.

Some would say, "I don't believe that a loving God would send anyone to hell." That is absolutely true. He does not send anyone to hell. Man sends himself to hell by refusing God's grace and the free gift of eternal life that Christ purchased for us on the Cross. God has gone to great lengths to STOP man from going to hell. The entire Bible from Genesis to Revelation is God's Master plan designed to help man escape the judgment that their sin deserves. God allowed His Own Son, Jesus Christ, to go to hell and pay for the sin of all mankind so that man would not have to go there himself. And now God stands at the door of your heart and knocks, begging you to let Him into your life.[286] You must make the choice. If you reject Him and choose to go your own way, you will go to hell. If you choose to follow the Lord, heaven will be your eternal home. As God tells us in Deut. 30:19, *"Choose life."*

---

[285] Matthew 7:13
[286] Revelation 3:20

If one really knew what hell is, they would do everything in their power to avoid it. Hell is a fiery place of burning torment and punishment. The Hebrew word "sheol" is defined as "hades, the world of the dead; subterranean, grave, hell, pit." The Greek has three words for hell. One is "Gehenna" (valley of the son of Hinnon.) This is a "place or state of everlasting punishment." Another is "Hades", which is "the place of departed souls, grave, hell, unseen." The final word is "tartaros", (the deepest abyss of Hades). Its meaning is to incarcerate in eternal torment, cast down to hell."

The Bible describes hell as being "down" in the lower part of the earth:

> *"For a fire is kindled in mine anger, and shall burn unto the **lowest hell**, and shall consume the earth with her increase, and set on fire the foundations of the mountains."* (Deuteronomy 32:22)

Job and Ezekiel state:

> *"...deeper than hell", "They shall go down to the bars of the pit, when our rest together is in the dust." "When I shall bring you down with them that descend into the pit... and shall set you in the low parts of the earth, in places desolate of old, with them that go down to the pit..."*[287]

Hell is also a place of darkness:

> *"...foaming out their own shame; wandering stars, to whom is reserved the blackness of darkness forever..." "...even to the land of darkness and the shadow of death; A land of darkness, as darkness itself; and of the shadow of death, without any order, and*

---

[287] Job 11:8, 17:16, Ezekiel 26:20

where the light is as darkness." "...cast out into outer darkness: there shall be weeping and gnashing of teeth."[288]

Mark 9:43-48 describes hell as a place of eternal death, fiery torment, and punishment:

> *"into **hell, into the fire that never shall be quenched: Where their worm dies not, and the fire is not quenched**... And if your foot offends you, cut it off: it is better for you to enter halt into life, than having two feet to be cast into **hell, into the fire that never shall be quenched: Where their worm dies not, and the fire is not quenched.** And if thine eye offend you, pluck it out: it is better for you to enter into the kingdom of God with one eye, than having two eyes to be cast into **hell fire: Where their worm dies not, and the fire is not quenched."***

Here Jesus is saying, *whatever* you have to do to stop sinning, do it, so that you will not have to go to hell. Any sin, attitude or motive that is not pleasing to God, get rid of it, or the consequences are disastrous AND ETERNAL! Psalm 11:6 and Revelation 20:10 describe hell as a place of fire and brimstone:

> *"Upon the wicked he shall rain **snares, fire and brimstone, and a horrible tempest**: this shall be the portion of their cup." "And the devil that deceived them was cast into the **lake of fire and brimstone**, where the beast and the false prophet are, and shall be **tormented day and night for ever and ever."***

---

[288] Jude 13, Job 10:21, Matthew 8:12

Jesus Himself gives us a graphic example of what hell is like:

"There was a certain rich man, which was clothed in purple and fine linen, and fared sumptuously every day: And there was a certain beggar named Lazarus, which was laid at his gate, full of sores, And desiring to be fed with the crumbs which fell from the rich man's table: moreover, the dogs came and licked his sores."

*"And it came to pass, that the beggar died, and was carried by the angels into Abraham's bosom: the rich man also died, and was buried; And **in hell he lifted up his eyes, being in torments**, and saw Abraham afar off, and Lazarus in his bosom. And he cried and said, Father Abraham, have mercy on me, and send Lazarus, that he may dip the tip of his finger in water, and cool my tongue; for **I am tormented in this flame."***

"But Abraham said, Son, remember that you in your lifetime received your good things, and likewise Lazarus evil things: but now he is comforted, and you are tormented. And beside all this, between us and you there is a great gulf fixed: so that they which would pass from hence to you cannot; neither can they pass to us, that would come from thence."

*"Then he said, I pray you therefore, father, that you would send him to my father's house: For I have five brethren; that he may testify unto them, lest they also come into this **place of torment**. Abraham said unto him, They have Moses and the prophets; let them hear them.*

And he said, Nay, father Abraham: but if one went unto them from the dead, they will repent. And he said unto him, If they hear not Moses and the prophets, neither will they be persuaded, though one rose from the dead."[289]

Notice that the rich man was not described as doing any overt, evil sin. He seemed to be a caring, family oriented individual, as he was concerned for the welfare of his brothers. However, his lifestyle showed that he did not have time for God or others outside of his own sphere. He simply lived for himself and ignored God. Being "good" by man's standard does not earn one the right to go to heaven. One must be Godly. That is, have God as the focus of one's life.

After death one does not cease to exist. The spirit continues to live eternally, either in heaven or in hell. In this case, the rich man's spirit, being conscious, felt the torments and pains of hell. The choices he made while alive sealed his eternal destiny forever. This is reality, and a somber warning from God's Word.

Most people feel that if *anyone* does go to hell, it will be only the very wicked. They believe that if their good deeds outweigh their bad, they will somehow make it into heaven. God, however, does not "grade on the curve." Only the pure in heart will see God. And that eliminates all of us, for Psalm 14 states:

"The LORD looked down from heaven upon the children of men, to see if there were any that did understand, and seek God. They are all gone aside, they are all together become filthy: there is none that doeth good, no, not one."

---

[289] Luke 16

God looks at the heart of man. Though one may not have murdered anyone, Jesus said if there is hatred in your heart, you are the same as a murderer. If there is lust in your heart, it is as if you have committed that immoral act. (Matthew 5) Pride is a sin that is an abomination to God. Pride causes man to justify his sin and try to make himself look right:

> *"There is a generation that are pure in their own eyes, and yet is not washed from their filthiness."* And that, *"Every way of a man is right in his own eyes: but the LORD ponders the hearts."*[290]

They are right in their own eyes, but not in God's. Sin must be confessed and repented of, not covered up and justified.

Many religious people will be in hell because they have rejected God's only way to heaven (that is, through Jesus Christ-John 14:6). They didn't obey the simple Gospel message to believe on the Lord Jesus Christ to be saved. Instead, they trust in their good works or church membership to get them to heaven. But only true faith in Jesus will get you there.

Many will go to hell because they love the world more than Jesus. They will not make a public stand for Jesus Christ for fear of being rejected or persecuted. Some will be in hell simply because they ignore God. Scripture tells us plainly who will be in hell: *"The wicked shall be turned into hell, and all the nations that forget God." "You cast the wicked down into destruction. How are they brought into desolation, as in a moment! they are utterly consumed with terrors."*[291]

---

[290] Proverbs 21:2, 30:12
[291] Psalm 9 & 73

God will judge righteously. He judges according to His Holy Word, not what is politically correct or socially acceptable. Sexual sin shall be judged: *"Even **as Sodom and Gomorrah**, and the cities about them in like manner, giving themselves over to **fornication**, and going after strange flesh, are set forth for an example, **suffering the vengeance of eternal fire.**"* (Jude 7)

As Paul tell us in Romans 2, there will be wrath upon those who rebel against God:

> *"But after your hardness and impenitent heart you treasure up to yourself wrath against the day of wrath and revelation of the righteous judgment of God; Who will render to every man according to his deeds: To them who by patient continuance in well doing seek for glory and honor and immortality, eternal life: But unto them that are contentious, and do not obey the truth, but obey unrighteousness, **indignation and wrath, tribulation and anguish**, upon every soul of man that doeth evil…"* Hell is a place of perpetual suffering and anguish. It's horrible!

Proverbs 28:17 warns *"A man that does violence to the blood of any person shall flee to the **pit**; let no man stay him."* Hell is called the "pit" which in the Hebrew means "hole, cistern, dungeon." Hell is a dungeon… a prison, where souls are tormented.

Religious hypocrites will go to hell: *"Even so you also **outwardly appear righteous** unto men, but within you are **full of hypocrisy and iniquity**… You serpents, you generation of vipers, **how can you escape the damnation of hell?**"* (Matthew 23:28, 33)

Those who know the truth but do not do it are much more accountable to God for their disobedience. "Christians" who tote

Bibles and quote scriptures but live like the devil will be punished more severely than those who never knew the Word of God.

Just going to Church will not keep you out of hell. Even Judas Iscariot attended the House of God, but his heart was not right within him: *"a man mine equal, my guide, and mine acquaintance. We took sweet counsel together, and **walked unto the house of God** in company... let them **go down quick into hell**: for wickedness is in their dwellings; you, O God, shalt bring them down into the **pit of destruction**: bloody and deceitful men shall not live out half their days"* (Ps. 55: 14-23)

Those who do not believe the Gospel of Jesus Christ will go to hell:

> *"...when the Lord Jesus shall be revealed from heaven with his mighty angels, In flaming fire taking vengeance on them that know not God, and that obey not the gospel of our Lord Jesus Christ: Who shall be punished with **everlasting destruction** from the presence of the Lord, and from the glory of his power;"*[292] Hell is a place of perpetual death.

Those who continue in willful sin are destined for hell: *"For if we **sin willfully** after that we have received the knowledge of the truth, there remains no more sacrifice for sins, but a certain fearful looking for of **judgment and fiery indignation**, which shall devour the adversaries... For we know him that has said, Vengeance belongs unto me, I will recompense, said the Lord."*[293]

---

[292] II Thessalonians 1:7-9
[293] Hebrews 10:26

Those who do not think that they need God in their lives will go to hell. Riches can cause men to become proud and think that they do not need God. They become "lovers of pleasure, more than lovers of God" and are consumed only with the temporal things of life:

> *"Woe unto them that rise up early in the morning, that they may follow strong drink; that continue until night, till wine inflame them! And the harp, and the viol, the tabret, and pipe, and wine, are in their feasts: but they regard not the work of the LORD, neither consider the operation of His hands...* *Therefore, **hell has enlarged herself**, and opened her mouth without measure: and their glory, and their multitude, and their pomp, and he that rejoices, shall **descend** into it."*[294]

One does not have to be a "terrible sinner"—a murderer or adulterer—to go to hell. You can simply be one who *"regards not the work of the LORD."* You do not acknowledge God in your everyday life, and do not honor Him as the Creator of the universe…the One who holds your very breath in His hands. Pride does not acknowledge God or the need to serve Him. It blindly indulges in pleasures of this world without giving thanks to the One who made it. Hell is a real place. As more and more billions of souls descend into that pit of torment it literally has to "enlarge" itself to contain them all. Hell is a place beneath the earth, and therefore those souls "descend" into it.

I Timothy 6:9, 10 states: *"But they that will be rich fall into temptation and a snare, and into many foolish and hurtful lusts, which drown men in **destruction and perdition**. For the love of money is the*

---

[294] Isaiah 5:11-14

root of all evil..." Utter destruction is the end for those who are deceived by the lusts of flesh, lusts of the eyes, and pride of life.

"For many walk... that they are the enemies of the cross of Christ: **whose end is destruction** *... who mind earthly things."*[295]

There is a payday coming for those who despise God's grace and the opportunity to receive eternal LIFE through Jesus Christ. It will be death... not cessation of existence, but cessation of enjoying the presence of God—His love, righteousness, peace, and joy in the Holy Ghost. Death will be filled with all that God IS NOT: chaos, hate, malice, fear, unbelief, torment, evil, perversity, darkness, and lies... perpetually.

"The wicked... spend their days in wealth, and in a moment go down to the grave. Therefore, they say unto God, 'Depart from us; for we desire not the knowledge of your ways. What is the Almighty, that we should serve him? and what profit should we have, if we pray unto Him?' ... he shall **drink of the wrath of the Almighty.** *"*[296]

How presumptuous man is to think that he will not have to give account of himself before God. Our God is a consuming fire. How dare mortal man mock and spurn the God who gave them life. They will not always do so, for there is a day of reckoning. Those who do not repent of their pride and turn to God will have to face God's wrath. Many put their trust in wealth instead of in the God who richly gives us all things to enjoy. We need a reality check in light of eternity. God is God, and you are not!

---

[295] Philippians 3:18, 19
[296] Job 21:12-20

Sin in one's life will keep them out of heaven: *"But the fearful, and unbelieving, and the abominable, and murderers, and whoremongers, and sorcerers, and idolaters, and all liars, shall have their part in the **lake which burns with fire and brimstone: which is the second death.**"*[297]

Hell is not symbolic...it is a real place. The lake of fire has burning brimstone into which all sinners will be cast forever. It was never God's will for man to be there. It was created for satan and his angels--not for man. But if man chooses to follow satan there, that is where they will end up. The only way to escape the judgment of hell is for your name to be written in the Lamb's book of life:

> *"And I saw a great white throne, and him that sat on it, from whose face the earth and the heaven fled away; and there was found no place for them. And I saw the dead, small and great, stand before God; and the books were opened: and another book was opened, which is the book of life: and the dead were judged out of those things which were written in the books, according to their works. And the sea gave up the dead which were in it; and death and hell delivered up the dead which were in them: and they were judged every man according to their works. And death and hell were cast into the lake of fire. This is the second death. **And whosoever was not found written in the book of life was cast into the lake of fire.**"* (Rev. 20: 11-15)

When Jesus died on the Cross for our sin, He made the way possible for us to escape hell. He suffered God's wrath for our sins so

---

[297] Revelation 21:8

that we would not have to. Because of His great love for us, He endured the torments of hell and ransomed us from death. Consider the following prophetic scriptures that describe what He went through for us:

> *"For you will not leave my **soul in hell**... The **sorrows [pains] of hell** compassed me about: the snares of death prevented me. The **sorrows of death compassed** me...He brought me up also out of a **horrible pit**... Your fierce wrath goes over me; your terrors have cut me off."* [298]

God is holy and righteous, and cannot allow sin to go unpunished. Out of love for us, He allowed His Beloved Son to be punished for our sins. Jesus became a Ransom for sin, freeing us from the penalty of death and hell. Because of His great love for us, Jesus willingly gave Himself for our sins, and endured God's WRATH and judgment in hell.

As Hebrews 2:9 states, "Jesus tasted death for every man." And WHY did He do it? So that He could cast you into hell? NO!!! It was so that you would not have to go there! God has done everything in His power to keep you OUT of hell. The only thing that He cannot do is to force us to receive the gift of eternal life that He offers to all. That is our choice. His Blood can deliver us from the pit of hell: *"**You have in love to my soul delivered it from the pit... You have cast all my sins behind Your back.**"[299] "**...by the Blood...covenant I have sent forth...prisoners out of the pit...**"[300]* Thank God for the Blood of Jesus!

---

[298] Psalm 16, 18, 40, 88, 89
[299] Isaiah 38:17
[300] Zechariah 9:11

WOMEN IN MINISTRY

There are many who question whether or not women should be in the ministry. Some cite certain Biblical passages and argue that women are not allowed to publicly speak or minister in Church. However, the Bible is replete with examples of women who not only ministered, but were in places of authority in God's economy. The following are some examples:

Huldah The Prophetess

Huldah was a prophetess during the time when kings were ruling over Israel. She dwelt at the Jerusalem college of the prophets and was in a place of great respect in the spirit realm. Kings and men of God (priests in Temple ministry) came to her for the inspired, prophetic counsel of God:

> *"So Hilkiah the priest, and Ahikam, and Achbor, and Shaphan, and Asahiah, went unto* **Huldah the prophetess***, the wife of Shallum the son of Tikvah, the son of Harhas, keeper of the wardrobe; (now* **she dwelt in Jerusalem in the college***;) and they communed with her...But to* **the king of Judah which sent you to inquire of the LORD***, thus shall ye say to him... I will gather thee unto thy fathers, and thou shalt be gathered into thy grave in peace; and thine eyes shall not see all the evil which I will bring upon this place. And they brought the king word again."*[301]

---

[301] II Kings 22:14

Deborah The Judge

Judges 4:4 tells of Deborah the prophetess: *"And **Deborah, a prophetess**, the wife of Lapidoth, **she judged Israel at that time**:*

> *"And she dwelt under the palm tree of Deborah between Ramah and Bethel in mount Ephraim: and the children of Israel came up to her for judgment. And she sent and called Barak the son of Abinoam out of Kedesh-naphtali, and said unto him, Hath not the LORD God of Israel commanded, saying, Go and draw toward mount Tabor, and take with thee ten thousand men of the children of Naphtali and of the children of Zebulun? And I will draw unto thee to the river Kishon Sisera, the captain of Jabin's army, with his chariots and his multitude; and I will deliver him into thine hand. And Barak said unto her, If thou wilt go with me, then I will go: but if thou wilt not go with me, then I will not go..."*

Deborah led Israel both spiritually and politically. She gave exact prophetic instructions concerning the impending war that gave Barak the courage to fight the enemy of Israel. Her counsel was so trusted that Barak refused to go to war except Deborah accompanied the army. Because they submitted to her prophetic, inspired leadership, God gave deliverance to the nation.

Miriam, Prophetic Praise Leader

Miriam (Moses' sister) is another example of a woman being in spiritual leadership. She was a "prophetess" that led public praise and worship in the congregation ("the Church" in the wilderness)[302] after God wrought deliverance for them at the Red Sea:

---

[302] Acts 7:38

*"Then **sang Moses and the children of Israel this song** unto the LORD, and spoke, saying, I will sing unto the LORD, for he hath triumphed gloriously: the horse and his rider hath he thrown into the sea...And **Miriam the prophetess,** the sister of Aaron, took a timbrel in her hand; and all the women went out after her with timbrels and with dances.   And Miriam answered them, Sing ye to the LORD, for he hath triumphed gloriously; the horse and his rider hath he thrown into the sea."[303]*

Redemption Preached By Anna

In the New Testament women are also mentioned as publicly ministering in the place where God's people assembled.   Anna the prophetess is mentioned, announcing Jesus' arrival:

*"And when the days of her purification according to the law of Moses were accomplished, they brought him [Jesus] to Jerusalem, to present him to the Lord... And there was one **Anna, a prophetess**, the daughter of Phanuel, of the tribe of Aser: she was of a great age, which departed not from the **temple,** but served God with fastings and prayers night and day. And she coming in that instant gave thanks likewise unto the Lord, and **spoke of him to all them that looked for redemption in Jerusalem."[304]***

Anna publicly announced in the Temple that Jesus was the coming Redeemer (Messiah) sent to deliver Israel.   She preached the Good News to all those that were in the House of God.

---

[303] Exodus 15
[304] Luke 2

Jesus Commissions Mary

Another woman who shared the good news of Jesus was Mary Magdalene. She was the first person that Jesus revealed Himself to after His resurrection from the dead:

> *"The first day of the week cometh Mary Magdalene early... Mary stood without at the sepulcher weeping... she turned herself back, and saw Jesus standing, and knew not that it was Jesus...Jesus said unto her, Mary. She turned herself, and said unto him, Rabboni; which is to say, Master. Jesus said unto her,* <u>*Touch me not; for I am not yet ascended to my Father:*</u> *but* **go to my brethren, and say unto them, I ascend unto my Father, and your Father; and to my God, and your God.** *Mary Magdalene came and told the disciples that she had seen the Lord, and that he had spoken these things unto her."*[305]

Mary was the first to witness Jesus' resurrection from the dead. The amazing thing about this account was that Jesus said, *"Touch Me not...for I have not yet ascended to My Father."* Jesus had defeated death, hell and the grave, but had not yet presented His Holy Blood before the throne of God. That was why Mary was forbidden from touching Him at that point. Jesus was so moved with compassion for Mary's broken heart that He interrupted that Heavenly ascent to the Father to appear to Mary and to comfort her.

After He ascended to the Father, He returned and appeared to men and women. Only *then* did He allow (and even encouraged) them to touch Him. He wanted them to know that He was flesh and bone,

---

[305] John 20

not just a spirit.[306]   When Jesus commanded Mary to tell the other disciples the Good News that He was risen, she became the first evangelist of the church--commissioned by Jesus Himself!   The disciples did not believe her.   Later, Jesus strongly rebuked the disciples for their unbelief and hardness of heart because they believed not those (including Mary) which saw Him after He was risen from the dead.[307]

Priscilla The Teacher

Another important woman in ministry in the New Testament was Priscilla. She and her husband Aquila had been discipled by Paul and were his traveling companions. Paul actually stayed in their home and worked as a tent maker while preaching in Corinth. Paul discipled them during that time and considered them mature enough to be instated as pastors in Ephesus:

> *"And Paul after this tarried there yet a good while, and then took his leave of the brethren, and sailed thence into Syria, and with him **Priscilla and Aquila;** having shorn his head in Cenchrea: for he had a vow. And he came to **Ephesus, and left them there...**"*[308]

It was very unusual in the Greek culture to have a woman's name to precede her husband's name. It is therefore very noteworthy that three times in scripture Priscilla's name precedes Aquila's. (See Acts 18:18, Romans 16:3, II Timothy 4:19.) Even in today's society a husband and wife are addressed as "Mr. and Mrs._____," with the husband's title coming first.   Greek scholars note this unusual placement of her name, and state that her name preceding her husband's indicates that she had a more dominant position in ministry than Aquila.

---

[306] Matthew 28:9, John 20:27
[307] Mark 16:14
[308] Acts 18:2, 18

In the book of Acts, we note that the writer was inspired to put the predominant person's name before others, such as "Paul and Silas" and "Peter and John."

Priscilla had a very active ministry in the Church. Acts 18 tells of Apollos coming to Ephesus trying to share insights about the Messiah. When Priscilla and Aquila heard him and realized that he had an incomplete knowledge of the Gospel, *"they"* both took him aside and taught him, expounding to him the way of salvation more completely. The teaching of Priscilla and Aquila resulted in Apollos being established as one of the most powerful ministries of the New Testament Church. Paul states that Priscilla was one of his helpers in ministry.[309]

Phoebe The Overseer

Other women are also mentioned in scripture as being "laborers" in the ministry with Paul. Romans 16 lists *Phoebe*, Tryphena and Tryphosa, and Mary, as women that labored in the Lord. Phoebe is especially interesting. The fact that her name was the first listed in Romans 16 was not insignificant. First placement of a name often implies predominance. It is very interesting that male ministers, (*Apostles*, Andronicus and Junia), were greeted *after* her name.[310]

Phebe was called a *servant* of God who was a *succourer* of many in the Church:

> *"**I commend unto you Phoebe** our sister, which is a **servant** of the church which is at Cenchrea: That ye receive her in the Lord, as becomes saints, and that ye assist her in whatsoever business she hath need of you:*

---

[309] Romans 16:3
[310] Romans 16:7

*for she hath been a **succourer** of many, and of myself also."*

Phoebe is called a "servant" of the church, which is the same title that Apostle Paul, Apostle Peter, Apostle Jude, Apostle James, and Apostle John designated for themselves in their epistles to the churches.[311] She had a position of authority in the Church of Cenchrea, as inferred by the term *"succourer."* **Succourer** ("prostatis" in the Greek) is the feminine derivative of "proistemi", which means "one who stands before-in rank-, presides, maintains, to be over, rules."[312]

Her position apparently included presiding over the Church as a protectress (a term equated to the position of bishop or overseer in the Church.) She traveled to the various churches, and Paul admonished the Church in Rome to *"assist her in whatsoever business she had need of"* when she came there. Paul validated her ministry saying that Phoebe had been a *"help to many in the Church, of myself also."* [313]

Scriptural Precedence

With these many scriptural examples of women in public ministry one may wonder why some Churches preach against allowing women to minister or to have any place of leadership in the church. The reason is partly due to the misinterpretation of certain scriptures that have been taken out of context. To get a true and complete understanding on any subject in scripture, one must take the whole counsel of God on the subject so as to *"rightly divide the Word of Truth."*

First, we must acknowledge that the Apostle Paul and Luke validated women in ministry in their books, Acts and Romans. All

---

[311] Titus 1:1; James 1:1; II Peter 1:1; Jude 1; Revelation 1:1
[312] James Strong, Strong's Exhaustive Concordance of The Bible, (Madison, NJ: Abingdon, 1981), 984
[313] Romans 16:2

scripture is given by inspiration of God, so these books are *"profitable for doctrine, for reproof, for correction, for instruction in righteousness."*[314] These books accurately record God's word and principles by which the church is to be instructed and governed.

Those who teach or preach against women ministers are disregarding this counsel of scripture. To disregard any scripture (i.e., not accepting the whole counsel of God) can lead to spiritual error. One must accept all of what God says on a matter, even if a church's teaching or one's own dogma does not embrace it. Jesus said that the *"traditions of man can make the Word of God of no effect."* To stay in truth, we must heed *all* of what God's Word says on a matter.

Women Shouldn't Speak?

Why do some reject women teaching or operating in public ministry? There are two scriptures that are most commonly quoted as reasons for not allowing women to minister in Church. However, if one keeps these scriptures in context, it is evident that neither of them actually teach excluding women from public ministry. One is I Corinthians 14:34, which says, *"let your women keep silence in the churches; for it is not permitted unto them to speak"* and the other is I Timothy 2:12, where Paul instructs, *"I suffer not a woman to teach, nor to usurp authority over the man, but to be in silence."*

Upon first examination, it would appear that Paul is making a blanket prohibition of women ever speaking (teaching, preaching, prophesying) in the Church. But, if that *were* true, then Paul contradicted himself by validating all the women who were in public ministry in the Churches that he established (see Romans 16.)

---

[314] II Timothy 3:16

Context Brings Clarity

If one keeps the scriptures in context so as to determine exactly what Paul is addressing, then these scriptures do reconcile with the rest of God's Word. Proper context gives insight to these statements, and takes away confusion and misunderstanding regarding women speaking. Here is I Corinthians 14:

> *"Let the prophets speak two or three, and let the other judge. If anything be revealed to another that sits by, **let the first hold his peace.** For **you may all prophesy one by one, that all may learn,** and all may be comforted. And the spirits of the prophets are subject to the prophets. **FOR GOD IS NOT THE AUTHOR OF CONFUSION**, but of peace, as in all churches of the saints. **Let your women keep silence in the churches:** for it is not permitted unto them to speak but they are commanded to be under obedience, as also said the law. **And if they will learn anything, let them ask their husbands at home: for it is a shame for women to speak in the church... Let all things be done decently and in order."***

Decently And In Order

Paul's entire purpose for the 14th chapter of I Corinthians was to give instruction for keeping order in the Church services. First he had to correct those who were prophesying. They were so eager to do so that they often would begin speaking when others were prophesying. He commanded them to prophesy one by one so there was no interruption and that everyone could hear the message.

Paul states "You may all prophesy..." which included the women, but it must be done decently and in order. Other abuses in the church included a free-for-all atmosphere in which people were speaking exclusively in tongues (with no interpretation). He told them this would bring confusion or disdain to new believers. He instructed that if one had a message in tongues, but there was no interpreter, they should pray for interpretation or remain silent.

Hey Levi!

Then, there was the issue of the women calling out to their husbands on the other side of the church in the middle of services. It was cultural for the men and women to sit on different sides of the assemblies. The women (who were frequently uneducated in scripture), interrupted the services by trying to ask their husbands questions while the Word of God was being shared. Without a P.A. system for the speaker, the excessive noise of the women speaking out caused the Church Body not to be able to hear the Word of God. As a result, the church was not being edified.

Paul admonished the women (and then all the church), to do things in an orderly way so that the message of God could be shared without interruption. When Paul instructed the women **to be silent**, it was _not_ in the context of them _ministering the Word_. He was addressing them interrupting the services with questions. He instructed the wives to be quiet during the service, and if they want to ask questions, wait and ask their husbands when they got home from church.

The whole point of this instruction was to stop the confusion and unnecessary noise so that whoever was ministering could do so without being interrupted. The prohibition was not for women publicly ministering the word (for he said "you may all prophecy"), but for women talking and interrupting the services.

In fact, Priscilla and her husband, Aquila, were members of the Corinthian church at one time. They were instrumental in teaching and mentoring Apollos, the much celebrated Apostolic teacher in the early church.[315] She was not forbidden to teach.

Women and *Woman*

I Timothy 2 also needs to be taken in context to be properly understood. Here it says:

> *"I will therefore that men pray everywhere, lifting up holy hands, without wrath and doubting. In like manner also, that **women** adorn themselves in modest apparel, with shamefacedness and sobriety; not with braided hair, or gold, or pearls, or costly array; But (which becomes women professing godliness) with good works.*

> *Let the __woman__ **learn in silence with all subjection**. But I suffer not a **woman** to teach, nor to usurp authority over the man, but to be in silence, For __Adam was first formed, then Eve__; And Adam was not deceived, but the woman being deceived was in the transgression. Notwithstanding she shall be saved in childbearing, if **they** continue in faith and charity and holiness with sobriety."*

Woman or Wife?

Notice that first the instructions are for "men" (plural) and then for "women" (plural) regarding their appropriate behavior as Christians. Here men are admonished to pray, and women are

---

[315] Acts 18

admonished to dress modestly and maintain good works. This applies to all women.

Then the admonition changes to "woman" (singular), and "man" (singular.) What many do not know is that the term for "man" and "husband" is the same in the Greek ("aner"). The term for "woman" and "wife" is also the same in the Greek ("gune"). One must look at the *context* of what is being said in order to know whether to interpret "gune" as the general term "woman" or the specific term "wife."

Man And Wife

The first part of the scripture admonishes all women to dress modestly and do good works. This is rightly translated "women" (not "wives"). But, when the context changes from the plural "women" to the singular "woman", the term needs to be translated "**wife**", not "woman." The context of what Paul was addressing here (vs. 11-15) had to do with the specific relationship of a **wife with her husband**. Here, the first husband and wife (Adam and Eve) are referenced.

Then Paul gives them a promise that the *wife* will safely bear children if they both walk in love and sobriety. This context is obviously referring to the marriage relationship. The point here is that God has established a special order in marriage that must be recognized. A wife should give proper respect to the position of authority that the husband has over her. And, in the marriage relationship, the husband is to love his wife as Christ loves the Church.[316]

---

[316] I Corinthians 11:3, Ephesians 5:22-24, & Colossians 3:18

Marriage Relationship, Not Church Protocol

Marriage is the context referred to here in which the _wife_ should not _"teach nor usurp authority"_ over the _husband_. If the husband and the wife keep God's order in marriage (with faith, love and holiness) the wife will be protected.[317] A wife should not downplay the husband's scriptural authority by arguing or trying to correct the husband. I Peter 3:1-5 states if a husband is not being obedient to the Word of God in some area, the wife should not try to browbeat him, but live a Godly example before him. She will win him over with her respectful behavior, not with her words. Following God's order will result in peace, rather than contention, in the home.

What scripture is actually saying here is: _"Let the **wife** learn in silence with all subjection. But I suffer not a **wife** to teach, nor to usurp authority over the **husband**, but to be in silence."_ This does not mean that women are never allowed to teach. If that were the case, then Paul's son in the faith, Timothy, would have been very unlearned, for it was his mother and grandmother who gave him his scriptural training.[318]

Paul did not say that _women_ could not minister and teach, for he trained many women ministers himself (e.g., Priscilla, Phoebe, etc.) What he did say was that a _wife_ should not try to take the spiritual authority away from her husband in the marriage relationship by trying to teach and correct _him_. The best way for her to win her husband over is by a Godly example. If she gets out of order and tries to usurp his authority, she can be deceived like Eve was. It was in this context of _marriage_ that Paul admonished the wife not to teach or usurp the husband's authority in the home--not a prohibition against women ministering spiritual gifts in the Church.

---

[317] I Timothy 2:15
[318] II Timothy 1:5

They All Spoke

In Church women are at liberty to be used in ministry, for *"in Christ it is neither Jew or Greek...neither male nor female, but you are all one in Christ."* (Galatians 3:28) All of the members of Christ's Body are to function and minister in the way and with the gifts that God has distributed to them. The New Testament clearly sanctions women speaking and ministering in the public setting of the Church.

At the first Church service on the Day of Pentecost all one hundred and twenty believers were filled with the Spirit and spoke in tongues and prophesied.[319] Among those were many women, including Mary, the mother of Jesus. Peter did not sit the women down and say "you can't prophesy in Church! You must remain silent!" No. Rather, he confirmed in the last days the Holy Ghost would be poured out, and daughters and handmaids (women) would prophesy.

Those who try to silence anointed women from proclaiming the Word of the Lord are fighting against God's agenda for His Church. The Word of God teaches that women can minister, be in a place of spiritual authority, and use the spiritual gifts endowed to them by God.

---

[319] Acts 1:14, 2:4,17,18

THE CHRISTIAN AND THE CHURCH

There are many professing Christians who do not see the need to regularly attend Church. They have various reasons for not attending. Some believe that they can worship the Lord just as well at home as in the confines of the four walls of a church. Others have had bad experiences in the church, and have withdrawn fellowshipping in Church on that basis.

However, the Bible (which is God's direct will and testament to us) tells us that true Christians should be in Church. Certainly we can and should worship the Lord at home, but that does not preclude the necessity of attending a legitimate church body that gathers together on a regular basis. If one avoids church because of having had a bad experience, they must overcome it by forgiveness. Then they can search out a Body with which they can feel comfortable fellowshipping.

It's A Command

The first and most important reason for attending Church is that Christ commands us to do so. God tells us in Hebrews 10:25 not to stop attending church: *"not forsaking the assembling of yourselves together, as the manner of some is; but exhorting one another: and so much the more, as you see the day approaching."* Prophetically we can see the day of Christ's return approaching. Therefore--*especially now*—we should not forsake church. We all need the spiritual encouragement only found when the corporate Body of Christ gathers together.

If You Love Me, Obey Me

Obedience to God's command is evidence of your love for Him. In John 14:21 Jesus says, *"He that has My commandments, and keeps them, he it is that loves Me."* Conversely, one who does not obey His commands does not love Him: *"He that loves Me not keeps not My sayings; and the word which you hear is not mine, but the Father's which sent Me."*[320] God expects us to obey Him and assemble with other believers in Church.

Jesus Went to Church

Jesus considered worshipping in the congregation very important. In Hebrews 2:12 Jesus says *"I will declare Your name unto My brethren, **in the midst of the church will I sing praise** unto Your name."* If Jesus Himself worshipped in the church, how much more should we! The Apostle Paul admonishes the Corinthians Church saying, *"When you come together [in Church], brethren..."*[321] Notice he did not say, *"If* you come together." It is expected that you will, in obedience to God's command, gather together with other believers in Christ.

A Church By Any Other Name

Here is might be appropriate to define what "Church" means. The term "Church" in the Greek is "eklesia." It is translated "assembly" and "Church" throughout the New Testament. It literally means "out-called," referring to people "called out" from their previous locations to meet together as a body for some purpose. As true believers in Christ, we have been called out of the world. When we gather together in Church, we are *called out* in order to meet together as the Body of Christ.

The "Church," therefore, does not refer to a building, denomination, or group of religious people. It is a gathering together

---

[320] John 14:24
[321] I Cor. 14:26

of true believers who are called out from the world (separated from the world) and gather together to worship God in Spirit and in truth. God is seeking such a people to worship Him.[322]

church Or The Church

We are to avoid those who, though religious, deny God's Spirit and power and live like the world.[323] They are not the true Church. We must discern and differentiate between true believers and those in spiritual error, as Jude 17-19 states:

> *"...remember the words which were spoken before of the apostles of our Lord Jesus Christ; how that they told you there should be mockers in the last time who should walk after their own ungodly lusts. These be they who separate themselves, sensual, having not the Spirit."*

There are those who separate themselves from legitimate ministry in order to find a "comfort zone" religion—somewhere where they will feel comfortable with their drinking and partying and fornication. The look for a seeker-friendly church that preaches a smooth "gospel" that offends no one. Then they feel license to walk after their own lusts instead of the Spirit of Truth since the seeker-friendly churches often say nothing about repentance or sin. The Apostle John writes that those who leave the Truth are not truly part of God's "called out ones" (Church):

Church Is Not Burger King (Have It Your Way)

> *"They went out from us, but they were not of us; for if they had been of us, they would no doubt have*

---

[322] John 4:23, 24
[323] II Timothy 3:1-6

continued with us; but they went out, that they might be made manifest that they were not all of us. But you have an unction from the Holy One, and you know all things.[324]

Therefore, is behooves true believers to search out legitimate ministries with which to fellowship on a regular basis. It may not be in the largest building in town, but God has a church--a remnant--with which believers can assemble. If one is serious about following Christ, they will obey His commandment to assemble with believers to worship, pray, and to fellowship.

Edifying The Church

Apart from being commanded by Christ to attend church, one should want to attend because of the spiritual benefits provided there. I Corinthians 14:26 states that the gifts of the Spirit will manifest resulting in the Body being edified. The Apostle Paul states in that God put gifts in the Body of Christ to help build up and encourage the Church to grow in spiritual maturity. Those gifts will strengthen the Church so that the evil one cannot deceive them:

> *"some apostles; and some prophets; and some evangelists; and some pastors and teachers **for the perfecting of the saints**, for the work of the ministry, for the edifying of the body of Christ: till we all come in the unity of the faith, and of the knowledge of the Son of God, unto a perfect man, unto the measure of the stature of the fullness of Christ: That we henceforth be **no more children**, tossed to and fro, and carried about with every*

---

[324] I John 2:19, 20

wind of doctrine, by the sleight of men, and cunning craftiness whereby they lie in wait to deceive."

Ministry Amiss

The leadership ministry gifts that God has put in the Body are in place to help nurture the Body spiritually, and to protect it from doctrinal error. They are to be the servants of the Body of Christ to equip the saints to effectively go out into the world and fulfill the Great Commission: "Go into all the world and preach the Gospel to every creature." Notice that the leadership was not called to build their own kingdom, but Christ's! When leaders in ministry are overly indulgent in building their own kingdom on this earth (mansions, ministry business endeavors) instead of concentrating on souls, something is terribly wrong. Their purpose is to build up the Body of Christ—not use the Body of Christ to finance their personal retirement "kingdom."

You Have Talent

In addition to leadership using their gifts to encourage the Body of Christ, each member of the Body has gifts that are necessary for local churches to grow and be healthy spiritually. You have a talent that God has entrusted within you. It may be a testimony of God's grace in your life, or perhaps the gift of helps whereby you can bless others with practical abilities and hands on help. It is a gift that you are to share with others in the Body. Romans 12 tells us:

> "*For as we have many members in one body, and all members have not the same office: So we, being many, are one body in Christ, and every one members one of another. **Having then gifts differing according to the grace that is given to us,** whether prophecy, let us prophesy according to the proportion of faith; Or ministry, let us wait on our ministering: or he that*

teaches, on teaching; Or he that exhorts, on exhortation: he that giveth, let him do it with simplicity; he that rules, with diligence; he that shows mercy, with cheerfulness."

Power In Numbers

Paul makes it very clear in that one should not isolate themselves from the rest of the Body:[325]

"But now has God set the members every one of them in the body, as it has pleased him. And if they were all one member, where were the body? But now are they many members, yet but one body. And the eye cannot say unto the hand, I have no need of you: nor again the head to the feet, I have no need of you. Nay, much more those members of the body, which seem to be more feeble, are necessary."

The point is that you have gifts from which the Body of Christ needs to benefit. Likewise, the Body of Christ has gifts from which you need to benefit. No one is complete by themselves in the Church. The local Body has been ordained by God to benefit each member in particular.

Call For The Elders

Another benefit from attending a Church is that healing is available by one calling for the elders:

*"Is any sick **among you**? let him call for the **elders of the church**; and let them pray over him, **anointing him with oil** in the name of the Lord: And the prayer of*

---

[325] I Corinthians 12:18-21

faith shall save the sick, and the Lord shall raise him up; and if he has committed sins, they shall be forgiven him. "[326]

God has ordained elders to be over local bodies. Titus 1:5 states: *"For this cause left I you in Crete, that you should set in order the things that are wanting, and ordain **elders** in every city, as I had appointed you."* Notice that in every city there are to plural "elders" ordained, not "an elder" for the local church.

Originally, they met in individual homes, so these elders would oversee and minister throughout a city. One man was not in charge, but a presbytery—a group of oversees. Often there would be prophets, teachers and apostles in one body, all ministering their gifts for the corporate and mutual edification of all.[327] Having multiple overseers (pastors, teachers, etc.) allowed for more effective oversight of the assemblies of believers. There was not the "one man show," mega-church mentality, but multiple leadership gifts operating for the health of the Body of Christ. It is easy for a little lamb to get overlooked by a shepherd who has a mega-flock. But with multiple elders, individual members can be better protected and fed.

Submit To The Elders

One must be submitted to a local body so that the elder can discharge their God-given duty to feed and protect the flock. I Peter 5:5 states *"Likewise, you younger, **submit yourselves** unto the elder. Yes, all of you be subject one to another, and **be clothed with humility**: for God resists the proud, and gives grace to the humble."* The implication here is that if one refuses to submit to God-ordained

---

[326] James 5:13, 14
[327] Acts 13:1-4

leadership, they are proud. They are rebelling against the order that God set in the Church.

In Hebrews 13:17 it tells us to *"Obey them **that have the rule over you**, and submit yourselves: for they watch for your souls, as they that must give account, that they may do it with joy, and not with grief: for that is unprofitable for you."* This means that there is legitimate authority that God has given elders in the church. They are ordained to lead you. If you do not submit, you are bucking God's authority. This does not mean elders are to act as tyrants and lord their authority over people--belittling them, intimidating (which amounts to witchcraft). Rather, they are to use their authority to build up the Body of Christ.

Qualifications Of Elders

Given such a sacred trust to lead the flock demands that the elders adhere to very high qualifications. Paul tells Timothy that overseers are to be blameless in lifestyle and character:

> *"If a man desires the office of a bishop, he desires a good work. A bishop then must be **blameless**, the **husband of one wife**, vigilant, sober, of **good behavior**, given to hospitality, apt to teach; Not given to wine, no striker**, not greedy of filthy lucre;** but **patient**, not a brawler, **not covetous;** One that **rules well his own house**, having his children in subjection with all gravity; (For if a man knows not how to rule his own house, how shall he take care of the church of God?) **Not a novice, lest being lifted up with pride he fall into the condemnation of the devil.** Moreover, he must have a **good report of them which are without;** lest he fall into reproach and the snare of the devil.* "[328]

---

[328] I Timothy 3:1-8

Don't Be A "Morning Star"

What was the *"condemnation of the devil?"* lucifer was the anointed cherub—the "star of the morning" who wanted to be exalted like the Most High.[329] satan was anointed. he had gifts and talents operating through him. People may have true gifts from God, but use them with impure motives (greed, self-exaltation, control). Some use God's gifts (perhaps the gift of healing) for money, selling prayer cloths, or other seed-faith "trinkets."

Others may use control measures like false prophecies, manipulation, and fear to keep congregants from leaving. Small congregations are susceptible to that type of cult mentality, warning the members that they will be cursed if they leave the church. Pure witchcraft! (I should say, *impure...*) Then there are "super-star" ministries that try to have the spotlight and cameras on themselves. They want men to follow them and exalt them. They want to be a star. They are in danger of falling like lucifer. God will not share His glory with anyone. We are foolish if we try to take it for ourselves.

Tickle The Ears, Pad The Pocket

Think about these qualifications: Elders are not to be greedy of filthy lucre, and they are to have a good report with them without (the people of the world). Then consider some of the major ministries on television. The self-indulgent life-styles and huge amassment of money for their own coffers is a sign that they are off-course. When their personal wealth acquired from "ministry" is so excessive that they warrant a 60 Minutes prime time investigative report on their opulent life-style, then something is terribly wrong. They no longer are above reproach. They do not have a "good report" with those without. They

---

[329] Ezekiel 28

may legally get by with the IRS and stay out of prison, but it doesn't undo the damage that their greed has done to the true preaching of the Gospel. They have lost all credibility.

People in the world will turn off TV preachers thinking that they are all charlatans— "All they want is my money." And, in many cases, they are right. They are motivated by greed or they are trying to please man for popularity. I get concerned when a Christian author has a best-selling book that the world likes. If they are not getting saved from reading it, then the message is skewed. The mentality is: "Whatever sells—whatever can be promoted to make a buck is okay." They are not concerned that the Truth is not going forth. Just make them feel good so that they will want to buy your next book. To them, ministry is no more than a vocation—a means of a paycheck--not a sacred calling from God.

Test The Fruit

A true man of God will only do and say that which pleases God.[330] Paul said, *"If I yet please man, I should not be a servant of Christ..."* Jesus said to beware of false prophets. If all men speak well of you, then something is wrong. Popular prophets are false prophets. Jesus said that you would know them by their fruit… love, joy, peace, patience, gentleness, goodness, faith, meekness, and self-control. He did not say you would know them by their Rolls Royce, their private jet, or their mansion. You would not know them by their gifts of healing or seemingly accurate prophetic words. You will know them by their fruit…their love for God and people.

The True Church

---

[330] Galatians 1:10

Thankfully, there are many ministers and pastors who sincerely do care for the flock. The book of Acts is the ultimate pattern for New Testament churches. It was founded on the Words of Christ and the anointed directives of the Holy Spirit through the Apostles. It was a vibrant, alive church that operated in the power of the Holy Ghost. Here is how it began:

"And when the day of Pentecost was fully come, they were all with one accord in one place. And suddenly there came a sound from heaven as of a rushing mighty wind, and it filled all the house where they were sitting. And there appeared unto them cloven tongues like as of fire, and it sat upon each of them. And ***they were all filled with the Holy Ghost,*** *and began to speak with other tongues, as the Spirit gave them utterance."*

Blessings For Obedience

Notice that all who gathered with the Church that day had the benefit of God's power by being filled with the Holy Ghost. According to I Corinthians 15 and Acts 1, over five hundred believers in Christ witnessed His resurrection. They were commanded not to leave Jerusalem, but to wait for the Promised Holy Ghost. Less than one fourth of the Church bothered to obey. Only the obedient few who faithfully assembled together received God's blessing that day.

Unity Brings Increase

Acts 2 says that because the believers were "together" in unity, it caused the Church to increase:

"Then they that gladly received his word were baptized: and the same day there were added unto them

*about three thousand souls. And they **continued steadfastly in the apostles' doctrine and fellowship, and in breaking of bread, and in prayers**. And fear came upon every soul: and many wonders and signs were done by the apostles.*

*And all that believed **were together**, and had **all things common**; sold their possessions and goods, and parted them to all men, as every man had need. And they, continuing daily with **one accord** in the temple, and breaking bread from house to house, did eat their meat with gladness and **singleness of heart**, praising God, and having favor with all the people. And the Lord **added to the church daily such as should be saved.***"

In Acts 4 the Holy Ghost moved powerfully because of the Church's corporate prayer. Being in one accord allowed for God's power to manifest and all of the Church's needs were provided:

*"And when they had prayed, the place was shaken where they were **assembled together**; and they were all filled with the Holy Ghost, and they spoke the word of God with boldness. And the multitude of them that believed were of **one heart and of one soul**: neither said any of them that ought of the things which he possessed was his own; but they had all things common.*

*And with **great power** gave the apostles witness of the resurrection of the Lord Jesus: and **great grace was upon them all**. **Neither was there any among them that lacked**: for as many as were possessors of lands or* *houses sold them, and brought the prices of the things that were sold.*"

Unity brings power, grace, and provision for the church. The world was never intended to be the source for the church needs being met. God can meet those needs within the Body. The church was on fire and met *"daily in the temple, and in every house, they ceased not to teach and preach Jesus Christ."*[331]

That is the New Testament pattern. What has happened to the zeal of the church in our day? Have soccer practices or TV comedies taken precedence over being in the very presence of Almighty God? Lord, help us to remove any idols that are in our hearts!

Changed From Glory To Glory

The Church in Antioch had teachers consistently discipling the church for an entire year. As a result, the Church became more Christ-like as their lifestyles emulated the Master:

> *"Then departed Barnabas to Tarsus, for to seek Saul: And when he had found him, he brought him unto Antioch. And it came to pass, that **a whole year they assembled themselves** with the church, and **taught much people**. And the disciples were called **Christians** first in Antioch."*[332]

Power In Corporate Prayer

When the church assembles together and prays sincere, effectual prayers, things change. We cannot just assume God is going to deliver unless we pray. The church may have gotten a bit lax in their

---

[331] Acts 5
[332] Act 12:26

prayers when Peter and James were cast into prison the second time. After all, the first time an angel supernaturally released them, and they were set free to keep preaching in the temple. However, this time, Herod beheaded James…and it looked like Peter was next in line. That got the church praying very earnestly for him and brought the deliverance by the angel:

> *"Peter therefore was kept in prison: **but prayer was made without ceasing of the church unto God for him.** And when Herod would have brought him forth, the same night Peter was sleeping between two soldiers, bound with two chains: and the keepers before the door kept the prison.*
>
> *And, behold, the **angel of the Lord came upon him, and a light shined in the prison: and he smote Peter on the side,** and raised him up, saying, Arise up quickly. **And his chains fell off from his hands.** And the angel said unto him, Gird thyself, and bind on thy sandals. And so he did… When they were past the first and the second ward, they came unto the iron gate that leads unto the city; which opened to them of his own accord: and they went out, and passed on through one street; and forthwith the angel departed from him."*

Peter was delivered because he was part of a vibrant church that knew the power of prayer. Though Peter certainly was praying, it says **"BUT prayer was made without ceasing of the CHURCH unto God for him."** This implies that if the church hadn't prayed, Peter would not have been delivered. **BUT** the church prayed for him… We need the intercession of the saints when we are weak or sick or discouraged.

Prayer support from the Body of Christ is vital. Being in church affords us a spiritual network of power and support.

Multitude Of Counselors

In addition to prayer support, the church can also be a source of spiritual confirmation and guidance. Proverbs says, *"in the multitude of counselors there is wisdom."* Though as a sheep of the Lord's flock we can all hear the Shepherd ourselves, yet, having others to confirm God's direction is needful. Paul knew God's call on his life, yet waited for confirmation to act:

> *"Now there were **in the church** that was at Antioch certain **prophets and teachers**; as Barnabas, and Simeon that was called Niger, and Lucius of Cyrene, and Manaen, which had been brought up with Herod the tetrarch, and Saul. **As they ministered to the Lord, and fasted, the Holy Ghost said, 'Separate me Barnabas and Saul for the work whereunto I have called them.'** And when they had fasted and prayed, and laid their hands on them, they sent them away. So they, being sent forth by the Holy Ghost, departed unto Seleucia; and from thence they sailed to Cyprus."*

Paul and Barnabas submitted to the leadership of the Holy Spirit through the local Body, even though they themselves were in leadership. Because they submitted to the elders in church, the Holy Spirit blessed their mission trip. It resulted in a number of churches being established.

Regular Meetings

The book of Acts reveals a pattern of the church meeting consistently and regularly. They did not limit church to one day a week, but often met daily to pray from house to house. At least once a week the Church met to break bread in communion (to "remember the Lord's death until He comes.") In Acts 20 it states that they met on the "Lord's day" [Sunday]:

> *"And upon the **first day of the week**, when the disciples came together to **break bread**, Paul preached unto them, ready to depart on the morrow; and continued his speech until midnight."*

We see that they did not have a sun dial (or clock) dictating when the service would end. It lasted until midnight, and then into the next morning. They allowed the Holy Spirit to dictate the flow of the service. It is fine to have regular times set, but we must be open to God's will to change and "interrupt" our service plans, even if it means cancelling our reservation at the diner. When times are desperate, church is not an obligation. It becomes an oasis of hope and strength.

Everyone Needs Church

Paul the Apostle needed to be in church. It was a source of encouragement and strength for him. In spite of all of the supernatural revelation that he received directly from the Lord, he needed to assemble with other believers. No one is so "spiritual" that they do not need church:

> *"Where we found brethren, and were desired to tarry with them seven days: and so we went toward Rome. And from thence, when **the brethren heard of us, they came to meet us** as far as Appii Forum, and The Three Taverns: **whom when Paul saw, he thanked God, and took courage.**"[333]*

---

[333] Acts 28:14,15

If one says that they do not need to be in church… that they can seek God by themselves, then they are deceiving themselves. God's Word says, *"Forsake not assembling together."* Period.

Spiritual Discipline In Church

No one likes the topic of spiritual discipline. Probably because there have been abuses and misuses that have destroyed or severely injured those who were supposed to benefit from it. Any "discipline" in church must be done in a spirit of love for those involved, and for the flock as a whole. It is not for the lay people to dole out, but for mature, spiritual leaders who have the best interest of the flock at heart, and the mind of the Lord regarding the issues at hand. The elders are simply servants of the church… under-shepherds ordained to feed the flock. But they do have spiritual authority to administer discipline when it is necessary. Sin cannot be tolerated. It defiles the Body. In the early Church, instant death occurred when there was sin in the camp:

> *"A certain man named Ananias, with Sapphira his wife, sold a possession, And kept back part of the price, his wife also being privy to it, and brought a certain part, and laid it at the apostles' feet. But Peter said, Ananias, why hath Satan filled thine heart to **lie to the Holy Ghost**, and to keep back part of the price of the land? Whiles it remained, was it not thine own? and after it was sold, was it not in thine own power? why hast thou conceived this thing in thine heart? thou hast not lied unto men, but unto God. And **Ananias hearing these words fell down, and gave up the ghost…"***

*"...when his wife, not knowing what was done, came in. And Peter answered unto her, Tell me whether ye sold the land for so much? And she said, Yea, for so much. Then Peter said unto her, How is it that **you have agreed together to tempt the Spirit of the Lord?** behold, the feet of them which have buried thy husband are at the door, and shall carry thee out. Then fell she down straightway at his feet, and yielded up the ghost...* "[334]*

Why was the judgment so severe and immediate? Because the power of God was moving. He was not going to allow sin in the camp that could contaminate and stop the flow of the Holy Ghost and the Church's growth. Many were added to the church as a result of God's moving. Another time Peter warned a new convert that if he did not repent of the impure motive of his heart (tried to purchase Holy Ghost power for himself), he and his money would perish.[335]

Sin In The Camp

In other cases, there was instruction to dis-fellowship with a "Christian" who would not repent of their sin. Why? Because like Achan of old, sin in the camp can bring ruin to a whole nation.[336] Joshua had to remove the sinner (Achan) from the assembly and eradicate him so that the armies of Israel could go forth and not suffer any more loss from the breach opened by sin. Sin is a spiritual cancer... an evil leaven that can infect and affect everything around it. Once a certain sin is allowed to remain in a church body, satan will use that breach to infiltrate further.

---

[334] Acts 5
[335] Acts 8
[336] Joshua 7

If a sexual sin (adultery, fornication, homosexuality) is winked at and not corrected, that sin will spread like cancer. I recall a church that had a wholesome congregation with solid marriages. An outside woman was hired to be director of an important facet of the church. She seduced a married man in the congregation, and they pursued an adulterous affair. He ended up divorcing his wife to marry the adulteress. The adulteress was never removed from her church position because of her "importance." As a result of that unchecked sin, many marriages in that church began falling apart like an epidemic. People were destroyed because of sin in the camp.

Restoration Of The Sinner

Apostle Paul gives us instructions on how to deal with sin in the church: *"Brethren, if a man be overtaken in a fault, ye which are spiritual, restore such an one in the spirit of meekness; considering thyself, lest thou also be tempted."*[337] First, the term "fault" means a "misstep." This infers that one is not intentionally, continually walking in a wrong way, but got "tripped up" in some manner. They have sinned, and they need to be restored. They must be approached in a loving, meek manner for the purpose of praying with them to bring restoration to that believer.

Spiritual Leaven

But then there are those who are continuing down a path of habitual sin without sincere repentance. That is considered spiritual leaven. That was the case in the Corinthian Church:

> *"It is reported commonly that there is **fornication among you**, and such fornication as is not so much as named among the Gentiles, that one should have his father's wife. And ye are **puffed up, and have**

---

[337] Galatians 6:1

not rather mourned, that he that hath done this deed might be taken away from among you.

For I truly, as absent in body, but present in spirit, have judged already, as though I were present, concerning him that hath so done this deed, In the name of our Lord Jesus Christ, when ye are gathered together, and my spirit, with the power of our Lord Jesus Christ, To **deliver such an one unto satan for the destruction of the flesh, that the spirit may be saved in the day of the Lord Jesus.**"

"Your glorying is not good. Know ye not that a **little leaven leavens the whole lump? Purge out therefore the old leaven**, that ye may be a new lump, as ye are unleavened. For even Christ our Passover is sacrificed for us: Therefore, let us keep the feast, not with old leaven, neither with the **leaven of malice and wickedness**; but with the unleavened bread of sincerity and truth."

"**I wrote unto you in an epistle not to company with fornicators: Yet not altogether with the fornicators of this world,** or with the covetous, or extortioners, or with idolaters; for then must ye needs go out of the world. But now **I have written unto you not to keep company, if any man <u>that is called a brother</u> be a fornicator, or covetous, or an idolater, or a railer, or a drunkard, or an extortioner; with such a one no not to eat.** For what have I to do to judge them also that are without? do not ye judge them that are within? But them that are without God judges.

Therefore, put away from among yourselves that wicked person."

Paul was very serious about this blatant disregard for God's holy Word. This was a "brother" (Brother X) who had been taught the truth that he needed to repent of fornication. He knew it was wrong, but the church did not bother to address it. He was comfortable living in sin and still going to church. After all, this was Corinth. Fornication is commonplace. It really isn't that bad, is it? And Brother X does so well in the praise team... The church cannot have him leave. *Really??*

Paul was not only grieved with the man involved in fornication, but he was equally grieved that the church arrogantly thought that they could simply ignore his sin issue.

Sin is not to be tolerated. Obviously a sinner coming to an evangelist church should be allowed opportunity to hear the Gospel and repent and get saved. But a "saint" is not to be allowed fellowship with the Body when they, after being approached in corrective love, defiantly continue in their sin. It brings a defiling influence into the Body of Christ. Paul was so serious about the need to purge sin from the church, that he was compelled to deliver "Brother X" over to satan so his flesh would be destroyed.

Paul would not tolerate placating to Brother X's lust and rationalizing why it wasn't so bad. Paul invited satan to attack him physically. How mean! NO! How loving! Paul cared enough to risk rattling people's sensibilities, hurting people's feelings, and becoming unpopular with the Corinth Church to rid them of spiritual death. And it was the most loving thing for Brother X. When he was dis-fellowshipped, he had to face the reality of the depravity of his gross sin, instead of feeling comfortable with it in the confines of the church.

As a result, it brought repentance to the church, and to the one entangled in sin.

Obviously this discipline is a last resort only to be pursued after one has personally gone to the one in sin in a spirit of love to bring correction and restoration. If he rejects a personal entreaty, then take another witness or two with **humility, compassion** and **love**. They should approach that one with a goal of restoration. If he refuses that correction, then bring it before the church body. If they still refuse to repent from willful sin, they are to be rejected by the church.[338] They have a spirit of rebellion, like the sin of witchcraft. Paul said, *"Those that sin, rebuke before all, that others also may fear."*[339] Paul did not attend a "seeker friendly church." He pleased God.

Pastors might say, *"Well, let the wheat and tares grow together... God will do the separating,"* (citing the parable in Matthew 13). That is a cop out. The "field" in that parable is not the church... it is the world. Believers are responsible to judge those who are within the church.[340] Pastors must be willing to do the unpleasant... to do "house cleaning," for the sake of the rest of the body, if not for the unrepentant sinning "saint." God said that judgment begins first at the church,[341] and if we will first judge ourselves, then we will not have to be judged. Some might say, "If we judge those who are practicing sin, we will lose a lot of the congregation." Peter lost two of his big "contributors," (Ananias and Sapphira). Follow God's pattern and see what God will do. Perhaps your church will "turn the world upside down," and bring revival to your city, as did the early church.[342] They had the fear of God with His power.

---

[338] Matthew 18:15-17
[339] I Timothy 5:20
[340] I Corinthians 5:12
[341] I Peter 4:17
[342] Acts 17:6

God has made it very clear in scripture that He ordained for the local Church to be a place of growth, nurturing, instruction (and discipline, if needed). God expects true believers to obey His command to "*not forsake assembling*," but to find a church to attend regularly. Believers are to use the gifts that God has uniquely bestowed upon them so that all of the Body of Christ may receive mutual edifying. Church is to be a place of blessing and strength for God's holy people.

BIBLICAL FINANCES

The Bible has much to say about finances. One of the principles of Biblical giving is that concerning tithing. Though some may say, "We are not under the Law, so we do not have to tithe…" I would have to concur in part, in that we do not follow Old Testament precepts to be justified. However, the principle of giving tithes was in place before the Law of Moses. We know that Jesus came to fulfill the righteousness of the Law for us. Scripture tells us that when we walk after the Spirit of God, we fulfill the Law:

"the righteousness of the Law might be fulfilled in us, who walk not after the flesh, but after the Spirit."[343]

The New Covenant has an even higher standard of righteousness than did the Law of Moses. Whereas Moses said, *"you shall not commit adultery,"* Jesus said,[344] *"Whosoever **looks** on a woman to lust after her has committed adultery with her already in his heart."*

The New Testament standard exceeds the demands of the Law. Jesus measures not just actions, but the intent of the heart. That makes us even *more accountable* to God, as the motives of our heart as well as our actions are judged. When one follows the Spirit of God, He will lead you not only to do God's commands, but many times to go above and beyond them. Whereas the Law required tithes and offerings, the New Testament followers were sometimes required to "forsake all" to follow Christ...[345]

---

[343] Romans 8
[344] Acts 2:45, Acts 4:32
[345] Mark 10:21, 29

Above And Beyond

An example of "going beyond" the tithe principle is found in the early church. They freely shared with each other by selling off their assets and giving them to the church to distribute to those in need. The principle that *following God's Spirit* will not only fulfill the letter of the Law of Moses, but *goes beyond those statutes* is confirmed here. However, let us just consider the minimal level of giving, which is tithes and offerings.

Abraham Gave

Tithing means "tenth," and so it implies that you give back to God ten percent of that which He blesses you with... financially, materially, talents, and time. This principle pre-dates the Law of Moses by over 400 years, as even Abraham knew it was appropriate to honor God with a tenth of all of his increase. The following demonstrates Abraham's obedience in giving:

Abraham's nephew, Lot, lived in the wealthy (albeit, evil) city of Sodom. There were renegade marauders (regional "kings" with their armies) that would often invade neighboring cities to plunder their land and goods. There was a league of these marauding "kings" that conspired against the city of Sodom and the nearby cities with which Sodom had confederacy. When they invaded, they not only took all of the goods of the land, but also kidnapped the residents, including Lot and his family. Having heard of the attack, Abraham armed his trained servants (three hundred and eighteen men), and pursued the invaders north. With God's help he brought back all of the goods, as well as his nephew Lot, his wife, his daughters, and the other people who were kidnapped.

Offering Of Thanks

In gratitude for God saving his family, Abraham wanted to give God an offering of thanks:

*"And Melchizedec king of Salem brought forth bread and wine: and he was the **priest of the Most High God**. And he blessed him and said, Blessed be Abram of the Most High God, possessor of heaven and earth: And blessed be the Most High God, which has delivered thine enemies into your hand. **And he gave him tithes of all.**"*[346]

Abraham was a man of faith who honored God with all that he had. As a result, God moved and wrought deliverance for his family when the enemy had kidnapped them. Because Abram knew that Melchizedek was the priest of the Most High God, it is likely that he made a vow to the priest to petition God for help in Lot's rescue. As the priest of God, Melchizedek likely prayed on Abraham's behalf for the safety and deliverance of his family members. After God brought them all back, Abraham gratefully gave Melchizedek a tithe of all the spoils.

Jesus Our High Priest

Jesus is called a *"Priest forever, after the order of Melchizedek."*[347] If Abraham can give the man that foreshadowed Jesus' Priesthood ten percent of his increase, surely we can give the High Priest of Heaven (Jesus, the Son of God), at least that amount! Giving financially to support the work of God is a means by which we can honor and thank God for His goodness toward us. He delivered us from the power of the enemy, and has brought us into His marvelous light! We owe Him our very lives! Jesus, our High Priest, is worthy of much more than tithes!

---

[346] Genesis 14:11
[347] Hebrews 5:6

But, tithing is at least a beginning place to start when considering the principle of giving. The Prophet Malachi gives a strong rebuke and admonition for the people of God concerning it:

Will You Rob God?

*"Will a man **rob God**? Yet you have robbed me. But you say, Wherein have we robbed you? **In tithes and offerings. You are cursed with a curse**: for you have robbed Me, even this whole nation. **Bring ye all the tithes into the storehouse**, that there may be meat in Mine house, and prove Me now herewith, said the LORD of hosts, if I will not open to you the windows of heaven, and **pour you out a blessing, that there shall not be room enough to receive it. And I will rebuke the devourer for your sakes**, and he shall not destroy the fruits of your ground; neither shall your vine cast her fruit before the time in the field, said the LORD of hosts. And **all nations shall call you blessed: for you shall be a delightsome land**, said the LORD of hosts."[348]*

Though this is a serious rebuke, there is a wonderful promise of provision with it! Consider first what God says: "***You have robbed Me...***" Robbery against God is a very serious offence. Robbery is done personally—it is not "theft," in which one secretly steals. To rob someone is to *personally* take something away from someone else. Robbing God is taking that which is His, right in front of His face! I do not want to commit a crime against Almighty God!

Prove God

God then gives us a challenge: "Prove Me." If one will step out in faith and obedience to honor God with their finances (tithes and

---

[348] Malachi 3:8

offerings), God promised to pour out a *blessing that we would not have room enough to contain.* That is huge! So the choice is ours: blessing or curse.

The curses listed in Deuteronomy are daunting! They touch every area of one's life. satan likes to "kill, steal, and destroy," and when we shut the door to God's blessings, we open the door to the devil's curses. All of the curses are allowed to come upon us if we disobey God.

Curses For Disobedience

The curses include every type of pain and sickness, family heartache and loss, mental distress, fear, confusion, financial and personal loss, invasion, war, famine, and even cannibalism! Why open the door to the enemy stealing every happiness and security in your life? Simply obey God and tithe!

Fear

Fear is a reason that some do not give to God. They look at the economy and believe that they cannot afford to give. They try to secure their future by storing up what they possess. However, this is flawed reasoning. When the economy is bad, that is *really* when you need to incorporate God's supernatural provision and blessing into your life. You do so by obedient faith. Isaac knew this principle. God gave him a promise that if he would stay in the land of Canaan during the time of famine (rather than flee to Egypt), God would bless him in the land.[349]

Isaac Sowed

It took an act of faith for Isaac not to leave for the more productive land of Egypt when Canaan was experiencing a severe

---

[349] Genesis 26

famine. But, he stayed in faith and worked the fields, sowing his seed. It seemed a foolish waste of seed when everyone else's crops were failing from the drought, yet he sowed anyway. God showed Himself faithful to His promise and gave Isaac a *hundred fold return* on the seed that he had sown. Faith in God's ability to provide prevailed! Had Isaac looked at the natural circumstances, he would never have sown his seed in that arid land. But because he trusted God's promise, he obeyed and was greatly blessed with provision.

Sow In Famine

Our land is in a spiritual famine, and eventually that will lead to a natural famine. Now is the time to trust God's promise and put Him first in your finances. Through obedience to His command to honor Him with your finances, God will open the windows of heaven for you! Sowing and reaping is a spiritual principle that that Paul taught the Corinthian Church:

> *"... For you know the grace of our Lord Jesus Christ, that, though He was rich, yet **for your sakes He became poor, that you through His poverty might be rich...***
>
> ***He which sows sparingly shall reap also sparingly; and he which sows bountifully shall reap also bountifully.*** *Every man according as he purposes in his heart, so let him give; not grudgingly, or of necessity (out of compulsion): for **God loves a cheerful giver.** And God is able to make <u>all grace abound toward you</u>; that you, always having all sufficiency in all things, may abound to every good work: (As it is written, He has dispersed abroad; <u>he has given to the poor: his righteousness remains forever.</u>*

God Will Meet Your Needs

God promises to meet your financial need as you sow into His harvest field by supporting the Gospel. Local churches that preach the Gospel and have a vision for world evangelism are good places to sow one's seed. I do not recommend donating for waterparks and the like that waste God's money on vain pursuits. Sow into that which focuses on soul winning for Jesus.

Love Gives

A true saying is, "You can give without loving, but you cannot love without giving." Jesus said, *"Where your treasure is, there will your heart be also."* If you love God, you will be willing to give Him anything. Under the Law the children of Israel were *required* to give tithes and offerings. Under grace the Holy Spirit motivates our giving, which could very well exceed the mandatory tithe. The early church was very generous. In Acts 2 (after being filled with the Holy Ghost) they sold their possessions and shared the proceeds and their food with one another.

By Faith, Give

Giving is not only a measure of *love* for God and others, but is also a measure of your *faith* in God. *"By faith Abel offered to God a more excellent sacrifice than Cain..."*[350] When you trust God as your provider, you are not trusting in the limited amount that you may have in your hand, but in the resources of the eternal God, Who owns the cattle on a thousand hills. Your faith in God's care and ability to provide, pleases Him. It shows that you trust His character. You believe that He will not withhold any good thing from you, as you walk uprightly. Stinginess is a sign that one *does not trust God* to replenish what they give to others. But the Bible says, *"the liberal soul shall be*

---

[350] Hebrews 11:4

made fat."[351] You open the floodgates of heaven when you give in faith. You do not give *in order* to get, but give out of love and obedience.

Cheerful Giver

Faith allows you to be a "cheerful" giver, for you know that God will meet all of your needs according to His riches in glory by Christ Jesus. You will not give cheerfully if you <u>do not</u> believe that God will provide for you. Meditate on His promises of provision so that when you give, you do so in faith. Then, God is able to make all grace abound to you.[352] His provision will empower with more resources so that you can increase in your giving (i.e. "abound unto every good work.") We are to be conduits of God's blessings, not stopped-up pools hoarding what we receive for ourselves. It is more blessed to give than to receive. Give from a pure heart of love and faith. Then God will in turn bless you, not only financially, but spiritually!

> *"God loves a **cheerful giver**. And God is able to make **all grace abound toward you**; that you, **always having all sufficiency in all things, may abound to every good work:** (As it is written, He has dispersed abroad; he has **given to the poor: his righteousness remains forever.** Now he that ministers seed to the sower both minister bread for your food, and **multiply your seed sown,** and **increase the fruits of your righteousness**...*"[353]

Floodgates Of Blessings

Notice that the purpose of one getting increase on the seed (financial giving) that they have invested is to get *more seed* to sow

---

[351] Proverbs 11:24, 25
[352] II Corinthians 8 & 9
[353] II Corinthians 8:7-10

into *more good works* (such as giving to the poor). The financial increase was to make the giver a conduit of blessing to the needy in the world, not to squander it upon gold-plated faucets to prove to the Christian community how "spiritual" you are because you have more money in the bank than anyone else. God help us to give with a right motive. God is not stingy. He wants us to be blessed. But He wants our driving concern not to be about ourselves, but to bless others with acts of kindness. If you see your brother in need and close your heart of compassion, how does the love of God dwell in you? They will know we are Christians by our love one to another. Love is tangibly seen when we are generous and give.

Fruit Of Righteousness

One aspect of giving is that one's "fruit of righteousness" will increase. The fruit of the Spirit (love, joy, peace...)[354] will abound in you when you give to help others. That is amazing! God will bless us spiritually when we give of our finances. We see this principle working in the life of a military man named Cornelius. God was very impressed that this Roman Centurion had begun praying to the God of Israel, and giving much alms to the poor. His sincere, generous giving so touched the heart of God that He sent an angelic messenger to Cornelius. The basis for this non-Jew to *hear the Gospel first* was because he had honored God by giving alms to the poor. ("He who has mercy on the poor lends to the Lord...and the Lord shall repay him.")[355] God said that Cornelius' almsgiving became a *"memorial before God in heaven."*

Memorial Before God

God remembered Cornelius after the New Covenant was ratified by the Blood of Jesus. He sent an angelic messenger, as well as the Apostle Peter to preach the Gospel message to Cornelius and his

---

[354] Galatians 5:22-23
[355] Proverbs 14:21

house. As a result, all of his house was saved. You can build a memorial before God if you will, in faith and love, share with the poor and support the work of the Gospel.

Another beautiful testimony of how giving touches the heart of God is when the "sinner" woman anointed Jesus' feet with ointment. It is said that she spent almost an entire year's wages on that precious ointment. Because of her love and appreciation for Jesus extending His grace and forgiveness to her, she lavishly poured all the ointment out upon Jesus in an act of worship. That act was especially precious, as it would be the only ointment that Jesus' body would have for His burial. Though the crowd rebuked her for her extravagant giving, Jesus commended her.

She Has Done What She Could

He said, *"She has done what she could: she is come beforehand to anoint My Body for the burying. Truly I say unto you, wheresoever this Gospel shall be preached throughout the whole world, this also that she has done shall be spoken of for a memorial of her."*[356] Have you *"done what you could"* for the One who redeemed your life from eternal destruction with His Blood? How can we not give Him everything that we have and all that we are? God sees your sacrificial giving to Him as precious… It a cherished memorial in heaven of your love for Him.

Giving is an important principle for every believer to practice. It is God's means by which He can validate your trust in Him, and whereby He can in turn bless your finances. However, the highest purpose for giving is that of an act of worship and love for Him.

---

[356] Mark 14:8, 9

DIVORCE AND THE CHURCH

Sadly, divorce and re-marriage is rampant in America and throughout the world today. That which used to be a societal taboo is now very common place, including within the walls of the Church. Even well known "preachers" are on their second and third marriages because the first one(s) "just didn't work out." Marrying and giving in marriage is a sign that points to Jesus' soon coming: "*For as in the days that were before the flood they were eating and drinking, **marrying and giving in marriage**, until the day that Noah entered into the ark, And knew not until the flood came, and took them all away; so shall also the coming of the Son of man be.*"[357]

Evil And Violence

In Noah's time men's thoughts were "*only evil continually*" and society was filled with violence.[358] Jesus' statement infers that society's excessive preoccupation with eating, drinking, and marrying is indicative of an evil generation. Obviously, marriage in itself that is not evil, for, "*marriage is honorable in all*" and ordained by God.[359] Man can make the institution of marriage an evil thing by perverting it. Gay "marriage" is certainly a perversion of God's plan for marriage.

Another evil trend of society is the cycle of "marrying and giving in marriage" (marriage/divorce/re-marriage). Breaking the covenant of marriage through divorce is evil. It does violence to that sacred institution that God ordained. How many tabloid stars are married for just a couple of years (at best), and then file for divorce, while they actively seek out another "significant other?" They have no commitment. Their prenuptial agreements attest to their lack of

---

[357] Matthew 24:37, 38
[358] Genesis 6:5-10
[359] Hebrews 12:4

commitment. They anticipate divorce even before they marry. That is what God opposes:

> *"The Lord has been witness between you and the wife of your youth, against whom you have dealt treacherously; yet she is your companion, and the wife of your covenant. And did not He make one? Yet, He had the residue of the Spirit. And why one? That He might seek a godly seed. Therefore, take heed to your spirit, and let none deal treacherously against the wife of his youth. For the LORD, the God of Israel, said that* **He hates putting away: for one covers violence** *with his garment, said the LORD of hosts: therefore take heed to your spirit, that you deal not treacherously."* (Malachi 2:14-16)

Breaking Covenant

God says here that divorce (*"putting away"*) is an act of violence. To make a vow to be one with an individual and then to break it rips apart a unit... spiritually, emotionally... in every way. The implication here is that the husband divorces the wife out of convenience for another woman (he therefore, "dealt treacherously" with her.) In other words, he turns in the old model ("wife of your youth") for a new model ... like trading cars. His lust causes him to negate the covenant of marriage for another woman. The hurt of abandonment in the wife and children is the "violence" he inflicts. Of course, the treachery is not limited to the husband. An adulteress wife inflicts the same violence on a marriage covenant. God is a God who keeps covenant.[360]

---

[360] Deuteronomy 7:9

Covenant Commitment

To manifest a Godly nature, Christians should keep their covenants. Ecclesiastics 5:5 states that it is better never to vow a vow, than to vow and not keep it. Don't enter into the covenant of marriage lightly. It is a vow to God and man. God expects us to keep our vows, and certainly marriage is the most important earthly vow we can make.

Sadly, the convenience mindset of the world has crept into the Church. Some Christians have adopted the mentality of "well, if it doesn't work out, I can always divorce." With that lack of commitment, it won't work. Love (God's love) is willing to give unconditionally. It is a commitment to love that supersedes your own temporal feelings or emotions. It doesn't pack up the bags and leave if things don't go the way he or she wants. Obviously, divorce is not God's perfect will. God desires marriage to reflect the type of unconditional love that Christ has for the Church:

Husband, Love Your Wife

*"Husbands, **love your wives, even as Christ also loved the church, and gave himself for it**... So ought men to love their wives as their own bodies. He that loves his wife loves himself. For no man ever yet hated his own flesh; but nourishes and cherishes it, even as the Lord the church: For we are members of his body, of his flesh, and of his bones. **For this cause shall a man leave his father and mother, and shall be joined unto his wife, and they two shall be one flesh.** This is a great mystery: but I speak concerning Christ and the church. Nevertheless, let every one of you in particular so love*

*his wife even as himself; and **the wife see that she reverence her husband.**[361]*

Christ's love is unconditional and eternal. That kind of love is what God intended for marriage.

Divorce Happens

Unfortunately, we are not in a perfect world and, as human beings, we are prone to make mistakes. Divorce happens... even to Christians. In Jesus' day, divorce was very prevalent, even among the religious Jews. If a wife didn't please the husband (even for a small reason), he could use a loophole in the Law of Moses to write her a bill of divorcement. With it, he could severe the marriage with little consequence. Jesus was questioned about divorce. Here is His response:

> *"The Pharisees also came unto Him, tempting Him, and saying unto Him, 'Is it lawful for a man to **put away his wife for every cause?'"** "And He answered and said unto them, 'Have you not read, that He which made them at the beginning made them male and female, and said, 'For this cause shall a man leave father and mother, and shall cleave to his wife; and they twain shall be one flesh?' Therefore, they are no more two, but one flesh. **What therefore God has joined together, let not man put asunder."***

> *"They say unto Him, 'Why did Moses then command to give a writing of divorcement, and to put her away?' He said unto them, 'Moses, because of the hardness of your hearts suffered you to put away your*

---

[361] Ephesians 5:25-29

*wives; but from the beginning it was not so. And I say unto you, **whosoever shall put away his wife, except it be for fornication, and shall marry another, commits adultery: and whoso marries her which is put away doth commit adultery.**' His disciples say unto Him, 'If the case of the man be so with his wife, **it is not good to marry.**'"[362]*

Not Good To Marry?

The very fact that the Pharisees bothered to ask Jesus about His opinion on divorce was because they knew in their hearts it was not God's will. It was wrong to deal with a wife in a treacherous way, (even though it was technically allowed by the Law). We can see that even Jesus' disciples were of the mindset that divorce was a normal option for married people. Their response, *"If the case of the man be so with his wife, it is not good to marry"* lets us know their opinion was if one could not easily divorce his wife, then perhaps it was best not to marry at all! In other words, their mindset previously had been that divorce was always an option if a marriage got "rocky." Jesus taught that when God puts a union together, the only reason divorce should be allowed is in the case of infidelity. This puts major constraints on divorce between believers. What About...

The Only Reason?

Did Jesus really mean that unfaithfulness on the part of one's spouse is the *only* reason that one can divorce? This brings into question many extenuating circumstances. What about a situation in which abuse exists? Marital abuse can take many forms: mental, emotional, and/or physical. Is the wife (or husband) just to sit as a doormat and *take it*? Some Church leaders dogmatically insist that one

---

[362] Matthew 19:3-9

must stay in an abusive marriage, and condemns those that opt to leave. However, the Bible states *"God has called us to peace."*[363] If one is in an abusive situation (particularly physical abuse) they need to leave that abuser. They can separate and pray for the abusive spouse long distance. If the abusive person will not repent, divorce is an option. God loves His children. He does not expect you to tolerate abuse. One must always follow the path of love and forgiveness, but that does not mean one must be a whipping post for the devil.

What God Has Joined Together

Why then, does Christ's statement seem to be so absolute regarding divorce? One needs to keep what Jesus said in context. He said *"What GOD has joined together, let not man put asunder."* God does not join together unbelievers, or a believer with an unbeliever. The Bible clearly says, *"How can two walk together unless they agree?"* and we are not to be "unequally yoked" together with unbelievers.[364]

That which Jesus refers to is a marriage that God has put together (in which both parties are true believers in Christ). In that case, the husband and wife are subject to God's Word and commands, as they both have God's Spirit. There is no need to dissolve a marriage between two believers, as God's Spirit can work in each individual's heart to resolve their differences. As they submit to Jesus' Lordship, repentance and reconciliation can be wrought. If it entails a time of separation for the husband and wife to work out their issues, that is acceptable. Divorce between two, true believers should not be necessary.

---

[363] I Corinthians 7:15
[364] II Corinthians 6:14

Know Them By Their Fruit

What constitutes a "believer" is another issue. Jesus said, *"You shall know them by their fruit."* If one does not manifest the fruit of the Spirit (love, joy, peace, patience, kindness…)[365], and they are not led by the Spirit of God, they are not of God: *"For as many as are led by the Spirit of God, THEY are the sons of God."*[366] Does this mean one has to be perfect to qualify as a "believer?" No. But it means that they will not continue in sinful, hurtful behavior. If they do fail, they will *sincerely repent* and ask for forgiveness both from their spouse and from God.

A marriage that does not have God as the center, does not have *love* as its foundation--for, *"God is love."* Love is *"patient, kind, keeps no record of wrong, believes the best of others…"*[367] Without Christ residing in the heart, there is no enduring love…only temporal lust. The lust of the eyes, the lust of the flesh, and the pride of life[368] are motivations that dominate those in the world—those who are not yet born from above. Lust is the fleshly counterfeit of God's love--which is always selfless and giving.

Those motivated by lust focus on satisfying their own desires. If their spouse loses the ability to fulfill their insatiable appetites, they feel justified in severing the relationship by infidelity or divorce. Lust is totally self-centered. A marriage based on God's love, however, will persevere through a relationship's ups and downs. It is founded on the principles of Christ, which include mercy, forgiveness, and unconditional love. Jesus' disciples are to deny themselves and pick

---

[365] Galatians 5:22-24
[366] Romans 8:14
[367] I John 4:8; I Corinthians 13:4-8
[368] I John 2:16, 17

up their crosses daily.[369] Just because everything is not going your way in a marriage does not give you the liberty to "exit stage left."

Christian Divorce

Why then do many "Christian" marriages end in divorce? Again, one must qualify what a "Christian" marriage is. One dedicated Christian wife (a church secretary) was regularly abused by her "Christian" husband. This was in spite of her earnest efforts to effect change through prayer and marriage counseling. He would not repent of his abuse, which continued for years. She finally obtained a divorce. Was this man a true Christian? Not by any stretch of the imagination. Yes... he at one time had made a profession of faith, and he was very active in church activities. But his lifestyle was not consistent with that of a true believer. Again, you will *"know them by their fruit."* This woman was not in sin when she divorced her husband.

Jesus said that a "brother" (one purportedly to be a fellow believer in Christ) is to be considered a heathen if they refuse to repent from sin after being admonished by the Church:

> *"Moreover if your brother shall trespass against you, go and tell him his fault between you and him alone: if he shall hear you, you hast gained your brother. But if he will not hear you, then take with you one or two more, that in the mouth of two or three witnesses every word may be established. And if he shall neglect to hear them, tell it unto the church: but if he neglect to hear the church, let him be unto you as a heathen man and a publican."[370]*

---

[369] Matthew 16:24
[370] Matthew 18:15-17

Likewise, Paul states that one can reject a "brother" who willfully continues in sin after he has been admonished twice: *"a heretic after the first and second admonition reject; knowing that he that is such is subverted, and sins, being condemned of himself."* (Titus 3:10, 11.)

These instructions were for those who were in the church, (considered "brothers") but who refused to repent when confronted with their sin. They were to be considered a "heathen."

Let Not The Wife Depart

Paul states that in the case in which two legitimate believers are having some marital contention, they are not to divorce:

> *"And unto the married I command, yet not I, but the Lord, **Let not the wife depart from her husband**: But and if she depart, **let her remain unmarried, or be reconciled** to her husband: and let not the husband put away his wife."*[371]

Here Paul reiterates what Jesus taught regarding two believers in a marriage (those whom "God has joined together"). They should not divorce. If there is incompatibility, then a separation with the view to reconciliation is in order. Divorce is not a legitimate option for a husband and wife who are true followers of Christ. They need to forgive and love. God expects them to keep their vows.

Do Not Put Her Away

Then Paul addresses another marriage situation in which one is unequally yoked (i.e., a believer married to an unbeliever). He gives

---

[371] I Corinthians 7:10, 11

his instructions to the churches with the apostolic[372] anointing he had to give clarity on issues that Jesus did not specifically address in His teaching:

> *"But to the rest speak I, not the Lord: If any* **brother has a wife that believes not, and she be pleased to dwell with him, let him not put her away.** *And the woman which has a* **husband that believes not, and if he be pleased to dwell with her, let her not leave him.** *For the unbelieving husband is sanctified by the wife, and the unbelieving wife is sanctified by the husband: else were your children unclean; but now are they holy."*

Let The Unbeliever Depart

> *"But if the unbeliever depart, let him depart. A brother or a sister is not under bondage in such cases: but God has called us to peace. For what do you know, O wife, whether you shall save your husband? or how do you know, O man, whether you shall save your wife. But as God has distributed to every man, as the Lord has called every one, so let him walk. And so ordain I in all churches."[373]*

Paul first addresses believers married to unbelievers in a *peaceful* marriage relationship. They should remain married, knowing that their children are sanctified by the believing parent. If, however, the unbeliever contentiously opposes the faith of the believer, then the believer is not under bondage or obligation to remain married to them. Paul said *"let the unbeliever depart, for God has called us to peace."* If they are going to fight against you following Christ, let them go.

---

[372] I Corinthians 14:37
[373] I Corinthians 7:13, 14

There are cases in which one must forsake family members in order to follow Jesus:

For The Gospel

"Jesus answered and said, truly I say unto you, There is no man that has left house, or brethren, or sisters, or father, or mother, or wife, or children, or lands, for my sake, and the gospel's, But he shall receive a hundredfold now in this time, houses, and brethren, and sisters, and mothers, and children, and lands, with persecutions; and in the world to come eternal life. (Mark 10:29)

"If any man come to me, and hate not his father, and mother, and wife, and children, and brethren, and sisters, yes, and his own life also, he cannot be my disciple. And whosoever doth not bear his cross, and come after me, cannot be my disciple." (Luke 14:26, 27)

If an unbeliever gives the believer an ultimatum, "Jesus or me," then one must follow Jesus. Divorce is authorized in such cases. Paul said believers who divorce their unbelieving spouses for legitimate reasons are not in bondage, but are free to marry someone in the faith.[374]

Believers Sanctify

To the extent that a believer can continue to stay married to and live in relative peace with an unbeliever, however, they are to do so. They should not divorce. God honors covenant, and can bless a household for the believer's sake. God sanctifies unbelievers through the believer's faith, which allows their children to be blessed of God.

---

[374] I Corinthians 7:15, Romans 7:2, 3

This was the case of Timothy, Paul's spiritual son in the Lord. He had a believing Jewish mother who was married to an unbelieving Greek husband. Timothy was blessed through his mother's faith.[375]

But, if the unbeliever is antagonistic (actively opposes the believer's faith in Christ), the believer is not obligated to stay married to them. Some who remained married to a contentious unbeliever (faithfully praying for their salvation), have had the good pleasure of eventually seeing them come to Christ. However, as verse 16 states, you cannot be sure that they will get saved. In cases like this you should seek Godly counsel and pray to hear God's direction for your particular situation. He will be faithful to lead you.

The Bible Teaches

To summarize, the Bible teaches that believers (whom God has put together) should not get divorced. They can separate with a view to reconciliation if they have compatibility issues. But as true believers, they should be able to work out their differences. The exception is if one of the partners has committed fornication (including pornography...) Then divorce is permitted (but not necessarily mandated). In the case of a believer married to an unbeliever, as long as they can live in relative peace, then the believer should not divorce the unbelieving spouse. But, if the unbeliever contentiously opposes the believer's faith, then divorce is an option for the believer.

If a believer is married to a so-called "believer" who contentiously continues in grievous sin (in spite of being admonished by the church authority) they are to be considered an unbeliever. This includes a man who will not provide for his own house, or who is

---

[375] II Timothy 1:5; Acts 16:1-3

abusive.[376] In those cases, the true believer is authorized to divorce the contentious one as an unbeliever.

Stay Where You Are At

Paul gives practical teaching to those who become believers: *"as the Lord has called every one, so let him walk."* Whatever state one is in when they are saved, they should remain in that same situation. If one is married to their third wife when they are saved, they should not think that they must divorce her and be reconciled to the first wife. As new believers in Christ, the past is forgiven and forgotten. Start new wherever you are at. Remain in the marital status in which you are called.

If You Must Divorce

If the situation necessitates divorce (abandonment, abuse, infidelity) then the believer has not sinned. They can divorce and remarry as God directs. The Bible states that Joseph was a "just man" when he planned to divorce Mary for what he perceived to be a legitimate reason (infidelity).[377] So divorce in itself is not a sin. The motive behind a divorce can be sinful. If it is simply motivated by lust (trade in the old model for a new one), then it is sinful. But if the unbelieving spouse fights the believer's faith, then divorce is authorized, and it is not sinful.

God's Perfect Will; God's Permissive Will

God ordained marriage to be a beautiful reflection of His love for the Church. Unfortunately, in our imperfect world, divorce is a common reality. As followers of Christ, we should walk in love and follow peace in all of our relationships, especially that of marriage. We are to consider the marriage vow to be a binding covenant, as does God. Divorce should not be considered as an easy option to get out of a

---

[376] I Timothy 5:8
[377] Matthew 1:19

relationship simply because one does not feel fully gratified. God hates divorce. It is devastating to all those involved. However, in some cases, divorce is unavoidable. God's Word makes allowances for the believer to divorce in those cases.

ETERNAL SECURITY ERROR

Few doctrines have had the net effect of sending more "Christians" to hell than the false teaching of eternal security. That doctrine, also known as "once saved, always saved," teaches that once a believer is born-again, they can never lose their salvation. In other words, if they ask Jesus to be Lord of their life, and then afterward engage in a lifestyle of sin, they believe that they will still go to Heaven. They think they may lose rewards for sinning, but that their destiny in paradise is secure--regardless of how they live. Their "ticket to Heaven" is non-rescindable and non-transferable. Plainly speaking, eternal security adherents believe that one can live like the devil and still make Heaven. This is grievous error. Scripture, in fact, teaches no such thing.

Proof??

Let us first consider why some people have believed this doctrine. There are a couple of scriptures often quoted to defend eternal security teaching. When these scriptures are taken in *context*, however, they do not prove eternal security at all. When taken in context, those particular scriptures actually *refute* eternal security. One such scripture is John 10:28: *"And I give unto them [My sheep] eternal life; and they shall **never perish**, neither shall any man pluck them **out of my hand**. My Father, which gave them me, is greater than all; and **no man is able to pluck them out of my Father's hand**."* That sounds eternally secure. If you are God's sheep, you will never perish because you can't be plucked out of God's hand!

But let us keep this scripture in context: *"Jesus answered them...**My sheep hear my voice**, and I know them, and **they follow Me**: And I give unto **them** eternal life; and **they** shall never perish, neither shall any man pluck them out of my hand. My Father, which gave them*

232

me, is greater than all; and no man is able to pluck them out of my Father's hand."

Notice that there is a condition. To be considered *God's* sheep one must **hear His voice** (which includes His written Word and the Holy Spirit's leading), and then they must **follow it.** If one is going their own way, then they do not qualify as Jesus' sheep. Only sheep (those who know and follow the voice of the Shepherd) receive eternal life. It is the *sheep* that cannot be plucked out of the Father's Hand. Sheep readily follow the Shepherd. Goats do not.

What is the Condition?

Another scripture often quoted is *"[Jesus] became the author of **eternal salvation**..."* That sounds clear. Jesus' salvation is eternal. His salvation last forever. However, read the entire verse in context: *"He became the author of eternal salvation **unto all** **them that obey Him.**"* (Hebrews 5:9) Again, we see that there is a condition for those who expect their salvation to be eternal. It is obedience to the Lord. True faith always has corresponding actions.

Jesus' Lordship- True Disciple

When one becomes born again, they relinquish Lordship (rule) of their life to Jesus. A true disciple of Jesus denies their self, takes up their cross daily, and follows Him. There is a spiritual change on the inside of a born-again believer. They have been set free from satan's[378] dominion and are brought into the Kingdom of God's Dear Son. They are no longer controlled by the spirit of disobedience, but by the Spirit of God. God's Spirit literally works in them "both to will and to do His good pleasure."[379]

---

[378] Colossians 1:13
[379] Philippians 2:13

As Paul writes, *"It is no longer I that live, but Christ who lives in me; and the life that I now live in the flesh, I live by the faith of the Son of God, Who loved me and gave Himself for me."*[380] One cannot follow the old pattern of sin (as one who has not been born again) and expect to go to heaven. The true *"grace of God **that brings salvation** teaches us to deny ungodliness and worldly lusts and live soberly, righteously, and Godly in this present world."*[381] True Christianity is not easy "believism" (just belief in God). Even the devil *"believes and trembles."* (James 2:19) True faith will have corresponding actions. In other words, because you *have been* born again, you will "walk the walk" and desire to please God.

Saved By Works??

Just to clarify, your *works* do not save you. But your works confirm that you have been saved. Being born again results in a changed life, changed desires, and changed motivations. Your outward actions and lifestyle manifest the changes that have been wrought in you. It is error to think that anything that you do (good works, following church rules and regulations) can save you. If you could earn your salvation by your own works instead of by the Blood of Jesus Christ alone, then you relegate His Blood as being insufficient and not precious enough to fully pay for your sin.

This type of legalistic mentality of works is blasphemous. It negates the power of Jesus' Blood to atone for sin. There is nothing you can DO to earn your salvation, for it is *"by grace [God's unmerited favor] are you saved through faith; and that not of yourselves; it is the gift of God; NOT of works that any man should boast."*[382] Good works

---

[380] Galatians 2:20
[381] Titus 3:11
[382] Ephesians. 2:8,9

do not save you. They are simply evidence of the faith you receive at salvation. True faith results in a Godly lifestyle.

New Creation

The new nature that God gives us at salvation makes us free from the Law of sin and death. We do not *have to* sin any longer. We still have the flesh, which is contrary to our born again spirit, and wars against us daily. If we yield to the flesh and sin, God will forgive us. We must, of course, sincerely repent and confess our sin. Then *"He is faithful and just to forgive us our sin and to cleanse us from all unrighteousness."*[383] Our regenerated conscience will convict us that we have done wrong. God will graciously restore us back into fellowship with Him as we acknowledge our sin and repent. He does not "kick us out of the family" for falling into sin.

Blood Of Sprinkling

There are areas in all of our lives that are not perfect… attitudes, motives, etc. We may not be aware of sin in our heart, but God's grace is sufficient to cover us even then. If we are sincerely following the Lord Jesus, there is an automatic covering of His Blood to cleanse us, even from unknown sins. God made provision for sin done in ignorance, *"the Blood of sprinkling"*:

> *"And the LORD spoke unto Moses, saying, Speak unto the children of Israel, saying, If a soul shall* **sin through ignorance** *against any of the commandments of the LORD concerning things which ought not to be done, and shall do against any of them: If the priest that is anointed do sin according to the* **sin of the people***; then let him bring for his sin, which he*

---

[383] I John 1:9

hath sinned, a young bullock without blemish unto the LORD for a sin offering."

"And he shall bring the bullock unto the door of the tabernacle of the congregation before the LORD; and shall lay his hand upon the bullock's head, and kill the bullock before the LORD. And the priest that is anointed shall take of the bullock's blood, and bring it to the tabernacle of the congregation: And the priest shall dip his finger in the blood, and **sprinkle of the blood** *seven times before the LORD, before the vail of the sanctuary."*[384]

Jesus' Precious Blood

This of course is an Old Testament shadow of what the Blood of Jesus does for us. His Blood cleanses us, even when we are not aware that we need cleansing. Peter tells us that we are redeemed with the *"precious Blood of Christ..."* And we are sanctified by God's Spirit *"unto obedience and sprinkling of the Blood of Jesus Christ."*[385] As our High Priest, Jesus sprinkles us with His Atoning Blood when we fall into sin through ignorance. The fact that the sin is done in "ignorance" (unwittingly, a mistake), and it is not a sin of volition (a willful act of defiance and rebellion against God's Word) allows for this Blood of sprinkling to be applied for sin cleansing.

Walking In The Light

In this case, one is not willfully practicing sin. They are walking in the light that they have of God's Word, but they have inadvertently fallen short in an area. (Isn't that all of us!) When God's

---

[384] Leviticus 4:1-6
[385] I Peter 1:2, 19

Spirit reveals and convicts us of sin, we must repent and confess it to be cleansed:

> "This then is the message which we have heard of him, and declare unto you, that God is light, and in him is no darkness at all. If we say that we have fellowship with him, and walk in darkness, we lie, and do not the truth: **But if we walk in the light, as he is in the light, we have fellowship one with another, and the <u>blood of Jesus Christ his Son cleanses us from all sin.</u>** If we say that we have no sin, we deceive ourselves, and the truth is not in us. If we confess our sins, he is faithful and just to forgive us our sins, and to cleanse us from all unrighteousness."[386]

The true follower of Christ is walking in the light of God's Word, where the Blood of sprinkling cleanses from all sin. When the conviction of God's Spirit shows us an area of sin (so that it is no longer a matter of ignorance), we must repent and confess it to God for forgiveness. However, if we become rebellious and try to justify the sin revealed to us by God's Spirit, then we are not walking in the Light. Not until we truly repent and confess our sin can we be cleansed. The Blood of sprinkling cleanses us as we walk in the Light.

Don't Harden Your Heart!

If rebellion against God's Word becomes a pattern—an ongoing practice of sin—then we are in grave danger of hardening our hearts toward the Spirit of Truth and Grace. He is the One who convicts us of sin. By refusing to repent and follow the Spirit, we desensitize ourselves to God's working in our life. *"As many as are led by the*

---

[386] I John 1:5-9

Spirit of God, they are the sons of God." Conversely, if one is not led by the Spirit of God, they are not a son of God.

God will not force us to love Him or follow Him. He does not leave us, but we can choose--by our own rebellion-- to leave Him. God's Spirit will not always strive with man.[387] When you refuse to allow the Holy Spirit to convict you of sin, you are actually insulting (*"doing despite to"*) His goodness and grace. For a Christian to continue in a lifestyle of willful sin (shunning the conviction of the Holy Ghost and ignoring God's Word), it means that Jesus is no longer the Lord of their life: *"Know you not, that to whom you yield yourselves servants to obey, his servants you are to whom you obey; whether of sin unto death, or of obedience unto righteousness?"*[388] If you continue in willful sin, you have become satan's servant, not God's.

Discipline For Repentance

Because of God's great love for His children, He will correct and chasten them to bring them into alignment with His will and His Word.[389] God first will patiently extend great mercy and goodness to His children to try to evoke reciprocal love, (and thereby, obedience) in them. It is the goodness of God leads us to repentance. God may send messengers to warn His children of their error. If that does not work, He may even allow the destruction of the flesh (sickness or calamity) into a wayward believer's life to try to bring about repentance.[390] But in the end, each person must choose whether or not they are going to follow Jesus as Lord or satan and sin.

If You Continue In The Faith...

---

[387] Genesis 6:3
[388] Romans 6:16
[389] Hebrews 12:6-8
[390] I Corinthians 5:5

These scriptures show it is possible for believers to leave Christ by not continuing in the faith:

I Timothy 5:11, 15- *"But the younger widows refuse: for when they have begun to wax wanton against Christ, they will marry; Having damnation, because they have **cast off their first faith**...For some are already turned aside after satan."* We see here that some of the young women who *had* faith in Christ decided to cast off that faith and turn to follow satan instead. They started with Jesus, but their unchecked lust caused them to leave God and follow the devil.

Romans 11:20-22- *"Well; because of unbelief they were broken off, and you stand by faith. Be not high-minded, but fear: For if God spared not the natural branches, take **heed lest He also spare not you**. Behold therefore the goodness and severity of God: on them which fell, severity; but toward you, goodness, **<u>if you continue in His goodness</u>: otherwise you also shalt be cut off."*** Paul warned the Church that they must continue in the true faith of Christ, or they risked being cut off from God (even as the Israelites were). One must *continue* with Jesus!

Hebrews 3:12-14- *"Take heed, **brethren,** lest there be in any of you an evil heart of unbelief, **in departing from the living God**. But exhort one another daily, while it is called To day; lest any of you be hardened through the deceitfulness of sin. For **we are made partakers of Christ, if we hold the beginning of our confidence steadfast unto the end."*** Paul is addressing the Christian "brethren." He somberly warned that any of the brethren could depart from the living God by hardening their hearts through sin. Being a partaker of Christ is contingent on one continuing to hold onto their faith. We must exhort each other, lest any of us depart from God.

Galatians 5:4-7- *"Stand fast therefore in the liberty wherewith Christ has made us free, and **be not entangled again** with the yoke of bondage. Behold, I Paul say unto you, that if you be circumcised, Christ shall profit you nothing. For I testify again to every man that is circumcised, that he is a debtor to do the whole law. Christ is become of no effect unto you, whosoever of you are justified by the law; **you are fallen from grace... You did run well;** who did hinder you that you should not obey the truth?"*

Here the Apostle Paul warned the Church in Galatia that they had *"fallen from grace."* He stated that they did begin right with God… they were running the Christian race well. But, legalism got them entangled in error, which in turn caused them to fall from grace. Religious pride (i.e., trying to be justified by their own works) resulted in their fall.

I Corinthians 9:27- *"But I keep under my body, and bring it into subjection: lest that by any means, when I have preached to others, I myself should be a castaway."* Paul did not consider himself exempt from the perils of being rejected by God. If he would not keep his flesh under subjection to the Holy Ghost, he himself could be castaway by God.

The term "castaway" here is "adokimos" in the Greek, which means "rejected, not standing the test, reprobate."[391] Paul said he (the **Apostle Paul!)** could be rejected by God as a reprobate if he did not take careful heed to his own spiritual walk. He knew that he must keep the flesh under subjection by actively putting to death the deeds of sin.[392] If apostles can become castaways, so can we!

---

[391] Vine, An Expository Dictionary, 173
[392] Colossians 3:5-8

Revelation chapters 1-3:

*"The Revelation of Jesus Christ, which God gave unto him, to **show unto His servants**... I have somewhat against you, because **you hast left thy first love**. Remember therefore from where **you are fallen**, and repent, and do the first works; or else I will come unto thee quickly, and will **remove thy candlestick** out of his place, except thou repent... because you allow that woman Jezebel, which calls herself a prophetess, to teach and to seduce **My servants to commit fornication**, and to eat things sacrificed unto idols. And I gave her space to repent of her fornication; and she repented not.*

*Behold, I will cast her into a bed, **and them that commit adultery with her into great tribulation, except they repent of their deeds...** hold fast, and repent. If therefore you shalt not watch, I will come on you as a thief... **He that overcomes**, the same shall be clothed in white raiment; and **I will not blot out his name out of the book of life**, but I will confess his name before my Father, and before his angels...because you are lukewarm, and neither cold nor hot, I will **spew you out of My mouth**...As many as I love, I rebuke and chasten: be **zealous therefore, and repent**."*

John the Revelator was given warnings to God's servants, the members of the seven churches of Asia. They were believers... real Christians, but most had gotten side-tracked in their walk with the Lord. Some had left their first love for Christ and the Great Commission. Jesus said they were "**fallen**" and needed to repent. If they did not, He would remove their candlestick. Those who allowed false doctrine and immorality into the church were warned that they would be **cast into**

great tribulation if they did not repent! The Sardis church was told that in order for their names not to be "*blotted out of the Book of Life*" they needed to repent and be overcomers. The lukewarm church was on the verge of being **spewed out** of the Body of Christ! The blessings of heaven were promised conditionally in every case: "*To those who overcome...*"

Conditions For Security

Being eternally secure with God is conditional. We do not have to worry about losing our salvation if we are faithfully following the Lord. This is what Jesus expects of His disciples:

"*My sheep hear my voice, and I know them, and they follow Me...*" (John 10:27)

"*For as many   as are led by the Spirit of God, they are the sons of God.*" (Romans 8:14)

"*[Jesus] became the author of eternal salvation unto all them that obey Him*" (Hebrews 5:9)

"*Then said Jesus to those Jews which believed on him, If you continue in my word, then are you my disciples indeed*" (John 8:31)

"*Not everyone that says unto me, Lord, Lord, shall enter into the kingdom of heaven; but he that does the will of my Father which is in heaven.*" (Matthew 7:21)

Strive For The High Calling

We cannot be perfect on our own. God knows that. But as long as we are honestly trying to follow Him (walking in the light as He is in the light) we will make it. God will give us grace to help us run this race. But those who throw caution to the wind and live any way that they want to after salvation are deceived.

These Shall Not Inherit The Kingdom Of God

You cannot enter the kingdom of God if you are living an unrighteous, ungodly life:

*"Know you not that **the unrighteous shall not inherit the kingdom of God**? Be not deceived: neither fornicators, nor idolaters, nor adulterers, nor effeminate, nor abusers of themselves with mankind [homosexuals], Nor thieves, nor covetous, nor drunkards, nor revilers, nor extortioners, shall inherit the kingdom of God."* (I Corinthians 6:9-10)

*"Now **the works of the flesh** are manifest, which are these; Adultery, fornication, uncleanness, lasciviousness, Idolatry, witchcraft, hatred, variance, emulations, wrath, strife, seditions, heresies, Envyings, murders, drunkenness, revellings, and such like: of the which I tell you before, as I have also told you in time past, that **they which do such things shall not inherit the kingdom of God.**"* (Galatians 5:19-21)

"He that overcomes shall inherit all things; and I will be his God, and he shall be my son. But the fearful, and unbelieving, and the abominable, and murderers, and whoremongers, and sorcerers, and idolaters, and all liars, shall have their part in the lake which burns with fire and brimstone:** which is the second death."* (Revelation 21:7,8

According to the Word of God, those who engage in sexual sin, lie, put other things before God (idolaters), murder, hate, are unbelieving or fearful, are in heresy, witchcraft, strife and envy, those who are drunkards, and the covetous *"shall not inherit the Kingdom of God."* The key to being eternally secure is really in the attitude of the heart. Do you love the Lord because He paid for your sins on the

Cross? If you truly believe that He loved you and gave Himself for you, you will love Him in return. And, if you love Him, you will obey His Word.[393] If we remember that Jesus has purged us from our sins (according to II Peter 1:5-10) we will have an abundant entrance to Heaven. When we diligently add the virtues of faith, knowledge, temperance, patience, godliness, brotherly kindness, and love to our lives, we will never fall.

Harden Not Your Heart

However, if we harden their hearts toward the Lord, and continue in willful sin, we set ourselves up for a great fall. Even if one has had a close walk with God, has received the Holy Ghost, and known the powerful Word of God, it is possible for them to fall away. If they fall into sin and harden their heart to the Spirit's conviction, He cannot bring them to repentance:

> *"For if we sin willfully **after that we have received the knowledge of the truth**, there remains no more sacrifice for sins, But a certain fearful looking for of judgment and fiery indignation, which shall devour the adversaries. He that despised Moses' law died without mercy under two or three witnesses: Of how much sorer punishment, suppose you, shall he be thought worthy, who has trodden underfoot the Son of God, and has **counted the Blood of the covenant, wherewith <u>he was sanctified</u>**, an unholy thing, and has done despite unto the Spirit of grace? For we know Him that has said, Vengeance belongs unto Me, I will recompense, says the Lord. And again, **The Lord shall judge His people.** It*

---

[393] John 14:21

is a fearful thing to fall into the hands of the living God." (Hebrews 10:26-31)

Notice that the writer says after one *"receives the knowledge of the truth…"* (that is, one has received Jesus, the Truth) and *"**was sanctified**,"* they could still incur the judgment of God! The frightening passage in chapter six tells us that one can be very spiritual, have God's power manifest greatly in one's life, and still backslide ("fall away"). Their end is to burn in hell.

Once An Enlightened Partaker, But Will Be Burned

> *"it is impossible for those **who were once enlightened**, and **have tasted of the heavenly gift**, and **were made partakers of the Holy Ghost**, And have tasted the **good word of God**, and the **powers of the world to come**, If they shall fall away, to renew them again unto repentance; seeing they crucify to themselves the Son of God afresh, and put Him to an open shame. For the earth which drinks in the rain that cometh oft upon it, and brings forth herbs meet for them by whom it is dressed, receives blessing from God: But that which bears thorns and briers is rejected, and is nigh unto cursing; **whose end is to be burned**."* (Hebrews 6:4-8)

With these sobering scriptures in mind, it behooves all of us to take account of our own lives. As Paul said, we must not neglect our salvation, but we must work out our own salvation with fear and trembling.[394] Can we be eternally secure of our salvation? Yes… if we stay close to Him. That personal relationship that you have with

---

[394] Hebrews 2:3, Philippians 2:12, 13

Christ on a daily basis will motivate you to love and obey Him, and not to engage in willful sin. This is how I John 3:6-10 explains it:

*"**Whosoever abides in Him sins not**: whosoever sins has not seen Him, neither known Him. Little children, let no man deceive you: **he that does righteousness is righteous**, even as He is righteous. **He that commits sin is of the devil;** for the devil sins from the beginning. For this purpose the Son of God was manifested, that He might destroy the works of the devil."*

God's Children Are Righteous

If someone calls themselves a Christian, and yet they are living a sinful life, they are not right with God. They are "of the devil." As such, they *will not* inherit God's Kingdom.

*"**Whosoever is born of God doth not commit sin**; for His seed remains in him: and he cannot sin, because he is born of God. In this the children of God are manifest, and the children of the devil: **whosoever does not righteousness is not of God, neither he that loves not his brother.**"*

If one is living a sinful lifestyle (as defined by the *Bible*, not our "politically correct" society), then they **will not inherit the kingdom of God**. Eternal security is for those who walk in the light of God's Word (as He is in the Light). Then their sins are covered by the Blood of Jesus.

Secure If You Walk In The Light

In summary, eternal security is a false doctrine. "Once saved, always saved" it is not supported by scripture. The few scriptures that *seem to* indicate salvation cannot be lost, actually reinforce the fact that there are conditions of obedience and faith required to retain one's eternal salvation. True salvation will be marked by a lifestyle of righteous living. There are many scriptures that warn believers about being "cut off" from salvation if they do not continue on with the Lord. Believers are warned in several New Testament passages that, if one engages in the various sins listed, they will not inherit the Kingdom of God. God warns that even those who once tasted of Spiritual gifts and God's power can fall away from the faith. If we walk in the light of God's Word, then the Blood of Jesus will cleanse us as we repent and confess our sins. One can be eternally secure in their salvation if they are following Jesus as Lord of their life.

CATHOLIC DOCTRINE- TRUTH OR CONSEQUENCES

As a six-year old I recall wearing a pair of red, furry ear muffs in the winter time. There was a thin, metal band connecting the two muffs. I would intentionally wear the muffs in such a way that the squared sharp part of the band would press on my ear, causing much discomfort. Why? Because my teacher, Sis. Mary Elizabeth Ann, taught us that if we would endure pain on earth, then we could help to take some of the suffering time off from those burning in purgatory.

I recall also that whenever I would hear an ambulance, I would immediately pray the "Hail Mary." We were taught that if we would implore Mary at such times that help would come to whomever was in a medical crisis. Mary was so important that on May Day we had the annual coronation of Mary at school (St. Paul's Catholic School). All the children would bring beautiful little "crowns" that they had made at home to place upon the statue of Mary in our classroom. I remember my mother had helped me fashion a beautiful little crown with pearls and jewel-like stones to place on the head of Mary's statue. At the daily morning Mass we often sang "Immaculate Mary, Your Praises We Sing" in adoration and worship of Mary.

I recall going to confession and placing a quarter in the little candle box and lighting a candle as an act of contrition. I would say the number of prescribed "Hail Mary's" and "Our Father's" that the priest deemed necessary for me to say to pardon my sins for the week. These were some of the memories of my Catholic upbringing. I believed in God and prayed, went to Communion and Confession, and figured that I was on my way to Heaven. However, nobody ever told me the scripture, *"You must be born-again to enter the Kingdom of*

God." I, like most sincere Catholics, did not know that I needed the born-again experience. I was headed for hell.

Tradition Or Truth

Most Catholics believe that water baptism, following the sacraments, and obeying the Ten Commandments eventually will grant them entrance into the kingdom of heaven. They are relying on the traditions taught by the church without actually knowing what the Bible teaches. However, after being enlightened as to what God's infallible Word teaches about the way of salvation, one can no longer can adhere to Roman Catholic beliefs. In many instances Catholic beliefs actually contradict the Holy Bible.

The Bible (not the traditions of the Catholic church) must be your basis for truth, for "all *scripture is given by inspiration of God, and is profitable for doctrine, for reproof, for correction, for instruction in righteousness: That the man of God may be perfect, thoroughly furnished unto all good works."* [395]

The Bible states, *"The Law of the Lord is perfect, converting the soul."*[396] Jesus, speaking to His Father, declares, *"Thy Word is truth."*[397] Therefore, the **Bible** is the source of truth. Unfortunately, there are many Catholic traditions which contradict the Bible. As Jesus said- *"In vain do they worship Me, teaching for doctrines the commandments of men... making the Word of God of none effect through your tradition."*[398] If a Catholic doctrine contradicts what the Bible says, then the Catholic doctrine is wrong. God's Word is always right: *"Let God be true, but every man a liar."* (Romans 3:4)

---

[395] II Tim 3:16
[396] Psalm 19:7
[397] John 17:17
[398] Mark 7:6-13

Bishop Of Rome?

One Catholic tradition that is not Biblical is the belief that Peter was the first Bishop of Rome. As his successor, the Pope, therefore (according to Catholic teachings) is infallible in matters of faith and morals. In truth, Peter never was the Bishop of Rome. He was the apostle to the Jews, as Galatians 2:7-9 tells us. Acts 18:2 states that Caesar ordered all Jews to depart from Rome. (This occurred in 49 A.D. under the reign of Claudius Caesar.) According to Acts 8:1, Peter's ministry was primarily to the Jews in Jerusalem.

When Roman occupation troops surrounded Jerusalem, then the believing Jews heeded Jesus' warning to flee from Jerusalem.[399] Many of them resorted to Babylon, where resided a very significant community of Jews. Peter's general epistle was written from there (I Peter 5:13.) In that epistle he writes to the Jews who were "scattered abroad" and list the provinces in the order they would naturally occur to one writing from Babylon.

At the conclusion of his life, Peter may have been martyred in Rome, but his ministry was centered elsewhere. He was not the Bishop of Rome. The Apostle Paul was the Apostle to Rome (Romans 1:1). When Paul sent greetings to the Church at Rome, he saluted all of the church leaders (Phoebe, Pricilla and Aquila, etc.), but never saluted Peter.[400] That was because Peter was not there. He was overseeing the Jewish community elsewhere.

Papal Infallibility

Papal infallibility has no scriptural basis, either. Peter (the supposed predecessor of the Papacy) was not infallible. Christ Himself had to rebuke Peter ("Get behind Me, satan; you desire the things of man, not the things of God.") Peter had given Jesus some satan-

---

[399] Luke 21:20, 21
[400] Romans 16:1-16

inspired advice right after Jesus confirmed that the Father had revealed to Peter that Jesus was the Christ.[401]   Later, the apostle Paul also had to rebuke Peter for spiritual error:

> *"But when Peter was come to Antioch, I withstood him to the face, because he was to be blamed. For before that certain came from James, he did eat with the Gentiles: but when they were come, he withdrew and separated himself, fearing them which were of the circumcision...*
>
> *But when I saw that they walked not uprightly according to the truth of the gospel, I said unto Peter before them all, If thou, being a Jew, live after the manner of Gentiles, and not as do the Jews, why do you compel the Gentiles to live as do the Jews?... Knowing that a man is not justified by the works of the law, but by the faith of Jesus Christ"[402]*

Peter was fallible. His so-called successors are as well.

Confess To God

Another tradition of Catholicism that is not scriptural is that one must go to a priest to confess one's sins and to receive absolution. The Bible states "There is one God and ONE MEDIATOR between God and men, the Man Christ Jesus."[403] We need no one but Christ to go between us and God. We go to Jesus (not a man) for forgiveness of sin: "If we confess our sins [to God], He is faithful and just to forgive us our sins and to cleanse us from all unrighteousness... and the Blood of Jesus Christ cleanses us from all sin."[404]

---

[401] Luke 21
[402] Galatians 2:11-14
[403] I Tim. 2:5
[404] I John 1: 7-9

Blood Atonement

Note that it is the Blood of Christ that cleanses us from sin--not an act of contrition (saying some prayers, lighting a candle, or any other good deeds that we can do). There are no religious sacraments or good works that one can do to merit or earn righteousness (i.e., right standing with God.) In fact, in God's eyes, all your righteousness is like filthy rags.[405] That is why one must trust Christ to give them the gift of His righteousness: *"For by grace [undeserved favor from God] are you saved through FAITH; and that not of yourselves; it is the gift of God; not of works, lest any man should boast."*[406] *"...a man is not justified by the works of the Law, but by the faith of Jesus Christ... for by the works of the Law shall no flesh be justified."*[407]

Neither being baptized into the Catholic Church, nor following sacraments (communion, confession, etc.) can make you righteous enough to enter into heaven. Jesus said that you *"must be born again to enter into the kingdom of God."*[408] One is born again (or "saved") by doing what Romans 10 says: "If you shall confess with your mouth the Lord Jesus and believe in your heart that God has raised him from the dead, you shall be saved. For with the heart man believes, resulting in righteousness; and with the mouth confession is made, resulting in salvation. For whosoever calls upon the Name of the Lord shall be saved." This is how one is "born-again," or regenerated.

Regeneration

The Catholic Church teaches that regeneration occurs when one is water baptized into the Catholic Church. Nowhere does the Bible say that being water baptized into the Catholic church is the means of salvation. But Catholics are taught wrongly that they must be baptized as Catholic to go to Heaven. Therefore, even infants receive this "sacrament." However, The Bible tells us that we are saved by faith,

---

[405] Isaiah 64:6
[406] Ephesians 2:9
[407] Galatians 2:16
[408] John 3:3

and that the confession of that heart-felt faith is how salvation is obtained. Obviously, babies cannot fully understand in order to believe or confess. God does not hold anyone accountable for their sin until they reach an age of understanding. Water baptism does not regenerate—faith does.

Body And Blood

Another Catholic tradition which scripture refutes is the doctrine of "transubstantiation." This doctrine states that in the Mass the priest changes the bread and wine into the literal, physical Body and Blood of Christ. The priest then (purportedly) re-offers His Body and Blood to God. However, Christ Himself stated that communion was to be done "in remembrance of me." It is a meal in which we remember Christ's sacrifice for our sin...not literally re-sacrifice Him. The elements are symbolic reminders of Christ's one time work on the cross. The bread and wine are not "miraculously changed," but remain bread and wine.

In instituting the first communion service (after blessing the wine), Jesus refers to it as "the fruit of the vine." [409] It was not changed into His literal Blood, but remained wine. In describing the communion service, the Apostle Paul refers to the element of Christ's Body taken in communion as "bread":

> *"For I have received of the Lord that which also I delivered unto you, That the Lord Jesus the same night in which He was betrayed took bread: And when He had given thanks, He brake it, and said, Take, eat: this is My body, which is broken for you: this do in remembrance of Me. After the same manner also He took the cup, when He had supped, saying, This cup is the new testament in My blood: this do ye, as oft as ye drink it, in remembrance of Me. For as often as ye eat*

---

[409] Matthew 26:26-29

*this bread, and drink this cup, ye do shew the Lord's
death till he come."*[410]

Paul said that which believers partake of is "bread," not
Christ's literal body. The elements do not change into another
substance (i.e., Christ's literal body). The purpose of Communion is a
"remembrance" of the one-time work on the Cross in which Jesus
suffered and died for our sins. Upon bowing His head and giving up
the ghost on the Cross, Jesus said, "It is finished."

The redemption was paid for once and for all.
Transubstantiation is not scriptural. Christ's literal body is not
sacrificed again at every Mass (as Catholicism teaches). Hebrews 9:26
states that Christ was "ONCE offered in the end of the world to put
away sin by the sacrifice of Himself." Jesus does not need to daily offer
Himself for our sins.[411] Jesus offered His Body and Blood one time—
not again and again at every Mass.

Purgatory? Or The Blood

What about purgatory? According to the Catholic Church,
purgatory is a place of suffering after death where one's sins are
"purged" (cleansed) by the flames. It can be likened to a temporary hell.
Once one has adequately been punished for their sins (according to
Catholic teaching), they are worthy to enter heaven. This doctrine is
blasphemous. To infer that one can pay indulgences, pray prayers, say
a Mass, or suffer enough in "purgatory" to atone for sin totally negates
the Cross of Christ. Essentially, one is saying that they do not need the
Blood of Jesus to cleanse from sin ... they can do it by their own good
works. If this were true, then Christ's sacrifice was in vain. But
scripture is very clear that only the Precious Blood of Christ can cleanse
and atone for sin:

---

[410] I Corinthians 11:23-26
[411] Hebrews 7:27

- *"forasmuch as ye know that ye were not redeemed with corruptible things, as silver and gold, from your vain conversation received by tradition from your fathers; but with the precious blood of Christ, as of a lamb without blemish and without spot" (I Peter 1:18, 19)*
- *"But God commends his love toward us, in that, while we were yet sinners, Christ died for us. Much more then, being now justified by His blood, we shall be saved from wrath through Him." (Romans 5:8, 9)*
- *"But if we walk in the light, as he is in the light, we have fellowship one with another, and the blood of Jesus Christ his Son cleanses us from all sin. If we say that we have no sin, we deceive ourselves, and the truth is not in us. If we confess our sins, he is faithful and just to forgive us our sins, and to cleanse us from all unrighteousness." (I John 1:7-9)*
- *"How much more shall the Blood of Christ, who through the eternal Spirit offered Himself without spot to God, purge your conscience from dead works to serve the living God... without shedding of blood is no remission." (Hebrews 9)*

Scripture states that after death sinners go to hell (see Luke 16:23), and Christians go to heaven to be with the Lord (II Corinthians 5:6-8). It is one or the other. Nowhere in the Bible is "purgatory" mentioned. That is because it does not exist.

Pay My Way?

For many years the Catholic Church sold "indulgences" (money paid to buy a soul out of "purgatory.") This blasphemous form of extortion brought great wealth to the Roman Catholic Church. In 1516 Pope Leo X set the price at 10 shillings per soul. Because of this unscriptural solicitation of monies, God refers to the Catholic Church as a "whore," Mystery Babylon. In Revelation 17 and 18 the great wealth of this false religious system is described, including the capture of men's "souls." The Bible says this religious system is seated in Rome (commonly called "the city of seven hills"), but has world-wide influence. God warns His people to "come out of her" so that they do not partake of His judgments.[412]

Mary Not The Mediator

Other unscriptural doctrines of the Catholic Church include the teaching that the Virgin Mary is exalted in the heavens as our "Mediatrix" (mediator). The Catholic church calls her the "Queen of Heaven" (the same title of the false goddess, Ishtar in the Babylonian religion.) Catholics believe that Mary was without sin and remains an eternal virgin. They also teach she is to be worshipped: "Mary is to be prayed to and worshiped in the churches" (Pope Pius XII, Oct. 11, 1954). But scripture says *"you shall worship the Lord your God, and Him only shall you serve."* (Matt.4:10) To pray to and worship Mary or any of the saints is idolatry, (which is strictly forbidden by God).[413]

Contrary to Catholic teaching, Mary is not our "Mediatrix" (mediator). The Bible clearly states that *"There is one God and ONE Mediator between God and men, the Man Christ Jesus."*[414] We need only go to Jesus to get to the Father. He said, *"I am the way the truth and the life; no man comes to the Father but by Me."*[415] Mary is not a Mediatrix. Our only mediator is JESUS. Mary is not exalted over any other member of the Body of Christ.

Mary Not Eternal Virgin

Additionally, Mary was not "without the stain of sin." The Bible states that *"all have sinned and fallen short of the glory of God"* and *"there is none righteous, no not one."*[416] Mary was a sinner, and one for whom Christ had to die. Additionally, she is not an eternal

---

[412] Revelation 18:4
[413] Exodus 20:3-5
[414] I Timothy 2:5
[415] John 14:6
[416] Romans3:23-Psalm l4

virgin. Matthew 1:18, 24, 25 state that Joseph did not "know" (i.e., have sexual relations) with Mary "until she brought forth her first born Son." After Jesus' birth, Mary and Joseph did have sexual relations and produced four other sons and at least three daughters:

> *"And when He was come into his own country, He taught them in their synagogue, insomuch that they were astonished, and said, Whence hath this man this wisdom, and these mighty works? Is not this the carpenter's son? is not His mother called Mary? and His brethren, James, and Joses, and Simon, and Judas? And His sisters, are they not all with us? Whence then has this man all these things? And they were offended in Him. But Jesus said unto them, A prophet is not without honor, save in His own country, and in His own house.*[417]

Jesus half-brothers did not believe in Him during His earthly ministry.[418] They were alienated from Him, as Psalm 69:8, 9 and John 2:17 prophesied: "I am become a stranger unto My brethren, and an alien unto My mother's children." Mary was not an eternal virgin. She had many other children after Christ. Catholic tradition again contradicts the Word of God.

The Truth Will Set You Free!

Jesus said, "You shall know the truth, and the truth shall set you free." Don't allow religious tradition to keep you from receiving the truth. The way to heaven is not through the Catholic Church. Salvation is only through faith in Jesus' work on the Cross as being ALL SUFFICIENT to cleanse you from sin. One must repent; confess their sins directly to God; and then ask Jesus to cleanse them of their sins and to become the "Lord" of their life. "*For whosoever calls upon the*

---

[417] Matthew 13:54-57
[418] John 7:3-5

name of the Lord shall be saved."[419] Jesus said, *"Behold, I stand at the door and knock; if anyone opens the door, I will come into him and will sup with him, and he with Me."*[420]

God loves all Catholics. He commands them to "Come out of her (that false, religious Babylonian system) My people," so they will not be judged during the Great Tribulation. That admonition is for all believers in Jesus. Being born-again is not a religious sacrament, but a Bible-based, personal experience between you and God. God bless!

---

[419] Romans 10:13
[420] Revelation 3:20

JESUS ONLY?

There is an offshoot of Orthodox Christianity called Pentecostal "Oneness" or, more commonly, "Jesus Only." This is a belief that there is only one God and that He is <u>one person</u> [Jesus], who manifests Himself as the Father, Son or the Holy Spirit. They deny the doctrine of the Trinity, which teaches there is one God Who manifests Himself as *three distinct persons*, namely, the Father, the Son, and the Holy Ghost. They believe there is only one person of the Godhead: Jesus. Therefore, they mandate that one must be baptized *only* in the name of Jesus (rather than the traditional "Father, Son and Holy Ghost").[421]

Semantics Or Substance

One might think that the difference is simply a matter of splitting hairs about words and semantics, and that it is not worth making it an issue of debate. After all, who can fully comprehend all the aspects of the Almighty, omniscient, eternal God! It would not be worth addressing except for the fact that "Jesus Only" people consider their particular belief and mode of *baptism* as essential to salvation. True Christianity teaches that we are saved by grace through faith in Jesus' redemption on the Cross and His resurrection...not by our own works.[422]

Baptism Prescription

"Oneness" teaches that unless one is water baptized in their prescribed way, they are going to hell. They see baptism as a *means* of salvation, rather than a public testimony of one's conversion. In other words, salvation is a result of "faith plus works" (the heretical recipe of many false teachers and denominations.) Oneness adherents believe Trinitarians are going to hell since they believe in the Father, Son and

---

[421] Matthew 28:19
[422] Ephesians 2:8

Holy Ghost, and baptize believers as such (rather than in the name of "Jesus" only). However, true salvation cannot be earned, merited or "worked for." It is a gift from God that is received by faith in Jesus' complete work on the Cross. It has nothing to do with any religious works that *we do*.[423] The two issues from which "Oneness" teaching divert from solid, Orthodox Christianity is their denial of the Trinity, and the assertion that water baptism in Jesus' name is necessary for salvation.

Jesus Is God

Oneness doctrine teaches that Jesus is the one, true God. That is absolutely true!

"In the beginning was the Word, and the Word was with God and the Word was God... and the Word became flesh and dwelt among us..." (John 1:1, 13) *"God was manifest in the flesh."* (I Timothy 3:16) *"Christ... for in Him dwells all the fullness of the Godhead bodily."*[424] Scripture clearly teaches that Jesus is fully God—God manifested in the flesh. In fact, in John 8:58 Jesus calls Himself the *"I Am"* (Jehovah) God. This was the name by which God revealed Himself to Moses in the burning bush.[425]

Truly, Jesus is the one, true God of the Bible. But is God only one Person? Scripture is replete with examples showing that this one true God manifests Himself as *three distinct persons*. Even in John 1:1 it shows that Jesus the Word was *"with God* [the Father]." In other words, more than one person of the Godhead was present at creation. In Genesis 1:26 the term "God" in Hebrew is "Elohim" (plural) when God says, *"Let Us make man in Our image, after Our likeness."* God refers to Himself in plural terms by using "Us" and "Our." He is not

---

[423] Galatians 5:4
[424] Colossians 2:8, 9
[425] Exodus 3:14

addressing angels. It was the Godhead that created man in His Own image, and that created the heavens and the earth. In creation God manifests Himself as three persons: The Father, the Word, and the Spirit.[426]

Separate But Equal

The plurality of God is evident, as well as the distinction in Personhood of the Trinity. Jesus many times referred to His Father as a separate Person from Himself. When Jesus came on earth as the God-man, He temporarily relinquished the use of certain Divine attributes that He shared with the Father and the Holy Spirit. The One True God is omniscient... knowing and seeing all. However, when God the Son was manifest on earth as a man, He allowed Himself to be limited in knowledge and glory. Jesus said, *"Who touched Me?"* and *"What is your name?"* when He ministered healing and deliverance in the eighth chapter of Luke.

Referring to Jesus' second coming, Jesus says, *"But of that day and that hour knows no man, no, not the angels which are in heaven, **neither the Son,** but the Father."*[427] Here He makes a distinction between Himself and the Father. The Father knew all, but not the Son.

A distinction is also found in John 17 when Jesus prayed to His Heavenly Father, and referred to the Father as *"Your"* and *"You"*, and Himself as *"I"* and *"Me."* Jesus requested of the Father that He would again glorify the Son with the glory they shared before creation. Jesus was not praying to Himself (as "Jesus only" doctrine purports), but to His Father in heaven. This clearly shows different, separate Persons of the Godhead.

---

[426] Genesis 1:1, 2
[427] Mark 13:32

Greater Than I

In John 14:8 Jesus again makes a distinction between Himself and the Father by saying, *"the Father is greater than I."* This in no way diminishes Jesus' deity or equality with the Father, for Jesus also said, *"I and My Father are one"* and *"I am in the Father and the Father in Me."* However, while on earth Jesus, allowed Himself to temporarily set aside the use of some of His Divine attributes. In this manner, Jesus could suffer as the Son of Man for us.[428] While on earth He said He could do nothing of Himself, but allowed Himself to be fully dependent on the Father to work through Him.[429]

Two "Lords"

An interesting passage that reveals the difference between the Divine Messiah (Jesus) and God the Father is in Psalm 2. Here scripture makes a distinction between the "Son" (the Messiah Who will reign over all the earth), and the Father (called "LORD"):

> *"I will declare the decree: the **LORD** has said unto **Me**, '**You are My Son**; this day have I begotten You. Ask of Me, and I shall give You the heathen for Thine inheritance, and the uttermost parts of the earth for Your possession.'"*

Psalm 110 also shows the Father and the Son as separate Persons, but calls both of them "Lord":

> *"The **LORD** [Father] said unto my **Lord** [The Son], 'Sit Thou at My right hand, until I make Thine enemies your footstool... the LORD has sworn and will*

---

[428] Philippians 2:7,8
[429] John 8:28

not repent, 'You are a priest for ever after the order of Melchizedek."

Here both the Father and the Son are called "Lord," but they have different functions. The Son would reign as a King and Priest, and sit at the right hand of the Father (the place of Messiah). Jesus is not sitting at the right hand of Himself, but of God the Father (a separate member of the Godhead). Notice also when Stephen the martyr was stoned. He looked up and saw Jesus as a separate person standing at the Father's right hand:

> *"But he, being full of the Holy Ghost, look up steadfastly into heaven, and saw the glory of God and Jesus standing on the right Hand of God, and said, 'Behold, I see the heavens opened, and the Son of man standing on the right hand of God.' ...and they stoned Stephen, calling upon God, and saying 'Lord Jesus, receive my spirit.'"* [430]

Again, the distinction between the Father and the Son is made, where the Son is at the Father's right hand. This does not diminish Jesus' Deity. Jesus the Son is God, just as the Father is God. When Stephen **calls upon God**, it says that he says, "***Lord Jesus***, *receive my spirit.*" Here, the Father and Son are shown in Heaven, and yet are distinct in their position and function.

Three In One

At Jesus' baptism, all three Persons of the Godhead (Father, Son, Holy Ghost) manifest as distinct Persons at one time:

> *"...it came to pass that **Jesus also being baptized and praying**, the heaven was opened, and the **Holy***

---

[430] Acts 7:55

Ghost descended in a bodily shape like a dove upon *Him and a Voice came from heaven [the Father],* which said, 'You are My Beloved Son; in You I am well pleased.'"[431]

How could God be only One Person? One Person was baptized in the river, One Person descended from Heaven in the form of a dove, and One Person spoke from Heaven. Three persons, yet one God!

If the name in which one is water baptized (the "formula" for baptism of "In the name of Jesus Christ") was so essential, then why did Jesus personally give command in Matthew 28 to baptize *"in the name of the Father, Son, and the Holy Spirit"*? The fact is, that the purpose of baptism is to publicly acknowledge Jesus as one's Lord, and one can do so either way. The words by which one is baptized do not save anyone. They are just public acknowledgment that one is saved by Jesus, the Son, who is a member of the eternal Godhead.

One But Triune

No one can fully comprehend the concept of the Triune God, but some have tried to use the analogy of an earthly element (H_2O) to understand the unity and yet distinction of the Godhead. Like the Trinity, H2O has 3 distinct manifestations: gas (steam); liquid (water); and solid (ice). Ice is not steam, neither is water, steam nor ice. They are 3 different forms, yet still they are all one element: H2O.

This analogy expresses the concept that 3 distinct entities (the Trinity) can be separate and yet the same. I John 5:7 states it best: *"For there are Three that bear record in heaven: The Father, the Word, and the Holy Ghost, and **these Three are One**."* In conclusion, scripture teaches that Jesus is God, but that God is not just one Person. God

---

[431] Luke 4:21, 22

manifests Himself as three distinct Persons: The Father, the Son and the Holy Ghost.

Baptism Subsequent To Salvation (*Not* Prerequisite!)

Now we must consider the issue of baptism. The "Oneness" doctrine considers baptism in the name of Jesus to be a prerequisite for salvation. Though baptism is important, it is NOT a means by which we are saved. One is saved by the confession of faith in the shed Blood of Jesus Christ. No religious works can earn salvation. As stated before, salvation is by faith alone:

*"For by grace are you **saved through faith,** and that not of yourselves; it is the gift of God: Not of works* [including baptism] *lest any man should boast."* [432] *"If you shalt confess with your mouth the Lord Jesus and **believe in thine heart** that God has raised Him from the dead, you shalt be saved."* And, *"For God so loved the world that He gave His Only Begotten Son, that **whosoever BELIEVES** in Him should not perish, but have eternal life."*

Salvation is the free gift of God received by faith in the Lord Jesus. Once we are saved we follow God's commands out of appreciation for His wonderful gift of eternal life. One who truly believes the good news of the Gospel will gladly follow the Lord's command to be water baptized. This outward work doesn't save you. It is simply a way to publicly testify one's commitment to Christ. In obeying Jesus' command of baptism, it shows you have a willing heart and a good conscience toward Jesus, and that you are truly following Him as Lord of your life:

"The like figure whereunto even baptism doth also now save us (not the putting away of the filth of the

---

[432] Ephesians 2:8,9; Romans 10:9-13; John 3:16

flesh, but the answer of a good conscience toward God,)
by the resurrection of Jesus Christ." (I Peter 3:21)

It is not the physical act of being water baptized that saves us, but faith in Jesus' finished work: His death, burial and resurrection. Baptism is an outward way of symbolically showing that we are spiritually raised from the dead with Jesus to new life.

In Mark 16:16 it declares *"He that **believes** and is baptized shall be **saved**; he that **believes not** shall be **damned**."* Believing or *not believing* are the determining factors as to whether one is saved or damned, *not* water baptism. Baptism does not save, but it is an outward testimony that one has believed and made Jesus the Lord of their life.

Converts Not Baptized

If water baptism *really* was a prerequisite to being saved, then Jesus was wrong when He told the thief on the cross, *"today you shalt be with Me in Paradise."* [433] According to "Jesus only" doctrine the thief went to hell since he was not water baptized in Jesus' name before he died. But Jesus was not wrong. The thief was saved and went to Paradise because of his faith in the Lord Jesus.

Also, if water baptism was the means by which one is saved (rather than being a testimony following salvation) then the Apostle Paul was amiss by not immediately baptizing all of his converts: *"For Christ sent me not to baptize, but to preach the gospel..."* and *"I thank God I baptized none of you."* (I Corinthians 1:4-7) But Paul was not amiss. He knew that his converts were already saved by faith in Jesus. Others baptized Paul's converts so that he could be free to preach the Gospel to others.

---

[433] Luke 23:44

Gentiles Saved *Without* Water Baptism

Acts 10 is a very telling passage that shows water baptism in Jesus' name does not save:

> *"Then Peter opened his mouth, and said... 'How God anointed **Jesus of Nazareth** with the Holy Ghost and with power: who went about doing good, and healing all that were oppressed of the devil; for God was with him. And we are witnesses of all things which he did both in the land of the Jews, and in Jerusalem; whom they slew and hanged on a tree: Him God raised up the third day, and shewed him openly... it is he which was ordained of God to be the Judge of quick and dead. To him give all the prophets witness, that through his name **whosoever believeth in him shall receive remission of sins.**"*

> *"While Peter yet spoke these words, the Holy Ghost fell on all them which heard the word. And they of the circumcision which believed were astonished, as many as came with Peter, because that on the Gentiles also was poured out the gift of the Holy Ghost. For they heard them speak with tongues, and magnify God. Then answered Peter, Can any man forbid water, that these should not be baptized, which have **received the Holy Ghost as well as we?** And he commanded them to be baptized in the name of the Lord."*

Purified By Faith

Peter acknowledged these Gentiles were saved, as they believed the message and were filled with the Holy Ghost, as Peter and the other disciples were on the day of Pentecost. Peter declared that God had *"purified their hearts by faith"* in Jesus.[434] They were already saved and filled with the Spirit *before* they were water baptized. Faith saved them, *not* water baptism.

In The Name

The "Oneness" doctrine not only erroneously teaches that water baptism saves, but that the specific words spoken at baptism brings "true salvation." Religious works (or words), however, do not save! "Oneness" teaches that believers must be baptized "in the name of Jesus Christ" to *really* be saved. (This reeks with the same error and religious spirit that infiltrated the early church. Then, false Jewish brethren tried to mandate circumcision, saying that unless one was circumcised according to the Law of Moses they could not be saved.[435] Paul vigorously opposed and renounced such false teaching, as we should today!)

It is true that Peter, on the day of Pentecost, is quoted as saying: *"Repent and be baptized every one of you in the Name of **Jesus Christ** for the remission of sins, and you shall receive the gift of the Holy Ghost."* (Acts 2:38) However, it is not a "religious mantra" or formula that saves us. It is faith in one's heart toward God.

Why Peter used the Name

One must keep in mind *why* Peter specifically used the name of Jesus when instructing the Jews to be baptized that day: Peter was speaking to the nation of Israel that had just denied that **Jesus** was the King of the Jews, and had crucified Him. The Jews were very familiar with the fact that God has a Son (the Messiah--see Ps. 2:7). But, they had denied that Jesus was that "Son." So, rather than quoting Jesus'

---

[434] Acts 15:7-9
[435] Galatians 2 & 5

exact words for baptism ("*in the Name of the Father, and of the Son, and of the Holy Ghost*" as Jesus commissioned in Matthew's Gospel), Peter used the **Son's name-- Jesus**. He told them they must repent and acknowledge that *Jesus* is God's Son (their Messiah) in order to be saved. That is why he preached to be baptized in Jesus' name. It was their acknowledgment that Jesus was the Messiah, the Son of God, whom they had rejected just days before.

Unto What Were You Baptized?

However, the usual, prescribed method of water baptism by the early Church was "in the name of the Father, the Son, and the Holy Ghost." The Apostle Paul makes this clear in Acts 19:

> "*Paul... finding certain disciples, he said unto them, 'Have you received the Holy Ghost since you believed?' And they said unto him, 'We have not so much as heard whether there be any Holy Ghost.' And he said unto them, 'Unto what then were you baptized?'*"

Here it is apparent that Paul assumed that these disciples had already been water baptized using the traditional phrase *"the Father, Son & Holy Ghost."* (Matthew 28) When Paul found out that they had never *heard* of the "Holy Ghost" (which was what they usually invoked when baptizing) he asked, "*Unto what then were you baptized?*" In other words, if you have never heard of the "Holy Ghost", then you must not have had the traditional, Christian baptism as Jesus commanded in Mathew 28. The point here is that the early Church normally baptized using the Trinity's Names—not "Jesus" only. Either way one is baptized is acceptable as long as one does not look to the mode of baptism as a means of receiving salvation.

Purpose of Baptism

The purpose of baptism is to publicly acknowledge the fact that one has been saved by faith in Jesus' death, burial and resurrection. The words spoken at baptism do not save… faith in Jesus does. Paul warns Christians not to depend on any outward religious works in order to be justified in God's sight. If they depend on circumcision, baptism, or any other "good works" to save them, they are in error and have fallen from grace.[436] It is only through faith in Jesus' Blood that we are saved. Adding any religious work to His Blood to merit salvation insults the Spirit of grace. Jesus' Blood alone is sufficient to save. To believe that water baptism saves you is a perversion of the Gospel of Christ; it is religious error of which we must be ware.

Baptism does not save: faith does

The Bible teaches that outward religious works do not save us (including our mode of water baptism). We are saved by grace through faith. One follows the Lord in water baptism after one is saved in order to make a public testimony of faith. The Bible also teaches that God is one, and yet manifests as three distinct Persons, namely, the Father, the Son, and the Holy Ghost. To deny the clear Biblical teaching of the Trinity by subscribing to "Jesus Only" doctrine is spiritual error. We must heed all of God's Word and *"Let God be true, and every man a liar."*

---

[436] Galatians 5:4

JESUS IS JEHOVAH

Scripture states that *"there shall be false teachers among you, who secretly will bring in **damnable heresies**, even **denying the Lord** that bought them, and bring upon themselves swift destruction."* (II Peter 2:1) To deny that Jesus is "Lord" (translated "Jehovah" in the Old Testament), is therefore a very serious error which results in damnation. One group that denies that Jesus is Lord is the "Jehovah Witnesses." They have made their own version of the Bible and have doctrines that actually contradict the Word of God. Many sincere followers of Jehovah Witness teachings do not realize that the founders of J.W. falsely claimed to be Bible scholars knowing the original languages of the Bible. Founder   Under oath in court at Hamilton, Ontario, Canada in 1913 founder Russell declared in support of his claims to be an expert Scripture scholar that he knew Greek. Handed a Greek New Testament, he was forced to admit that he did not know even the Greek alphabet. Neither did he know Latin or Hebrew. He wrote concerning the Bible, but every acknowledged Scripture scholar in the universities of the world today will agree that Russell's explanations are for the most part, quite contrary to the obvious meaning of the words of the Bible. Russell was never a scholar in the accepted sense of the word. New World Translation Bible contains many translation errors. In fact, the Watchtower refuses to reveal who their translators are. In the Douglas Walsh Trail in Scotland, one of their translators admitted his involvement in its translation and when given a simple Biblical Hebrew test, he was not able to translate it. Their New World Translation is filled with doctrinal error. A serious heresy of Jehovah Witnesses is the denial of Jesus' deity and the essential truths that salvation is received by faith, not religious works. They teach and promote anti-Christ doctrine by denying Jesus is Jehovah. The following study addresses their false teachings, and proves Biblically that Jesus is Jehovah.

I AM Is My Name

First of all, the Name "Jehovah" (Yahweh in Hebrew) is the title that God gives Himself: *"And God said unto Moses, 'I AM THAT I AM'; and He said, 'Thus shalt you say unto the children of Israel, I AM has sent me unto you.'"* (Exodus 3:14) *"I AM THAT I AM"* is translated as Yahweh in Hebrew, or "Jehovah" in English. Throughout the Old Testament, "Jehovah" is translated "LORD" in English versions of the Bible. It is the Title of the one true God. The fact that Jesus is this one true God cannot be denied. See the following passage in John 1. Clearly, the Word is God:

> *"In the beginning was the Word, and the Word was with **God**, and the Word was **God**. The same was in the beginning with God. All things were made by Him; and without Him was not anything made that was made ... And the **Word was made flesh,** and dwelt among us, (and we beheld His glory, the glory as of the Only Begotten of the Father) full of grace and truth."*

Jesus Is The Word

This reference of Jesus states He is the Word. We see in Revelation 19 that Jesus is called the *"Word of God,"* as well as *"KING OF KINGS, AND LORD OF LORDS."*

In John 1:1 it states that Jesus was with God (the Father) and that Jesus the Word was God. The term used for *"God"* for both the Father and the Son is *"Theos"* (Strong's Concordance # 2316.) However, the second "God" (referring to Jesus) has a slight difference. In the Greek, the writer wanted to stress *emphatically* that Jesus the

Word was God. So, the correct English rendering would be *"In the beginning was the Word, and the Word was with God, and the Word was absolutely God (the Supreme Deity.)"*

This is significant because Jehovah Witnesses try to negate Jesus' Deity by saying He is just "a [little] god," when in fact this passage teaches just the opposite.

Double Stress: Jesus Is GOD

Renown Greek scholar W.E. Vine states "...the absence of the article serves to lay stress upon, or give precision to, the character or nature of what is expressed in the noun. A notable instance of this is in John 1:1, "and the Word was God;" here a double stress is on theos, by the absence of the article and by the emphatic position. To translate it literally, 'a god was the Word,' is entirely misleading. Moreover, that 'the Word' is the subject of the sentence, exemplifies the rule that the subject is to be determined by its having the article when the predicate is anarthrous (without the article.)"[437]

The Holy Ghost in the writer John wanted to "double stress" that Jesus the Word is God. John 1:2,3 states that Jesus was in the beginning with God and that all things were created by Him (Jesus).

No God Before Or After

Referring to Jehovah God, Isaiah 43:10 states: *"You are My witnesses, says the Lord, and My servant whom I have chosen; that you may know and believe Me and understand that I am He: **before Me there was no God formed, neither shall there be after Me.**"*

Therefore, Jesus (being God), is the Lord Jehovah. He is not a "little god" formed later, as cults would falsely teach. Isaiah 44

---

[437] Vine, An Expository Dictionary, Vol. 2, p.160:

declares: *"Is there a God beside Me? yea, there is no God; I know not any."* Yet, Jesus the Word *"was God,"* according to Apostle John. He was also "with God" at creation. There is one God, Who is expressed or manifested as the person of the Father, the person of the Son (the Word), and the person of the Holy Ghost.[438]

Elohim

In the beginning, God the Father, God the Son, and God the Holy Spirit were jointly involved in creation. Genesis 1:1 states *"In the beginning God created the heaven and the earth."* The term "God" here (and in many other Old Testament reference) is *"Elohim."* In the Hebrew, Strong's Concordance (#430), it is a plural name for the Supreme God. Though there is only One True God, He is expressed in plural (three) Persons. Genesis 1 says:

"And God [Elohim] said, 'Let Us make man in
Our image, after Our likeness... so God created man in
His Own image, in the image of God created He him;
male and female created He them."

There are not three separate gods. There is one God, Who is expressed as three distinct Persons: Yet, they are inseparable, as being the one true God.

Jesus The Creator

Speaking of Jesus (the Word) John 1:3,10 says: *"All things were made by Him; and without Him was not anything made that was made ... He was in the world, and the world was made by Him."* Jesus is credited with creating the world (Hebrews 1:1-3): *"God ... has spoken unto us by **His Son**, ...**by Whom also He made the worlds**, Who being the brightness of His glory, and the express image of His person ..."* Colossians 1 declares that Jesus is Creator God:

---

[438] Matthew 28:19

*"...His Dear **Son:** in Whom we have redemption through His Blood, even the forgiveness of sins: Who is the image of the invisible God, the firstborn of every creature: for **by Him were all things created**, that are in heaven, and that are in earth, visible and invisible, ...all things were created by Him and for Him: and He is before all things, and by Him all things consist ... that in all things He might have the preeminence..."*

The Godhead In Jesus

Paul warned the Colossians to: *"Beware lest any man spoil you through philosophy and vain deceit, after the tradition of men, after the rudiments of the world, and not after **Christ. For in Him dwells all the fullness of the Godhead Bodily."*** Jesus is not a "little god." The fullness of the Godhead dwells in Him! As Paul further teaches in I Timothy, Jesus is "God in the flesh:

*"And without controversy great is the mystery of godliness: **God was manifest in the flesh** [in the Person of Jesus Christ], justified in the Spirit, seen of angels, preached unto the Gentiles, believed on in the world, received up into glory."*[439]

Who Raised Jesus From The Dead?

Further verifying Jesus' Deity (of the Godhead) is the Resurrection of Christ. Scripture states that **_God_ raised up Jesus from the dead** (Acts 2:32). We conclude that because Jehovah is the one true God, and besides Him there is no other, that **Jehovah** raised Jesus from the dead.

---

[439] I Timothy 3:16

Then, Galatians 1:1 declares that *"God the __Father__, Who raised Him [Jesus] from the dead."* Compare that to Romans 6:4, which says, *"...as __Christ was raised from the dead by the glory of the Father__."* From these scriptures, there is no doubt that the Father is Jehovah God, Who raised Jesus from the dead.

However, the Father was not the only member of the Godhead involved in Jesus' resurrection. Romans 8:11 states the *"__Spirit__ __raised Jesus from the dead__."* So, the Holy Spirit raised Jesus from the dead. He is Jehovah God, as well.

Then, in the Gospel of John it tells us that Jesus raised Himself from the dead:

> *"Therefore doth My Father love Me, **because I lay down My life,** that I might take it again. No man takes it from Me, but I lay it down of Myself. **I have power to lay it down, and I have power to take it again.** This commandment have I received of My Father."*[440]

Jesus confirms the fact that He raised Himself from the dead in John 2:

> *"Jesus answered and said unto them, 'Destroy this Temple, and in three days **I WILL RAISE IT UP.**' Then said the Jews, 'Forty and six years was this temple in building, and will You rear it up in three days?' But **He spoke of the Temple of His Body.** When therefore He was risen from the dead, His disciples remembered that He had said this unto them; and they believed the scripture, and the word which Jesus had said."*

---

[440] John 10:17,18

Here we see that Jesus is also "Jehovah God." He raised Himself from the dead. Even as the Trinity (all three Persons of the Godhead) all were involved in creation, so were they all involved in raising Jesus from the dead.

Jesus Is God

Jesus' Deity cannot be denied in scripture. Matthew 1:23 states: "*Behold, a virgin shall be with child, and shall bring forth **a son** and they shall call his name Emmanuel, which being interpreted is, '**God with us**.*'" Hebrews 1:6, 8 clearly teaches that Jesus is God:

> "*when he brings in the first begotten into the world, he says, 'And let all the angels of God worship him...But unto **the Son** he says, '**Your throne O God**, is for ever and ever: a scepter of righteousness is the scepter of your kingdom.*'"

Worship The Son

Here, Jesus the Son is called "God" and angels are commanded to worship him. Worship is reserved only for the one true God, as Christ Himself states: "*You shall worship the Lord your God, and Him only shalt you serve.*"[441] And yet, because Christ was "*God manifest in the flesh,*"[442] He freely received worship from those who encountered Him:[443]

- "*Where is he that is born **King of the Jews**? for we have seen his star in the east, and are come to worship him...And when they were come into the house, they saw*

---

[441] Matthew 4:10
[442] I Tim. 3:16
[443] Matthew 2; 8:2; 9:18; 14:33; 15:25; 28:9,10,17 (Also see Luke 17:15-18; 24:52; John 9:38; John 20:24-29; Revelation 1:17; and Rev. 5:11-13.)

277

the young child with Mary his mother, and fell down, and
worshipped him:"

- *"And, behold, there came **a leper and worshipped him**, saying, Lord, if thou wilt, thou canst make me clean. And **Jesus** put forth his hand, and touched him, saying, I will; be thou clean. And immediately his leprosy was cleansed."*

- *"behold, there came a certain ruler, and **worshipped him**, saying, My daughter is even now dead: but come and lay thy hand upon her, and she shall live. And **Jesus** arose, and followed him*

- *Then they that were in the ship came and **worshipped him**, saying, Of a truth thou art the **Son of God**.*

- *And as they went to tell his disciples, behold, **Jesus** met them, saying, All hail. And they came and held him by the feet, and **worshipped him**. Then said Jesus unto them, Be not afraid... And when they saw him, **they worshipped him***

Do Not Worship Creatures

Because Jesus is Jehovah God, He freely received the worship that is reserved for God alone. However, worship was forbidden[444] and refused by angels and apostles, as these passages show:

- *"And as Peter was coming in, Cornelius met him, and fell down at his feet, and **worshipped him**. But Peter took him up, saying, **Stand up**; I myself also am a man."*

---

[444] Acts 10:25,26; Acts 14:11-15; Rev. 19:10; and Rev. 22:9

- *And when the people saw what Paul had done, they lifted up their voices, saying… **The gods are come down to us in the likeness of men**…when the apostles, Barnabas and Paul, heard of, they rent their clothes, and ran in among the people, crying out, And saying, Sirs, **why do ye these things? We also are men…***

- *And I fell **at his feet to worship him**. And he said unto me, **See thou do it not: I am thy fellow servant, and of thy brethren** that have the testimony of Jesus: **worship God***

- *I John saw these things, and heard them. And when I had heard and seen, **I fell down to worship before the feet of the angel** which shewed me these things. Then he said he unto me, **See thou do it not**: for I am thy fellow servant… **worship God**.*

Why did Jesus received the worship that is reserved for God only? Because He is God manifested in the flesh. The flesh part of Jesus was fully man…the seed of David. But the spirit of Christ is fully God. He is the "Word made flesh," and is to be worshipped as God.

Before Abraham Was, I AM

The Son of God has been with the Father for eternity. Jesus did not begin His existence when He was born of Mary in the earth. He is the Self-Existent God. There are many manifest appearances of God in the Old Testament. We know that *"**No man has seen God** [the **Father**] **at any time**; the **Only Begotten Son**, which is in the bosom of the Father, **He has declared Him**."*[445]

---

[445] John 1:18

Any appearance of "The LORD" (Jehovah God) in the Old Testament was actually not the Father, but the Son manifesting. Old Testament appearances of God are called "Theophanies" (but more specifically, "Christophanies," --manifestations of God the Son):

- Isaiah 6:1, 5: *"In the year that king Uzziah died **I saw also the Lord (Jehovah)** sitting upon a throne, high and lifted up, and His train filled the temple...Then said I, 'Woe is me! for I am undone .... for **mine eyes have seen the King, the Lord of Hosts.** "*

- II Chronicles 18:18: *"... **I saw the Lord** sitting upon His Throne ..."*

- Genesis 12:7: *"And **the Lord (Jehovah) appeared** unto Abram, and said, "Unto your seed will I give this land: and there built he an altar unto **the Lord, Who appeared unto him.** "*

- Genesis 17:1-3: *"And when Abram was ninety years old and nine, **the Lord (Jehovah) appeared to Abram,** and said unto him, 'I am the Almighty God; walk before Me, and be you perfect. And I will make My covenant between Me and you, and will multiply you exceedingly. And Abram fell on his face: and God talked with him..."*

- Genesis 26:24: *"**And the Lord (Jehovah) appeared unto him** the same night, and said, 'I am the God of Abraham your father: fear not, for I am with you, and will bless you..."*

- Genesis 32:30: *"And Jacob called the name of the place Peniel: 'for **I have seen God face to face,** and my life is* *preserved.'" Genesis 35:9: "**And God appeared unto Jacob again...**"*

- Exodus 24:9-12: *"Then went up Moses, and Aaron, Nadab, and Abihu, and seventy of the elders of Israel: And **they saw the God of Israel**: and there was under His feet as it were a paved work of a sapphire stone, and as it were the body of heaven in his clearness. And upon the nobles of the children of Israel He laid not His hand: also **they saw God**, and did eat and drink. And the Lord said unto Moses, Come up to Me into the mount...."*

- Judges 13:22: *"And Manoah said unto his wife, 'We shall surely die, because **we have seen God.**' But his wife said unto him, 'If the Lord were pleased to kill us, He would not have received a burnt offering and a meat offering at our hands...'"*

- 2 Chron.1:7: *"In that night did **God appear unto Solomon** and said unto him, 'Ask what I shall give you.'"*

- Job 42:5: *"I have heard of You by the hearing of the ear; **but now mine eye sees You** ..."*

In the Volume of the Book it is Written of Me

Additional Old Testament Christophanies are found in Genesis 18:1; Genesis 26:2; 31:11,13; Genesis 28:13; Exodus 33:11; I Kings 22:19; Ezekiel 1:1, 26; 8:3; Judges 6:14; and II Chronicles 7:12. All of these sightings of the LORD (Jehovah) in the Old Testament were manifestations of God the Son. No man has ever seen God the Father, but the Son (Jesus) has "declared" Him. Jesus manifested the Lord God Jehovah, for He is the *"express image"* of God (Hebrews 1:3).

The Word Is Exalted Above The Name!

Christ's preeminence as God is confirmed throughout the Bible. Psalm 138:2 states *"For You has magnified Your **Word above all Your Name.*** " The Word (Jesus) is exalted above all of the various names of God (El Shaddai, Elohim, Jehovah) because Jesus, (the Word made Flesh) encompasses all the attributes expressed in the various names of God. *"For in Him [Jesus] dwells all the fullness of the Godhead Bodily."*[446]

Jesus is not inferior to Jehovah (as Jehovah Witnesses teach— relegating Him as an inferior, created being.) Jesus is the I AM --Self existent -- Jehovah God. He is everything God is in Bodily form.

No Other Name!

In fact, so exalted is Jesus the Son, that *"neither is there salvation in any other: for **there is none other name** under heaven given among men, whereby we must be saved."* (Acts 4:12) One must confess Jesus to be saved (born again.): *"That if you shall confess with your mouth the **Lord Jesus**... For whosoever shall call upon the Name of the Lord [Jesus] shall be saved."*[447]

The LORD Jehovah

Notice that one must confess **Jesus** is Lord to be saved. It is interesting that this passage in Romans 10 is quoting an Old Testament reference, Joel 2:32. The Old Testament reference is this: "And it shall come to pass, that whosoever shall call on the Name of the LORD shall be delivered (saved)" The term "LORD" in Joel 2:32 is "Jehovah." Romans quotes this scripture, and states that one must call on the Lord Jesus, confessing with your mouth that He is LORD. In other words, one must confess that Jesus is Jehovah (LORD) to be saved. Jesus is Jehovah God.

---

[446] Colossians 2:9
[447] Romans 10:9, 10, 13

Jesus The Savior

Jesus is also Savior. Paul calls Jesus, *"God our Savior"* in Titus 1:3, 4. Then look at this passage in Isaiah 43:11: *"I, even I, am the LORD (Jehovah); and **beside Me there is no Savior**."* Jesus is Jehovah the Savior. Then Isaiah 45:21 declares: *"...have not I the **LORD** (Jehovah)? and there is no God else beside Me; a just **God and a Savior; there is none beside Me**."*

Is God A Man?

Some might ask, "If Jesus is God, then why did He have to pray to His Father? (Luke 22:42); Why did He become weary? (John 4:6); and how could He be tempted?" (Matt. 4:1) The answer to this is that Jesus, (though He is Jehovah, equal with the Father) had to come to earth as the Son of Man. (Luke 6:5) *"God was manifest in the flesh ...*"[448] God had to partake of human flesh in order to pay for the sins of mankind as a Man. Paul expounds upon this in Romans 5:

> *"Wherefore, as **by one man sin entered into the world**, and death by sin; and so death passed upon all men, for that all have sinned: ... For if through the offence of one many be dead, much more the grace of God, **and the gift by grace, which is by one Man, Jesus Christ**, has abounded unto many...Therefore as by the offence of one judgment came upon all men to condemnation; even so by the **righteousness of One** the free gift [of righteousness] came upon all men unto justification of life. For as by one man's disobedience many were made sinners, so **by the obedience of One shall many be made righteous**."*

God In The Flesh

---

[448] I Timothy 3:16

The debt for mankind's sin had to be paid by man. God took on human flesh in the Person of Jesus: *"Behold, a virgin shall be with Child, and shall bring forth a Son, and they shall call His Name Emmanuel, which being interpreted is, 'God with us.'"* (Matthew 1:23) *"God was in Christ, reconciling the world unto Himself..."* (II Corinthians 5:19)

Temporarily Relinquished Glory

Though Jesus was God, He allowed Himself to temporarily set aside the use of certain attributes of Divinity in order to be able to pay for man's sin as a man. However, He was fully God before ever manifesting as the God-man in the flesh. In fact, in John 17:5 Jesus recounts:

> *"**the glory that I had with Thee** (with the Father) before the world was..."*

That was the glory He shared with the Father in His pre-incarnate state (before becoming "God in the Flesh" in the Person of Jesus.) Jesus shared the glory with the Father! Isaiah 42:8 states:

> *"I am the LORD (Jehovah): that is My Name: and **My glory will I not give to another**..."*

Jesus is one with the Father and so He partook of that glory.

Equal With God

What great humility the Son had by being willing to leave His exalted place in Heaven and to become Man! Though He was equal with God, yet He was willing to become the suffering Servant to bear the sins of all mankind:

*"Let this mind be in you which was also in Christ Jesus: Who, being in the form of God, thought it not robbery to be **equal with God**: but made Himself of no reputation, and took upon Him the form of a servant, and was **made in the likeness of men**: And being found in fashion as a man, **He humbled Himself, and became obedient unto death, even the death of the cross.***"

At Jesus' Name All Shall Bow!

"Wherefore God also has highly exalted Him, and given Him a Name which is above every name: that at the Name of Jesus every knee should bow, of things in heaven, and things in earth, and things under the earth; and that every tongue should confess that **Jesus Christ is LORD**, *to the glory of God the Father.*"[449]

The Father In Me Does The Work

Christ was temporary humbled for thirty-three years while He was on earth (*"being found in fashion as a man"*). During that time the use of certain Divine attributes (such as Omniscience, Omnipotence, Omnipresence) was set aside. Jesus declared that He was dependent upon His Father's power working through Him: *"Truly, truly, I say unto you, **the Son can do nothing of Himself**, but what He sees the Father do: for what things so ever He doeth, these also doeth the Son likewise."* [450] *"...If you loved Me, you would rejoice, because I said I go unto the Father: for **My Father is greater than I**."*

I And My Father Are One

---

[449] Philippians 2:5-11
[450] John 5:19; John 14:28

285

Though in the form of man, Jesus maintained that He was God, and in essence one with the Father:

> *"If you had known Me, you should have known My Father also: and from henceforth you know Him and have seen Him. Philip said unto Him, 'Lord, show us the Father and it will satisfy us.' Jesus said unto him, 'Have I been so long time with you, and yet have you not known Me, Philip? He that has seen Me has seen the Father; and how do you say then, "show us the Father?"*
>
> *Do you not believe that I am in the Father, and the Father in Me? The words that I speak to you I speak not of Myself; but the Father that dwells in Me, He does the works. Believe Me that I am in the Father, and the Father in Me: or else believe Me for the very works' sake.'"* (John 14:7-11.)

Jesus said, *"If you had known Me, you should have known My Father also."*[451] And He declared, *"He that believes on Me, believes not on Me, but on Him that sent Me. And He that sees Me sees Him that sent Me."*[452]

Jesus the I AM

Jesus so boldly declared His equality with Jehovah that the Jews wanted to stone Him:

> *"Your father Abraham rejoiced to see My day: and he saw it and was glad.' Then said the Jews unto Him, 'You are not yet fifty years old, had have you seen Abraham?' Jesus said unto them, 'Truly, truly, I say*

---

[451] John 8:19
[452] John 12:44,45

*unto you, before Abraham was, **I AM.**' Then took they up stones to cast at Him: but Jesus hid Himself, and went out of the temple, going through the midst of them, and so passed by."*

The reason the Jews were so incensed at Jesus was because He called Himself the "**I AM**" (Jehovah God). To them this was blasphemy. This was a direct quote from Exodus 3:14: *"And God said unto Moses, '**I AM THAT I AM'**: and He said, 'Thus shall you say unto the children of Israel, 'I AM has sent me unto you.'"*[453] Jesus called Himself the Self-Existent, **I AM** God--*Jehovah.* In John 5 it says that the Jews wanted to kill Jesus because He *"not only had broken the Sabbath, but said also that God was His Father, **making Himself equal with God.**"*

JESUS: Jehovah in the Old Testament
There are many scriptural cross references equating the Old Testament "Jehovah" with Jesus:

- Numbers 21:5-7 and I Corinthians 10:9 says tempting the LORD (Jehovah) is tempting Christ.
- Philippians 2:9-11 and Isaiah 45:21-23 state that every knee will bow to Jesus (Jehovah).
- Psalm 45:6,7 and Hebrews 1:8 says Jesus that sits in God's throne forever.
- Revelation 1:7-18, 21, 22 and Isaiah 41, 44, 48 call Jesus the "Alpha and Omega, the First and the Last," Jehovah God, Who created the heavens and the earth.

The anti-Christ spirit

---

[453] John 8:56-59

Those who have an anti-Christ spirit deny that Jesus is LORD (Jehovah).[454] In fact, unless one has God's Spirit, they cannot confess from their heart that Jesus is LORD.[455] II John warns us that in the last days there would be many deceivers who deny that Jesus is the Christ (God in the flesh, the Anointed One[456]). These false teachers are not to even be allowed into your home. We must *try the spirits, whether they be of God."* Test everything by the Word of God.

Jesus The Christ

Remember, Jesus Christ, of the seed of David, is also Jehovah God:

> *"For unto us a **Child is born**, unto us a Son is given; and the government shall be upon His shoulder: and His Name shall be, called Wonderful, Counsellor, **The Mighty God, The Everlasting Father,** The Prince of Peace. Of the increase of His government and peace there shall be no end, upon the throne of David, and upon his kingdom, to order it and to establish it with judgment and with justice from henceforth even forever."*[457]

God In The Flesh

Jesus came in the flesh, rose again in the flesh, ascended in the flesh, and will return in the flesh.[458] Acts 1:11 states: *"...**this same Jesus** which is taken up from you into heaven, **shall so come in like manner as you have seen Him go into heaven.**"* Jesus left in His glorified, flesh and bone, visible Body. When He returns He will return in His glorified, flesh and bone, visible Body. The founder of the

---

[454] I John 2:22
[455] I Corinthians 12:3
[456] Isaiah 61:1-3
[457] Isaiah 9
[458] John 1:14; John 2:20-22; Luke 24:39; 1 John 1:1.2; and Acts 1:2,3,9-11

288

Jehovah Witnesses organization (Watch Tower Society), Charles T. Russell, fell into grave error when he denied Jesus coming in the flesh, saying that Jesus returned spiritually in 1914.[459] That is anti-Christ heresy (that denies Jesus Christ coming in the flesh).

Sadly, Jehovah Witnesses deny that Jesus is Jehovah, and therefore cannot be born-again. We must guard against false teaching, and pray for those who have been taken by satan's snare.

---

[459] https://en.wikipedia.org/wiki/Jehovah's_Witnesses_beliefs

AMAZING FACTS IN THE BIBLE

The Bible is primarily considered to be a book of spiritual inspiration (and it is certainly that!) Yet, there are many amazing historical and scientific facts contained in Holy Scripture as well. Many of the scientific revelations contained in the Bible were not discovered by secular study until the 20th Century. The oldest book of the Bible, Job (written approximately 2,500 years B.C.), accurately describes undersea rivers and oceanic volcanic activity, the wind and sea currents, astronomy, and the rain cycle.[460] Job tells of the "circuit" of the earth (orbit) and that it "hangs on nothing." This was confirmed by modern science over four thousand years later.

The Rock Record

Science also confirms the account of creation as described in the Bible. The book of Genesis lists the order in which life on earth was created, with the fossil record bearing out that exact order in the layers of geological strata: (first, grasses; then fruit bearing plants; then fish and bird life; animals; and then man, being the crown of His creation).

World Wide Flood

The fossil record also confirms the Biblical account of a worldwide flood. The highest mountain peaks testify of a massive flood that covered the earth. For instance, shark teeth have been found at the very highest summits of mountains in California, and sea fossils have been found in the midst of deserts. The description of the flood in Genesis 7:11 says that *"the fountains of the great deep were broken up."* This is consistent with the evidence of the rapid layering of much sediment and lava from cracks in the earth's mantle from underwater volcanic eruptions. The fact that there was a cataclysmic, universal

---

[460] Job 8,9; 14:18, 19; 22:12, 13; 26:7-12; 36:27-30; 37:3-11; 38:4-11, 22-35

flood allowed for the rapid formation of rock strata. The flowing lava encased plant and animals, preserving them completely as intact fossils (not possible in the normal decay process). The fact that the same sandstone sedimentary layers are found consistently all over the world show that at one time the earth was covered with water. This allowed for massive deposits to form the same sedimentary strata worldwide.

Mount St. Helen's event

A scientifically observable example of underwater deposition of lava forming layers of rock in a relatively short period of time, occurred when Mount Saint Helens erupted. A nearby lake had layers of igneous rock form under water in just a matter of days. The layers resembled a mini Grand Canyon. If one looked at the lake bed without knowing that a volcano had quickly deposited the rock layers, one might assume that it took millions (or even billions of years) for those layers to form. In the normal sedimentary process of gradual deposition of mud and rock, it would take millions of years to form those rock strata. In actuality, it took only a few days.

The Rocks Don't Lie

Can we assume the possibility that the rock strata in the earth may have also formed rapidly, given the evidence that there was at one time a world-wide flood? We can not only assume, but conclude that the earth's rock layers *did in fact* form very rapidly. This is based on geological evidence in the rock layers themselves. Firstly, there had to be rapid accumulation of sediment to cover plant & animal life in order for their fossilized remains to be preserved intact. (The remains did not show decomposition and deterioration that would normally take place over a period of time of *gradual sedimentary accumulation* of hundreds of thousands of years.) The fossils had to be preserved quickly, before the plants and animals had time to deteriorate.

Poly-straight fossils

Another phenomenon proves the rapid formation of the earth's rock strata. That is the existence of *"poly-straight fossils."* These are fossils of plants that transverse vertically through several strata of rock. One very tall poly-straight fossil was discovered in its upright position extending through rock strata that supposedly took *5 million years* to deposit. That is a scientific impossibility. One particular plant fossil, for instance, was not a tree with a hard xylem, but a very tall, *reed type* plant with a flaccid (bendable) cambium or outer layer. The plant could not have maintained its upright position (allowing layers of sediment to accumulate on it) for even thousands of years, much less millions.

There are many of this type of fossilized plants that have been discovered. They traverse through many strata of rock layers, which shows that the layers of mud & sediment had to accumulate very quickly to preserve the plant and maintain its upright position. Rapid accumulation of sedimentary and igneous rock from underwater lava flow in a world-wide flood scenario *can* account for the poly-straight fossil phenomena. The "old earth" theory (presuming it took billions of years to form the rock layers) *cannot* account for poly-straight fossils being preserved and transcending through many strata of rock.

Dinosaur Prints?

There are other discoveries that indicate that the earth is very young, and that the earth's strata developed in a relatively short period of time. At one time, scientists thought the earth to be billions of years old. They believed that bacteria developed 3.5 billion years ago, and that 530 million years ago living systems began to develop. The Mesozoic Age, for example, supposedly spans 65 to 300 million years ago and has five divisions. According to their theory, dinosaurs died off 64 million years ago and man did not appear until 2.5 million years ago, with modern man only appearing 60,000 years ago. However, these arbitrarily assigned geological periods were not based on accurate dating methods. They were set by pure speculation and supposition.

Geology destroys "geological column!"

One example in point is a discovery in a 1950 Texas oil dig in which the Gulf Oil Company uncovered a fossilized human footprint in the "Permian Strata" of rock. The Permian age stratus is supposedly *250 million years old,* when (according to evolutionary theory) dinosaurs had not even developed. And yet, they found scientific evidence that human beings existed during that period.

In Glenrose, Texas in 2000 a human footprint was found in the rock layer with a large dinosaur footprint on top of it. There were water ripples in the strata, showing that these prints were made in mud, which had been quickly covered (perhaps by lava), which encapsulated both prints in the fossil record. These prints were in the Cretaceous strata of rock, purported to be 110 million years old. This totally shatters the entire evolutionary "Geologic column" that theorizes the relative age of man, dinosaurs, and earth being millions of years old.

The Heavens Declare The Glory Of God

Because of the complexities of the universe, many scientists now acknowledge that creation is not the result of an accidental cosmic explosion of gasses, but rather, the result of very complex and intricate design. The established laws of physics point to the fact that Intelligent Design had its Hand in it all. For instance, our solar system had to be designed so exactly in order to make life on earth possible. Jupiter's relative position with the Earth—it's fixed distance of 40 light minutes from the earth and 2 ½ times the size and its weight allows for it to shield the Earth from destruction of comets and asteroids that could destroy it completely. The exact position and mass of the planets have to be perfectly lined up in circular, horizontal orbits around the sun (unlike other galaxies) in order to allow for Earth's temperature and gravity to maintain life. This cosmic order points to a Creative Designer.

Giant Leap For Mankind

Another interesting fact regarding astronomy is that the Earth's moon proves that creation is very young. When NASA scientists planned for the first Lunar landing, they anticipated there would be hundreds of feet of fine dust accumulated on the moon's surface (given the rate at which dust accumulates, and their presumed age of the planets). The lunar module was equipped with disc landing pads to keep it from sinking in the moon dust. Upon taking one "small step for man, but one giant leap for mankind," scientists were surprised to find there was only around two inches of dust on the moon's surface, making the moon very young. This amount is consistent with the Biblical account of the Earth and moon being only thousands of years old, *not billions*.

God Said, "Let There Be..."

Additionally, the fact that the galaxies are moving apart and their relative temperatures prove that there was a *beginning* of matter, energy, space and time. Renowned astrophysicist Dr. Hugh Ross states that all matter, space and time came into existence at one time. Einstein's General Law of Relativity shows the universe had a beginning and that it expands away from each other. Temperature fluctuations show that the "Big Bang" model is correct as cosmic background radiation and the expansion of the universe demonstrate. In other words, there was a "Big Bang" (God said, "Let there be..." and BANG—it happened!) Astronomy observes the past by seeing light waves and radio waves—proving the Biblical account of creation: there was a beginning of matter, energy, space and time.

The Fool Has Said In His Heart, *"There Is No God"*

Astronomy proves that light separated from darkness instantaneously. (Sounds like Genesis 1, doesn't it?!) Astrophysics confirms there was a singular beginning of matter; and that matter had to be created. The cooling down of the universe, dark energy, the relation of the Milky Way, sun, moon and earth all point to Divine design. The inception of the universe was an instantaneous, carefully fine-tuned, intelligently controlled phenomenon... not a random explosion.

Scientists agree: Intelligent Design

Sir Isaac Newton said, "This most beautiful system of the sun, planets and comets could only proceed from the counsel and dominion of an intelligent Being." Dr. Charles Townes (recipient of the Nobel Prize for Physics and inventor of the Laser Beam) states, "Somehow intelligence must have been involved in the Laws of the Universe."

Dr. John Winhold, Professor of Physics from the renown, research university, Rensselaer Polytechnic Institute, tells us:

"I see the glory of God is on display in this physical world. I look at the fine workings--the internal structure of world... the microstructure of it. It is not a chaotic thing; it is an organized thing. There is great beauty, regularity and great detail in the fine workings of this world. We have atoms, we have nuclei, we have sub-nuclear or elementary particles. There is beautiful organization and regularity and structure even at the sub-nuclear level. God is the architect; He's the Author. It didn't just happen. It is God Himself displaying Who He is. The Creator is a Person that loves beauty. Physics is mathematical. The equations that describe all of nature have beautiful, mathematical organization. It is verification that God is the Lord of the universe."

295

Albert Einstein said, "Everyone who is seriously interested in the pursuit of science becomes convinced that a Spirit is manifest in the laws of the universe—a Spirit vastly superior to man, and one in the face of which, we, with our modest powers, must feel humble." The first and last Word on the subject is, "In the beginning, God created the heaven and the earth..." (Genesis 1:1)

Shall A Nation Be Born In A Day?

Other evidence of God's Divine power and wisdom come directly from the pages of the Bible. Bible prophecy is a confirmation of Divine Providence and foreknowledge in the affairs of man. Biblical prophecy is history written *before the fact,* hundreds (and sometimes thousands!) of years in advance. The book of Ezekiel has amazing examples of prophetic accurately regarding the future. During the Babylonian captivity, Ezekiel predicted that the Jewish people would be in captivity and without their own sovereign nation for over 2,500 years. Then, exactly on cue, the sovereign nation of Israel was established on May 14, 1948—exactly on the day that Ezekiel predicted over two thousand years before. That was Divine revelation!

History In Advance

Amazing predictions are also in the book of Daniel. This prophet saw all of the world's empires in sequential order. How could Daniel predict (hundreds of years before the fact), the world powers that would rise up after the Babylonian empire? He specified Alexander the Great's conquest of the world, his four generals that would replace him, and the subsequent Roman empire. How could he have known 600 years before the fact that "Messiah would be cut off" (Jesus killed), followed by the Romans destroying the Jewish Temple?

Over three hundred specific Bible predictions concerning Jesus' life, death and resurrection were fulfilled exactly as predicted in the

Old Testament. The statistical probability of these prophecies all being fulfilled in one man is 1 chance in 480 billion x 1 billion x 1 trillion… far beyond the realm of "chance." The Dead Sea scrolls validate that all of these ancient prophecies were written hundreds of years before their fulfillment. These were the Divine, prophetic revelations of the God of the Bible.

Bible Codes

In addition to the prophecies contained in scripture, there are amazing hidden messages encoded in the very text of the Hebrew Bible. Isaiah 53 has the name of the prophesied "Suffering Servant" imbedded in it. Every 12th letter in Hebrew spells "JESUS IS MY NAME." Through computer analysis researchers have discovered numerical sequences of names and dates that pertain to current events.

The name of the late Prime Minister Rabin, and even his assassin's name was encoded in the 3,500-year-old book of Exodus. In the ancient book of Deuteronomy are found references to the Holocaust, with the names, "Hitler", "Nazis," and the Auschwitz death camp named. Prime Minister, Benjamin Netanyahu, name is encoded in the text. The Bible is truly a Divinely inspired, prophetic book! One cannot use the Bible code as a form of divination, but it does confirm that the Author knew the beginning from the end.

Food for Thought

Medical truths and principles were revealed in the Bible long before the AMA discovered them. Kosher diet regulations of the Jews have been confirmed to minimize contamination and optimize nutrition. The regulation of *not mixing* meat and dairy allows for the benefits of iron from the meat to be absorbed in the body. (Mixing meat with dairy can cause anemia because the calcium in the dairy inhibits iron absorption.) They now know that shellfish (forbidden by the Law of Moses) not only often contains heavy metals, but bacterial infections. Also, the type of protein in shellfish is difficult for the human body to digest. Pork has many issues, including parasite infection, and cancer-causing properties.

The Great Physician

In the book of Leviticus there are medical principles, including quarantine and frequent hand washing that minimized the spread of disease. Not until the last two hundred years did medical science understand that disease was caused by micro-organisms. They then could appreciate the methods of purification spelled out in the Law of Moses to protect from cross contamination. These Biblical principles of cleanliness were millennia ahead of their time.

How could Abraham have known almost 4,000 years ago that the level of vitamin K (which aids in blood clotting) was at its very highest level in the human body on the exact day (the 8th day after birth) that God instructed the Hebrew males to be circumcised? Amazing!

Genetically Speaking...

Genetics also confirm the veracity of the Bible. The Biblical account of creation tells us that in the beginning God created one man and one woman, and that the world was populated by this one set of parents. DNA can trace the ancestry mitochondrial, which proves there was only one man and one woman from whom the whole world descended. Additionally, the 7+ billion Y genes show that all of the world's population came from one gene pool (DNA) source.

This is consistent with the Biblical account of the flood, in which the only gene pool was Noah's family who survived to repopulate the earth. Had the flood not occurred, the population would be so large today (in the trillions) that the earth could not support life. Today's population of seven billion people is consistent with the number of people who would be alive given the eight individuals who began reproducing after the flood 4,500 years ago. Science validates the Bible!

Simple Life?

The very complexity of cells is such that even bacteria are not "simple" life forms. Cells are specific and highly organized. In each cell there are 60,000 proteins in exact arrangement. If the proteins are not in the prescribed order, the cell begins to biodegrade in a matter of minutes. The odds that 60,000 proteins "self-organized" into effective arrangement to make cell function is 1 chance in 10 to the *4,478,000 power*. (Just 10 to the *50th power* mathematically has ZERO chance of occurring.) It is impossible for proteins-- the basis for all cells—to have "randomly" arranged. They did not evolve. Proteins for cells had to be Intelligently designed.

Evolutionary Impossibilities

What about mutations in genes? Do mutations result in "evolution?" No. Not evolution that causes change into a different species. That is the theory of "macroevolution" (the Darwinian Theory). Yes, **micro**evolution DOES occur within a species' genetic boundaries (which allows for adaptability). However, the changes are not due to new DNA being introduced, but existing DNA proteins that are allowed to express themselves given different environmental conditions. In other words, a moth species may have the genetic DNA to express itself in a variety of colors (even as we have DNA from parents & grandparents that could result in some offspring being dark haired, and others in the same family having red or blond hair.)

If the conditions for the moth in the jungle favored longevity due to its green color camouflaging it, then eventually the gene pool would favor and change to eliminate the expression of, say, a white colored moth with the same DNA pool. In other words, the green moths would tend to survive and reproduce better than their white colored moth "cousins" in the jungle environment. There is not a change of the DNA, but simply environmental conditions that tends to favor one trait over another. This is "microevolution;" that is, small changes of characteristics with certain dominant expressions manifesting more commonly with a species.

No Fossil Proof

However, there is no living or fossilized record of ANY entity changing from one species to another. That is macroevolution—which is only a theory with no scientific basis. In fact, macroevolution is genetically impossible. It is genetically impossible for a chimpanzee to become a human or a human to degenerate into a chimpanzee. There are 48,000,000 *differences* between the nucleotides of the DNA of a human and the nearest DNA of a chimpanzee. A series of only *three differences* in nucleotides causes fatality of a species or causes the following generation to be sterile. Genetically speaking, evolution is impossible. The genetic code dictates that "like begets like." The genetic seed (code) that you sow is what you will reap. There has never been evolution in which one species changes into another. The complexity of life-- even at the most "basic" level-- is such that it could not have occurred randomly. The whole ecosystem is so complex and interdependent that it had to be Intelligently designed by a Master Creator!

No Monkey In The Family Tree

Geology also destroys the theory of evolution since there has not been found _one_ transitional life form for _any_ species in the fossil record. In other words, there are no legitimate "missing links." Apes are still apes; humans are still human. If apes evolved into humans, then why do apes still exist? There are no transitional forms between apes and humans. The "great" missing link finds that anthropologists have promulgated have turned out to be chimpanzee bones, not an intermediary species. The human bones found in Germany with hunched backs turned out to be modern human skeletons with signs of severe rickets— (consistent with lack of vitamin D from limited sun exposure in the Black Forest area where the bones were discovered.)

Archeology

Finally, archeology completely validates the Bible. Biblical accounts of kings, peoples, & historical events have all been confirmed by recent archeological finds. Cities that some didn't believe existed (such as Sodom & Gomorrah at the bottom of the Dead Sea) have been discovered. Chariot wheels have been found in the midst of the Red Sea at the very place where the Bible records that the Egyptian army's chariot wheels came off (according to Exodus 14).

Some historians doubted the existence of the "Hittites," referenced in Genesis 23. In 1906 the Hittite capital was discovered with many historical tablets confirming it. There are cities that previously were only referenced in the Bible, but have now been discovered and excavated: Haran, Hazor, Dan, Megiddo, Shechem, Samaria, Shiloh, Gezer, Gibeah, Beth Shemesh, Beth Shean, Beersheba, and Lachish.

Archeology confirms the Biblical account of Israel's history in extra-Biblical finds: Hieroglyphic's found in Egypt of Shishak's invasion of Judah completely validate the Biblical accounts of I Kings and II Chronicles during the reign of Rehoboam. An Assyrian obelisk unearthed in 1846 references Israel's leader, Jehu, giving tribute to Assyria's Shalmaneser III (as 2 Kings 9-10 makes mention).

New Testament confirmation

The city treasurer, Erastus, was mentioned by name 3 times in the New Testament. Recently out of the ruins of Corinth they uncovered an ancient building stone with his name and title clearly engraved. In 1961 archaeologists discovered an ancient monument inscribed at the Roman amphitheater near Caesarea. The inscription reads "Pontius Pilate, Prefect of Judea." Prior to that, the name "Pontius Pilate" was only known from New Testament writings. Many, many other archeological finds continue to validate the Bible's accuracy one hundred percent.

Thy Word is Truth

All of these scientific facts validate that the Bible is Divinely inspired and true. But, when one knows the Author of the book, there is never any question of His integrity or veracity!

Much scientific information referenced is from contributing experts of the "Acts & Facts" publications (2000-2003) of the Institute for Creation Research, Dr. John D. Morris, founder.

ORIGIN OF THE BIBLE

The Holy Bible is our basis for truth. From the eternal truths of God's Word, we acquire the sound doctrine needed to successfully live the Christian life. Because the Bible has been interpreted and translated by man into different languages and versions, some question its accuracy and authority. Thankfully we have many ancient manuscripts of the Bible in the original languages that let us know that the Book that we cherish has been faithfully preserved. We can rest assured that the truths taught by the Bible are indeed the precepts of Almighty God.

Manuscript confirmation

Let us consider the reliability of the Bible text. The Bible has been scrutinized and validated more than any other book in history. There are thousands of ancient manuscripts written in the original languages (Hebrew, Greek, and Aramaic) that corroborate and substantiate our modern translations of the Bible. These manuscripts, collected from all over the ancient world, confirm through consistent uniformity of text the accuracy of both the Old and New Testament writings. The Old Testament has been fully validated by the Dead Sea scrolls. Those scrolls persevered in clay jars reveal there has been no change of the scripture for thousands of years! Two-thousand year old scrolls of Isaiah have virtually the same Hebrew text as modern Bibles. The New Testament also has thousands of corroborating manuscripts validating it.

Early Church Writings

In addition to Bible manuscripts, there are many additional extra-Biblical records that validate the New Testament. The early Church Fathers' ancient writings have been found to quote the New Testament extensively. From their writings alone one could construct a complete New Testament. Their writings verify that the New Testament we read is the same that they had.

Original Languages

Today there are many versions of the Holy Bible. Some are direct translations, some are paraphrased versions in modern vernacular for ease of reading and understanding. The principles of truth are still intact even with paraphrased versions. For those who want a literal reading of scripture (without the spin of human interpretation upon it) one must go back to the Hebrew, Aramaic, and Greek manuscripts in which scripture was originally written. To find an English version which most accurately translates these original languages, one must consider the ancient source manuscripts, and how the English versions were formulated from them.

As mentioned before, the Hebrew text of the Old Testament (Tanach) is undisputed by sound Bible scholars. The Septuagint's accuracy (Greek translation of the Tanach) was validated by Jesus, who quoted it. The Dead Sea Scrolls confirm the Old Testament text that we have.

New Testament Canon

The New Testament is also fully documented and validated. Since the time of the apostles the four Gospels and Apostolic letters to the churches (Epistles) were confirmed and were universally accepted as "scripture"—even contemporaneously. There is internal validation of the books and the authorship in the New Testament at the time that the Apostles wrote them. Peter, writing to the Hebrew Christians, told them that Paul's writings were to be heeded, and that he considered Paul's letters to the churches to be *scripture*:

> *"And account that the longsuffering of our Lord is salvation; even as our beloved* **brother Paul also according to the wisdom given unto him has written unto you; As also in all his epistles,** *speaking in them of these things; in which are some things hard to be*

*understood, which they that are unlearned and unstable wrest, **as they do also the other scriptures**, unto their own destruction.*"[461]

Paul the Apostle validates Luke's Gospel in writing to the church at Corinth when he states *"And we have sent with him the brother* [Luke]*, **whose praise is in the gospel** throughout all the churches; And not that only, but who was also chosen of the churches to travel with us with this grace...*"[462]

Luke's Gospel was one of the later Gospels written, and had already been universally accepted and acclaimed by all the churches when Paul wrote his letter to the Corinthians around 56 A.D. There was no doubt in the early church as to what constituted "scripture." As a result, they faithfully made copies on papyrus (a scroll made of paper-like material) or on the more expensive "parchment" (skins of animals). Paul made mention of the scriptural "books" that he had compiled, and requested specifically that Timothy bring him the "parchments."[463]

The early church was not confused about the New Testament canon. They had it established. To ensure the churches knew that the letters of inspiration that Paul wrote to them were legitimately from Apostle Paul, he signed all of his letters with his validating signature. He instructed the churches to look for his signature to verify the letters were his.[464]

Greek Manuscripts

The New Testament had a well-established canon, and there are tens of thousands of Greek New Testament fragments found throughout

---

[461] II Peter 3:15, 16
[462] II Corinthians 8:18
[463] II Timothy 4:13
[464] I Corinthians 16:21, Galatians 6:11, Colossians 4:18, II Thessalonians 3:17, Philemon
19

the ancient world. In addition to the Greek, New Testament manuscripts have also been found in Latin, Coptic, Syriac, Gothic and Arabic. Some fragments of the Gospel of John date possibly as early as the end of the first century. The early Churches were encouraged to share and read apostolic letters with each other.[465] Because the writings were considered scripture, many Christians faithfully made copies the Gospels and Epistles. That is the reason for the great number of Greek manuscripts available.

When the Greek New Testament manuscripts are collectively combined and examined, a consensus of the original content can easily be ascertained. If a particular manuscript had a missing part, the content could be determined by comparing it to hundreds of others that were more complete. The New Testament canon was so well-established that Greek scholars referred to the complete compilation of those ancient manuscripts as "Textus Receptus" (or the "received text"). It is from this "received text" the English Bible was originally translated.

"Enlightened" Ignorance

However, at the turn of the 19th century two "enlightened scholars," Westcott and Hort,[466] decided to include two old (but very inaccurate and corrupted) manuscripts in their translation of the New Testament. Those manuscripts, the Codex Vaticanus and Codex Sinaiticus, were singular works rife with textual mistakes, deletions, and inaccuracies. They were not consistent with the vast majority of "Received Text" manuscripts that corroborated each other in content and textual integrity. They erroneously thought the two codices were older than the Received Text and therefore more accurate.

---

[465] Colossians 4:16
[466] https://en.wikipedia.org/wiki/Revised_Version

Some scholars took great issue with that assessment, not only because the errors and inconsistencies of those codices were apparent, but the assumption of the codices' dating was wrong. Textus Receptus was derived from older, more abundant and accurate Byzantine manuscripts, dating from the early second century A.D.[467]

Inconsistencies with Revised Version

Because of the inconsistencies of the Codices Vaticanus and Sinaiticus, many did not consider them to be reliable sources from which to translate the New Testament. Some scholars give no credibility to the Revised English Bible (the translation derived from the corrupted Vaticanus and Sinaiticus Codices). The Vaticanus and Sinaiticus Codices are *singular manuscripts* without the thousands of corroborating manuscripts to substantiate them (as has Textus Receptus).

Though some would argue that there are not significant differences between the Revised English Bible and those translated from the Received Text, there are enough discrepancies that some scholars will only use translations from the "Received Text" (such as the King James Bible). It does not have the textual discrepancies of Revised English Bible versions.

Versions of Question

Some newer versions based on the questionable Revised English Bible include the New Revised Standard, the New English Bible, the Jerusalem Bible, the New American Standard, and the New International Version. Though these modern versions are in some cases easier to read, they are not as complete as versions translated from the Textus Receptus. When one reviews the emboldened text in the

---

[467] https://en.wikipedia.org/wiki/Textus_Receptus

scripture lists below (which indicate it was *omitte*d from the Revised Version), one can understand why many reject the newer versions as being incomplete Bibles:

REVISED STANDARD BIBLE OMISSIONS FROM THE TEXUS RECEPTUS (RECEIVED WORD OF GOD)

Matthew 6:4- *"and your Father which sees in secret Himself shall reward you **openly**."*

Matthew 6:13- *"And lead us not into temptation, but deliver us from evil; **For Thine is the kingdom, and the power, and the glory, forever. Amen.**"*

Matthew 6:18- *"and your Father, which sees in secret, shall reward you **openly**."*

Matthew 9:13- *"I am not come to call the righteous, but sinners **to repentance**."*

Matthew 12:47- ***"Then one said unto Him, 'Behold, Your mother and Your brethren stand without desiring to speak with You."***

Matthew 17:21- ***"Howbeit this kind goes not out but by prayer and fasting."***

Matthew 18:11- ***"For the Son of man is come to save that which was lost."***

Matthew 19:9- *"and shall marry another commits adultery: **and whoso marries her which is put away doth commit adultery**."*

Matthew 20:16- *"So the last shall be first, and the first last; **for many be called, but few chosen**."*

Matthew 21:44- ***"And whosoever shall fall on this stone shall be broken: but on whomsoever it shall fall, it will grind him to powder."***

Matthew 22:30- *"nor are given in marriage, but are as the angels of God in heaven."*

Matthew 23:14- **"Woe unto you, scribes and Pharisees, hypocrites! For you devour widows houses, and for a pretense make long prayer: therefore you shall receive the greater damnation."**

Matthew 24:14- *"there shall be famines, and pestilences, and earthquakes..."*

Matthew 25:31- *"and all the holy angels with Him..."*

Matthew 25:13- *"Watch therefore, for you know neither the day nor the hour wherein the Son of man cometh."*

Matthew 27:35- *"And they crucified Him, and parted His garments, casting lots: that it might be fulfilled which was spoken by the prophet, 'They parted My garments among them, and upon My vesture did they cast lots."*

Mark 6:11- *"for a testimony against them. Verily I say unto you, It shall be more tolerable for Sodom and Gomorrah in the day of judgment, than for that city."*

Mark 7:16- **"If any man have ears to hear, let him hear."**

Mark 9:24- *"and said with tears, Lord, I believe..."*

Mark 9:29- *"This kind can come forth by nothing, but by prayer and fasting."*

Mark 9:38- *"we saw one casting out devils in Your Name, and he follows not us: and we..."*

Mark 9:44- *"For every one shall be salted with fire, and every sacrifice shall be salted with salt."*

Mark 10:13- *"And they brought young children to Him..."*

Mark 10:21- *"and you shalt have treasure in heaven: and come, take up the cross, and follow Me."*

Mark 10:24- *"how hard is it for them that trust in riches to enter into the kingdom of God."*

Mark 11:10- *"Blessed be the kingdom of our father David, that cometh **in the Name of the Lord.***"

Mark 12:4- *"And again he sent unto them another servant; **and at him they cast stones, and...***"

Mark 12:23- *"In the resurrection therefore, **when they shall rise,** whose wife...*"

Mark 12:29- *"And Jesus answered him, The first **of all the commandments** is, 'Here O Israel...*"

Mark 12:30- *"and with all your strength: **this is the first commandment.***"

Mark 12:33- *"with all the understanding, and with all **the soul,** and with all the strength...*"

Mark 15:3- *"And the chief priest accused Him of many things: **but He answered nothing.***"

Mark 15:28: ***"And the scripture was fulfilled, which says, and He was numbered with the transgressors."***

Mark 16:17,18- [Note: 2 entire verses deleted by these "scholars" who reportedly denied the virgin birth of Christ Jesus, and did not believe the Biblical accounts of miracles]:

"And these signs shall follow them that believe; In My name shall they cast out devils; they shall speak with new tongues; they shall take up serpents; and if they drink any deadly thing, it shall not hurt them; they shall lay hands on the sick, and they shall recover."

Luke 4:8- ***"Get thee behind Me, satan;*** *for it is written..."*

Luke 4:18- *"...to preach the gospel to the poor; **He has sent Me to heal the brokenhearted,** to preach deliverance..."*

Luke 8:43- *"And a woman having an issue of blood twelve years, **which spent all her living upon physicians,** neither could be healed of any..."*

Luke 8:48- *"And He said unto her, Daughter, **be of good comfort;** your faith has made you whole"*

310

Luke 9:2- "*And He sent them to peach the kingdom of God and to heal **the sick.** *"

Luke 9:7- "*Now Herod the tetrarch heard of all that was done **by Him**; and he was perplexed...* "

Luke 9:54- "*...and consume them, **even as Elias did?** *"

Luke 9:55 56- "*But He turned, and rebuked them and said, **'you know not what manner of spirit you are of. For the Son of man is not come to destroy men's lives, but to save them.** ' And they went to another village.* "

Luke 10:19- "*...and over all the power of the enemy; and nothing shall **by any means** hurt you.* "

Luke 11:4- "*And lead us not into temptation; **but deliver us from evil.** *"

Luke 12:39- "*...if the good man of the house had known what hour the thief would come, **he would have watched,** and not have suffered his house to be broken through.* "

Luke 17:36- "***Two men shall be in the field; the one shall be taken,*** *and the other left.* "

Luke 19:45- "*and began to cast out them that sold therein, **and them that bought;** *"

Luke 20:23- "*But He perceived their craftiness, and said unto them, **'why tempt ye Me?** *"

Luke 22:20- "*Likewise also the cup after supper saying, This cup is the new **testament** in My Blood, **which is shed for you.** *" [Note: The New English Bible omits the entire verse]

Luke 22:68- "*you will not answer Me **nor let Me go.** *"

Luke 23:17- "***(For of necessity he must release one unto them at the feast.)***

Luke 23:38- "*And a superscription also was written over Him **in letters of Greek, and Latin, and Hebrew,** 'This is the King of the Jews.* "

Luke 24:1- *"which they had prepared, **and certain others with them.***"

Luke 24:3- *"And they entered in and found not the body **of the Lord Jesus.**"*

Luke 24:6- ***"He is not here, but is risen:*** *remember how He spoke unto you when He was yet..."*

Luke 24:12- ***"Then arose Peter, and ran unto the sepulcher; and stooping down, he beheld the linen clothes laid by themselves, and departed, wondering in himself at that which was come to pass."***

Luke 24:36- *"Jesus Himself stood in the midst of them and said unto them, **Peace be unto you.**"*

Luke 24:40- ***"And when He had thus spoken, He shewed them His hands and His feet."***

Luke 24:42- *"gave Him a piece of a broiled fish, **and of a honeycomb.**"*

John 4:24- *"God is a Spirit; and they that worship Him must worship **Him** in spirit and in truth."*

John 4:42- *"and know that this is indeed **the Christ**, the Savior of the world."*

John 5:4- ***"For an angel went down at a certain season into the pool, and troubled the water; whosoever then first after the troubling of the water stepped in was made whole of whatsoever disease he had."***

John 5:16- *"the Jews persecute Jesus, **and sought to slay Him**, because He had done these..."*

John 6:47- *"he that believes **on Me** has everlasting life."*

John 8:9- *"And they which heard it, **being convicted by their own conscience**, went out one..."*

Acts 8:37- *"**And Philip said, 'If you believe with all thine heart, you may.' And he answered and said, 'I believe that Jesus Christ is the Son of God.'**"*

Acts 9:5- *"I am Jesus, whom you persecute:* **it is hard for you to kick against the pricks.** *"*

Acts 9:6- *"****And he trembling and astonished said, 'Lord, what will you have me to do?'*** *And the Lord said unto him, 'Arise, and go into the city, and it shall be told you...* *"*

Acts 28:29- *"****And when he had said these words, the Jews departed and had great reasoning among themselves.*** *"*

Romans 4:1- *"that Abraham our father, as pertaining to the flesh,* **has found?** *"*

Romans 5:2- *"By Whom also we have access* **by faith** *into this grace wherein we stand, and...* *"*

Romans 8:1- *"There is therefore now no condemnation to them which are in Christ Jesus* **who walk not after the flesh,** *but after the Spirit.* *"*

Romans 10:15- *"them that preach the gospel of peace,* **and bring glad tidings of good things!** *"*

Romans 14:21- *"whereby your brother stumbles,* **or is offended, or is made weak.** *"*

Ephesians 3:14- *"For this cause I bow my knees unto the Father* **of our Lord Jesus Christ.** *"*

Colossians 1:14- *"In Whom we have redemption* **through His Blood,** *even the forgiveness of sins.* *"*

Colossians 3:6- *"For which things' sake the wrath of God cometh* **on the children of disobedience.** *"*

I Timothy 2:7- *"I speak the truth* **in Christ,** *and lie not;) a teacher of the Gentiles...* *"*

II Timothy 1:11- *"a teacher* **of the Gentiles.** *"*

Hebrews 2:7- *"You crowned Him with glory and honor,* **and did set Him over the works of Your hands.** *"*

I Peter 4:14- *"for the spirit of glory and of God rests upon you;* **on their part He is evil spoken of, but on your part He is glorified.** *"*

I John 4:19- *"We love **Him,** because He first loved us."*

I John 5:7- (Note: some versions combine and change verse numbers so it is not apparent that verse 7 is left totally out of some texts) ***"For there are three that bear record in heaven, the Father, the Word, and the Holy Ghost: and these three are one."***

I John 5:13- *"that you have eternal life, **and that you may believe on the Name of the Son of God."***

Revelation 1:8- *"I am Alpha and Omega, **the beginning and the ending,** says the Lord..."*

Revelation 1:11- *"Saying, **'I am Alpha and Omega, the first and the last**: and what you see write in a book, and send it unto the seven churches **which are in Asia;** unto Ephesus..."*

Revelation 2:9- *"I know **your works,** and tribulations..."*

Revelation 2:13- *"I know **your works,** and where you dwell..."*

Revelation 5:14- *"and twenty elders fell down and worshipped **Him that lives for ever and ever."***

Revelation 6:1- *"Come **and see."***

Revelation 14:5- *"for they are without fault **before the throne of God."***

Revelation 21:3- *"and God Himself shall be with them, **and be their God."***

This is an incredible amount of intentional omission of God's Word from the Revised English Version, and the newer translations based upon it. One must certainly question the accuracy of those versions that originated from embracing incomplete, corrupted manuscripts instead of versions translated from the complete "Textus Receptus" manuscript. Thankfully the King James version and a few others are based on the Textus Receptus that does not omit scripture passages from the text.

God sovereignly preserved the Old and New Testaments by leaving us abundant manuscripts in the original languages. The Holy Bible is perfect. God has faithfully preserved His Word for us. Truly, *"Forever, O Lord, Your word is settled in Heaven"*[468] and *"Heaven and earth shall pass away, but My words shall not pass away."*

---

[468] Psalm 119:89, Matthew 24:35

Dominionism: Demonic Deception

There is a prevalent teaching in "Christendom" today that is not Biblical. It denies some very core truths of the Gospel. It is the teaching called "Dominion Theology" or "Dominionism" (also known as "Kingdom Now"). The basic premise of Dominionism is that God has given Christians the mandate to take dominion over the worldly systems of the earth. The purpose of this dominion is to prepare the earth in order that Jesus can return to begin His 1000-year earthly reign. Unfortunately, the hidden agenda behind this deception is to prepare humanity (and even the "Church") for the anti-Christ system. Christians should be on their guard against this heresy!

In the Beginning

From where did adherents of Dominionism get their rationale to take over society? They cite Adam's commission in the beginning:

"And God blessed them and God said unto them,
'Be fruitful and multiply, and replenish the earth, and
subdue it, and have dominion over the fish of the sea,
and over the fowl of the air, and over every living thing
that moves upon the earth.'"[469]

God tells man to take dominion over the animal kingdom. Dominion Theology take this command to the extreme and attempts to apply the mandate of dominion to include all of human society, which certainly was not the intent of God's original command. Man was never called to dominate other men. However, Dominionists claim this mandate includes controlling all aspects of human society so that

---

[469] Genesis 2:28

unregenerate people are subjugated to Christian rule. In this way they believe "they will rule and reign with Christ" in this life.

Take It By Force?

The means by which this purportedly is to be done by "taking the kingdom by force" (that is, actively pursuing places of leadership over every facet of society). Their goal is to dominate the "Seven Pillars" or "Seven Mountains" of society: government, religion, media, family, business, education, and arts and entertainment. By doing this, they believe they will eventually control the world. They consider it their "Christian duty" to pursue dominance and leadership in all of these spheres. Once they have succeeded in completely dominating the world—putting society under their feet-- then Jesus will return to reign in the Millennium. They will have already "set up the kingdom" and He simply sits on the throne and enjoys the labor of these conquering spiritual *heroes*. They believe Jesus *cannot return* until they have done so.

Denies Christ's Imminent Return

This false teaching completely negates the teaching of Jesus and the Apostles concerning the imminent return of Jesus for the Church (also known as the "Rapture"). They often are adherents to Preterist teaching (the false teaching that the Book of Revelation is not going to be fulfilled literally… that it is simply a history of what took place in the first century in symbolic prose.)

This false teaching was first espoused by the Roman Catholic Jesuit, Luis de Alcasar (1554–1613), during the Counter-Reformation.[470] The fact that John the Revelator was given the book of the Revelation after 70 A.D. and was told to write "The things that

---

[470] https://en.wikipedia.org/wiki/Preterism

shall be hereafter"[471] negates the false Preterist teaching that the book of Revelation was all fulfilled by 70 A.D. A very cursory overview of the Book of the Revelation lets one know that none of great tribulation (Daniel's 70th week) has been fulfilled yet:

- There is no antichrist setting himself up in the Jewish Temple
- The two prophets Elijah and Enoch have not returned, preached, and been raised from the dead in the streets of Jerusalem
- Half the world's population has not yet been annihilated through war, disease, and famine (which happens before the half-way point of the tribulation time)
- All the world has not been mandated to take the mark of the beast.

None of it has been fulfilled. Preterists negate the literal interpretation of scripture. They deny God's clearly expressed truth in the Holy Word of God. Denial of God's Word leads to deception and, ultimately, perdition.

Why Lie?

Why would the Jesuits twist and try to re-interpret the Word of God? One could surmise that the obvious interpretation (very evident to the Protestants who were being martyred for the truth of God's Word during the Reformation) was that the Vatican was the harlot church seated on seven hills. The Book of Revelation states that the city on seven hills has a long history of shedding the blood of the saints.[472]

---

[471] Revelation 1:19
[472] Revelation 17:6, 9

318

For the Jesuit Alcazar to try to relegate that prophecy to first century history (negating the fact that it will be fulfilled in the future by antichrist's system) seems to be a ploy to distance the Roman Catholic church from its bloody history of persecuting the saints, and the complicity that it will have in the future support of the antichrist system.

It Shall Come To Pass

However, the prophecies of the Book of the Revelation will be fulfilled as written. The city on seven hills (the Vatican) will have a role in the forthcoming, religious deception of the world. Those who deny Jesus' literal coming at the Rapture and the futuristic fulfillment of the book of the Revelation oppose the very truth of God's Inerrant Word.

Avoid False Teachers!

The Preterist lie (denying prophecy, especially regarding that the Rapture will be literally fulfilled) has crept into the church. It is a cancer that must be excised. The Apostle Paul clearly denounced the false teachers who espoused the Preterist doctrine that denies the future resurrection of the church:

> "But **shun** profane and vain babblings: for they will increase unto more ungodliness. And their word will eat as doth a canker (cancer): of whom is Hymenaeus and Philetus; Who concerning the truth **have erred, saying that the resurrection is past already;** and overthrow the faith of some. Nevertheless, the foundation of God stands sure, having this seal, The Lord knows them that are his. And, Let everyone that names the name of Christ depart from **iniquity.** "[473]

---

[473] II Timothy 2:16-19

There are many errors with the false teaching of either putting off Jesus' imminent coming until pseudo-apostles "fix" this world and perfect it, or completely denying a forthcoming Rapture of the church.

Evil Mockers Deny Jesus' Coming

Denying Jesus' imminent coming is what evil, mockers of the Word of God do:

> *"But and if that __evil servant__ says in his heart, __My lord delays his coming__; and shall begin to beat the menservants and maidens, and to eat and drink, and to be drunken; The lord of that servant will come in a day when he looks not for him, and at an hour when he is not aware, and will cut him in sunder, and will appoint him his portion with the unbelievers."* (Matthew 24)

> *"Knowing this first, that there shall come in the last days* **scoffers**, *walking after their own lusts, And saying,* **Where is the promise of his coming? for since the fathers fell asleep, all things continue as they were from the beginning of the creation.** *For this they willingly are ignorant of... But the day of the Lord will come as a thief in the night... what manner of persons ought you to be in all holy conversation and godliness,* **Looking for and hasting unto the coming of the day of God...**" (II Peter 3)

What I Say To You, I Say To All: Watch!

Believers are to be actively looking (watching) for Jesus' imminent coming. All through the New Testament we are admonished to do so:

*"Watch therefore: for you know not what hour your Lord doth come. But know this, that if the good man of the house had known in what watch the thief would come, he would have **watched**, and would not have suffered his house to be broken up. Therefore, **you be also ready**: for in such an hour as you think not the Son of man cometh."* (Matthew 24)

Actively anticipating and looking for Jesus' return will cause believers to live in such a way that they will be ready when He comes. Implied here is that if one is not looking for His coming, they will not be ready. Putting off the day of the Lord will result in apathy and undue entanglement with the cares of this world. Jesus warns us against this mindset.[474]

Those Who Were Ready

Jesus admonishes believers over and over again to be ready for His coming. He warns that if they do not watch, they will not be ready:

*"While the bridegroom tarried, they all slumbered and slept. And at midnight there was a cry made, Behold, the bridegroom cometh; go you out to meet him...The bridegroom came; and **they that were ready went in with him** to the marriage: and the door was shut... **Watch therefore**, for you know neither the day nor the hour wherein the Son of man cometh."* (Matthew 25)

*"**Take heed, watch and pray**: for you know not when the time is. For the Son of man is as a man taking a far journey, who left his house, and gave authority to*

---

[474] Luke 8:14

*his servants, and to every man his work, and commanded the porter to watch. **Watch** therefore: for you know not when the master of the house cometh, at even, or at midnight, or at the cockcrowing, or in the morning: Lest coming suddenly he find you sleeping. And what I say unto you I say unto all, **Watch.**"* (Mark 13:33-37)

Evil Servant Does Not Anticipate

Luke chapter thirteen also admonishes Christ's servants to be ready. If they say in their hearts the Lord *delays* His coming (for *whatever "noble"* reason they rationalize), they are denying Christ's admonition to be watching and expecting His imminent coming.

Conditions To Be Ready

Jesus admonished His disciples that watching (actively anticipating Jesus' return) and praying always would ensure that they would be ready for His return at the Rapture. Then, they could be assured they would escape the "day of the Lord" (tribulation wrath):

*"And take heed to yourselves, lest at any time your hearts be overcharged with surfeiting, and drunkenness, and cares of this life, and so that day come upon you unawares. For as a snare shall it come on all them that dwell on the face of the whole earth. **Watch therefore, and pray always, that you may be accounted worthy to escape all these things that shall come to pass, and to stand before the Son of man.**"* (Luke 21)

Don't Sleep!

Paul the Apostle also warns us to watch for Jesus' appearing to escape the coming wrath:

"But you, brethren, are not in darkness, that that day should overtake you as a thief. You are all the children of light, and the children of the day: we are not of the night, nor of darkness. Therefore, let us not sleep, as do others; **but let us watch and be sober... for God has not appointed us to wrath, but for deliverance ("sozo") by our Lord Jesus Christ so that whether we are alive or dead at His coming, we will live (be resurrected) together with Him"** (I Thessalonians 5)

Paul reminds Titus that the active looking for Jesus' return for the saints at the Rapture is associated with righteous and godly living:

"we should live soberly, righteously, and godly in this present world; **Looking for that Blessed Hope, and the glorious appearing** *of the great God and our Savior, Jesus Christ."* (Titus 2:12, 13)

Staying ready and watching for Jesus' imminent appearing is commanded by God's Word.

Communion Reminds Us!

So important to a believer's spiritual life is this anticipation of Jesus' coming, that the Lord's Supper serves as a continual reminder of this blessed event:

"For as often as you eat this bread, and drink this cup, you do shew the Lord's death till He come." (I Corinthians 11)

The imminent return of Jesus for believers who are watching and waiting is clearly taught in scripture. Therefore, believers are to have a "pilgrim" mentality... knowing that we are not on this earth for long, but only passing through. This world is not our goal, as Peter admonishes us: *"Dearly beloved, I beseech you as __strangers and pilgrims__, abstain from fleshly lusts, which war against the soul."* (I Peter 2)

Looking For A City

Peter even addresses his letters to the "strangers" (aliens) of this world. The mindset of the apostles was not to take over this present world, but to be temporarily sojourning in it until Jesus comes. Paul admonishes us to look for a heavenly country, as did the heroes of the faith:

> *"These all died in faith, not having received the promises, but having seen them afar off, and were persuaded of them, and embraced them, and confessed that **they were strangers and pilgrims on the earth.** For they that say such things declare plainly that they seek a country."*

> *"And truly, if they had been mindful of that country from whence they came out, they might have had opportunity to have returned. But **now they desire a better country, that is, a heavenly: wherefore God is not ashamed to be called their God: for he has prepared for them a city."*** (Hebrews 11)

Reign As Kings??

Paul goes so far to say that true apostles are the "off scouring" of society (those who are brushed aside, as far as worldly stature and influence). They are not aspiring to "reign as kings" in this present world, as were the carnal Corinthians:

*"Now you are full, now you are rich, you have reigned as kings without us: and **I would to God you [really] did reign, that we also might reign with you**. For I think that God hath set forth us the apostles last, as it were appointed to death: for we are made a spectacle unto the world, and to angels, and to men.*

*"We are fools for Christ's sake, **but ye are wise** in Christ; we are weak, but ye are strong; ye are honorable, but we are despised. Even unto this present hour we both hunger, and thirst, and are naked, and are buffeted, and have no certain dwelling place; And labor, working with our own hands: being reviled, we bless; being persecuted, we suffer it: Being defamed, we entreat: we are made as the filth of the world, and **are the off scouring of all things unto this day."*** (I Corinthians 4:8-13).

So You Are a King??

Here Paul facetiously tells the proud Corinthian church that their prominent places in this life made them think they were already reigning as kings in Jesus' Kingdom (which they certainly were not!) Paul says that he wished that the Corinthians *really were* reigning as kings with Christ, for then it would be the Millennial Reign, and Paul would be reigning with them! Then he shows them what true apostles experience in this life: persecution, rejection, deprivation... Is that the message we hear from the Dominionism crowd? No. They are busy trying to build their kingdom now in this world. They are not looking for the return of Jesus.

Watch And Work

To sum it up, true believers are to be looking for Jesus imminent return, not to be trying to take over this present world through acquiring powerful positions in society. The mandate of Jesus, His great commission, was not, "Go into all the world and take over the government. Or media... or the economy. No. It was, *"Go into all the world and preach the Gospel to every creature."* (Mark 16:15)

Having received that mandate the early church went out and preached powerfully with signs and wonders! As a result, the entire known world was evangelized in their lifetime.[475] Jesus' disciples were never engaged in a takeover of society's pillars. They did not believe they would take over the world in Jesus' stead. They fully understood that the Kingdom would not be set up until Jesus personally returned and facilitated it Himself. They were engaged with the Great Commission of evangelism and looked forward to Jesus' return.

Spiritual Kingdom, Not Literal

While on earth Jesus told His disciples, *"My kingdom is not of this world."* They understood that in this dispensation Jesus reigns spiritually in the hearts of believers. Jesus said, *"The Kingdom of God is within you."* He has dominion in the spirit realm—and in the hearts of true believers. He rules over principalities and powers spiritually. We are to exercise spiritual authority over demonic entities.

Not By Power, But By God's Spirit

Nowhere in the Book of Acts do we see groups of believers demonstrating in political rallies trying to overthrow the heathen Roman government and take over society with natural power and influence. The only riots they caused were for preaching the Gospel.

---

[475] Colossians 1:5, 6

There certainly were believers in every strata of society back then, including high governmental positions, but taking over the government was not the goal of the early church. Their goal was to preach--whether in Caesar's palace, or a Philippian jail.

Light Shining in a Dark Place

Jesus did not teach we were to take over society with Crusader mentality, but rather, to be salt and light in this present dark world. He commanded His disciples to "give unto Caesar" due taxes, and the Apostle Paul taught believers to submit to government as an ordained power of God[476]... and this was in spite of the fact that that that government was comprised of idolatrous heathens!

The emphasis of the early church was to promote Jesus' spiritual Kingdom that rules in the hearts of born-again men. Society can change for good one heart at a time when Jesus' Kingdom reigns in the heart, not through political and economic pressure from "Crusaders" trying to strong-arm people's will into conversion by dominating society. That was the error of Constantine. Legislating faith resulted in a backslidden Church that was Christian in name only.

Of course, to the extent we can vote in righteous leaders, we should, for "righteousness exalts a nation." But, the Church's mandate is not to aspire for political, economic, and social domination, but to preach the Gospel. Once one is saved and has the Law of God written in his heart, he will want to keep God's righteous precepts.[477] He will not have to have legislation passed to force him to obey God.

Keep The Main Thing The Main Thing

---

[476] Romans 13:1-3
[477] Jeremiah 31:31

Paul's admonition to his spiritual son, Timothy, declares that believers in Christ's "army" should be pursuing "the main thing" of sharing the Word of God (not worldly social dominion):

"...be strong in the grace that is in Christ Jesus. And the things that you hast heard of me among many witnesses, the same commit you to faithful men, who shall be able to teach others also. You therefore endure hardness, as a good soldier of Jesus Christ. **No man that wars entangles himself with the affairs of this life;** *that he may please him who has chosen him to be a soldier."*

Spiritual Dominion

We are fighting spiritual forces that are trying to take men and women's souls to hell. We do not fight flesh and blood, but spiritual wickedness. We conquer satan by preaching and teaching the Gospel. It alone has the power to set sinners free.[478] Our focus should not be trying to change temporal institutions of the world—that is, not to be entangled with natural realm and worldly concerns, but to focus on promoting the eternal, spiritual kingdom of God.

Kingdom Now??

The idea that the Church is to dominate society IN ORDER THAT Jesus can come back to a world already subjugated to Christian rule is totally false. Scripture clearly teaches that this world will not get better, but will continue to get worse spiritually as we approach the "last days." The depravity of society is a sign that Jesus is coming back soon, as Paul warns Timothy:

"This know also, that **in the last days perilous times shall come.** *For men shall be lovers of their own*

---

478 II Timothy 2:2-4, Ephesians 6:11, 12

selves, covetous, boasters, proud, blasphemers, disobedient to parents, unthankful, unholy, Without natural affection, trucebreakers, false accusers, incontinent, fierce, despisers of those that are good, Traitors, heady, high-minded, lovers of pleasures more than lovers of God; Having a form of godliness, but denying the power thereof: from such turn away... "

"I charge you therefore before God, and the Lord Jesus Christ, who shall judge the quick and the dead **at His appearing and His kingdom***; Preach the word; be instant in season, out of season; reprove, rebuke, exhort with all longsuffering and doctrine.*

For **the time will come when they will not endure sound doctrine***; but after their own lusts shall they heap to themselves teachers, having itching ears; And they shall turn away their ears from the truth, and shall be turned unto fables. But watch you in all things, endure afflictions, do the work of an evangelist, make full proof of your ministry. For I am now ready to be offered, and the time of my departure is at hand. I have fought a good fight, I have finished my course, I have kept the faith: Henceforth there is laid up for me a crown of righteousness, which the Lord, the righteous judge, shall give me at that day: and not to me only, but unto all them also that* **love His appearing***."* (II Timothy 3, 4)

Last Day Society Not Getting Better

The sign that we are in the last day is not world dominion by Christians and a perfected Christian kingdom, but that society becomes even more depraved. Jesus said when the signs of the times are evident (such as increase of natural disasters, wars, and society becoming depraved like Sodom and Gomorrah), that believers should *"look up, for your redemption draws near."* He tells us this world will get darker and darker spiritually before Jesus returns to take true believers out.

Stay Awake And Escape!

Jesus promised if believers stay awake spiritually and pray they will **escape** the coming time of seven years of great tribulation judgments that will come upon the unrepentant world.[479] This is known as Jesus' appearing, or the "Rapture" of the Church. Notice that Paul said that Jesus would judge at two different times: "at His appearing AND His kingdom."

The appearing of Jesus refers to the Rapture of the Church when "The Lord Himself shall descend with a shout" and believers are "caught up" to meet the Lord in the air and to join Him in the heavenly mansions.[480] This imminent return of Jesus for believers is when the Church will stand at the Judgement seat of Christ to be judged for the works done while on earth. Another judgement is at "Jesus' Kingdom" when Jesus separates the goats and sheep (believers and unbelievers) at the end of His Millennial reign, also known as the Great White Throne judgement.

Resurrection First, Then Jesus Reigns

The world is not subjected to Christ's rule until Jesus personally returns to rule and reign on this earth. HE (not self-appointed pseudo-apostles) will put all rule and power under His feet:

> *"Now if Christ be preached that he rose from the dead, **how say some among you that there is no resurrection of the dead?** But if there be no resurrection of the dead, then is Christ not risen: And if*

---

[479] Luke 21:28-36
[480] I Thessalonians 4

Christ be not risen, then is our preaching vain, and your faith is also vain..."

"*...Then cometh* **the end, when He shall have delivered up the kingdom to God, even the Father;** *when* **He shall have put down all rule and all authority and power. For HE must reign, till HE has put all enemies under his feet. The last enemy that shall be destroyed is death...**" (I Corinthians 15:20-28)

Love Not This World

The only one who will rule over this world (prior to Jesus' reign at His return) is the antichrist. Those who are promoting one world religion, government, economy, media, etc. are actually playing into the antichrist's agenda. The number of a man, 666, means man is ruling, not Jesus Christ. Many sincere Christians have been fooled into thinking their call is to dominate the world in some sphere of social influence. There is no mandate from God for the church take over this world. The mandate for the church is to preach the Gospel. Any other agenda is error.

Come Up Hither!

The next event on God's prophetic timeclock is Jesus' return for His Church. Until then, believers are to preach the Gospel of Jesus Christ as they watch and wait for Him. The Book of the Revelation gives a clear outline of prophetic, future events. Chapters two and three are admonitions to the church to do the first works of the Church (evangelism) and to be ready for Jesus' coming. Chapter four depicts the Rapture of the church, "come up hither." Then in chapter five we see the church has already been judged for their rewards. They are seen seated on their respective thrones with their awarded crowns. The Church escapes the wrath to come.

Anti-Christ Sets Up Kingdom

Chapter six shows God's wrath beginning to be poured out upon the earth's inhabitants. By chapter thirteen (three and a half years after the Rapture) the anti-Christ is seen taking dominion over the world and causing all to take his "mark of the beast." Seven years after the Church's Rapture, Jesus returns with the armies of heaven (the Church) to combat the antichrist and his armies. This is futuristic. This was not fulfilled by 70 A.D., as Preterists espouse. Jesus then destroys the wicked and then HE and the church will rule the world with a rod of iron.[481]

The false "kingdom now" mentality says Jesus must delay His return until the church takes over this world's systems. No. The Church is to evangelize. Jesus will personally return, take dominion, and rule the world. We will then rule and reign with Him. But not before.

Witness To The World

Jesus' return is imminent. There is no waiting for the church to first "take dominion" over the world before He can come back. Sadly, the false teaching of Dominionism has the end effect of diverting sincere Christians from the Great Commission of preaching the Gospel into busying themselves trying to dominate spheres of politics, media, business, and so on. We are called to salt and light in whatever sphere of society God has ordained for us to be... We should not be *trying to dominate society, but rather illuminate this dark world* with the Gospel.

The foundational truth of the Church's Rapture is denied by Dominionists—and even mocked by some of their renown "teachers" (false prophets). They claim the Rapture is a man-made doctrine for weak, carnal Christians who simply have an "escape" mentality.

---

[481] Revelation 19:14

Count me in among those with "escape mentality"! I plan to escape. Jesus promised I could!

> "*Watch and pray always that you may be able to escape all these things...*" (Luke 21:36)

The truth is, the doctrine of the Rapture (the "Blessed Hope" of the Church) is clearly taught in scripture. (I Thessalonians 4:14-18, John 14:1-2, and Isaiah 26:19-21.) The true church will escape the coming wrath of God. This is an encouragement for believers to stay alert, and evangelize before Jesus returns to Rapture the Church.

> "*Therefore, my beloved brethren* [in light of the resurrection of believers at the Rapture] *you be steadfast, unmovable, always abounding in the work of the Lord, forasmuch as you know that your labor is not in vain in the Lord.*"[482]

World evangelism is the "labor" (goal and mandate) of the true Church of Jesus Christ. Jesus did not tell us to take over society and dominate the governments of this world. Dominion theology side-tracks the church from evangelism to social/political takeover. Note this quote from leading Dominionists who blatantly espouse the takeover of society *in lieu of evangelism!*

Prophetic Perspective??

"On 'Prophetic Perspectives with **Rick Joyner,**' leading Seven Mountains dominionist, **Lance Wallnau,** demonstrated the duty of Christians to occupy the "mountains" of government, media and economics. Referring to the parable of the strong man, Wallnau

---

[482] I Corinthians 15

suggests that these "mountains" of influence are currently being occupied by Satan:

> "Well, the church is the equipping place, **but the world system is where we haven't gone. We've been going into all the nations to plant churches. We haven't been going into all the nations to invade systems.**"

> "We have to start to bring the Word of God, the teaching of Christ, into the systems. What systems? The governments need to be led by people with principle. That's how you overthrow principalities, is people who have anointing and principles occupying high places. The media, right now the economics world, the media world and the government world is shaping every minute that you're bumping into when you have a conversation….and education."

> "What we need are believers going to the top of these systems because it's where the high places are that satan occupies the strong man's house. And if you want to plunder the strong man's house, you've got to go where the gates of Hell are located.'"

Wallnau stated in a presentation outlining the "seven mountains" theology that the church has been off-track by pursuing evangelizing people… They should be taking over the system:

> "**The reason why we're having a problem in the United States is because,** honestly, we have not been pursuing the discipling of the nation, **we've been pursuing the evangelizing of the people** and the building of ministries," he said. "And so we've

neglected entire territory that the Enemy was all too quick to go in and take possession of."[483]

Rick Joyner, affirms the top-down control model, going so far as to endorse the necessity of a temporary totalitarianism as an alleged transition to freedom in God's Kingdom:

"The kingdom of God will not be socialism, but a freedom even greater than anyone on earth knows at this time. [I like that part. However:] At first it may seem like totalitarianism, as the Lord will destroy the antichrist spirit now dominating the world with "the sword of His mouth" and will shatter many nations like pottery. However, fundamental to His rule is II Corinthians 3:17, 'Now the Lord is the Spirit; and where the Spirit of the Lord is, there is liberty.' Instead of taking away liberties and becoming more domineering, the kingdom will move from a point of necessary control while people are learning truth, integrity, honor, and how to make decisions, to increasing liberty so that they can. . . The kingdom will start out necessarily authoritative in many ways, or in many areas, but will move toward increasing liberty–so do all true churches and movements that are advancing toward the kingdom."

How scary! The false teachers of Dominion theology actually state that the Church should *not be* evangelizing, but taking over society! That is in direct opposition to Christ's commission. They espouse taking over the world's systems—government, economy, military, religion--in a totalitarian manner. That is not Christ's agenda. THAT is the anti-Christ's agenda! Joyner openly teaches against the Rapture of the Church. Additionally, in his book, <u>There were Two Trees</u> he states that Jesus is only a Spirit, not God in the flesh.[484] Both

---

[483]   http://www.rightwingwatch.org/content/martyrdom-and-dominion-jim-garlows-future-conference#sthash.0O98zguA.dpuf
[484] There Were Two Trees in the Garden, Rick Joyner

of these false teachings align with anti-Christ deception. Anti-Christ doctrine teaches that Jesus is not in the flesh. Jesus doesn't need to come back in the flesh because the "Vicar of Christ"[485]--the Pope--can dominate the earth in His stead.

The most dangerous aspect of Dominionism is the blatant denial of the written Word of God and the exaltation of their own "spiritual" interpretations that in many cases contradict scripture. Their "revelations" are elevated above God's Holy Written Word.

Whose Agenda?

Dominion Theology fits right into the anti-Christ agenda, and the doctrine of the Roman Catholic church. Many evangelical leaders have been courted by and given their allegiance to the Pope of Rome. They have even joined the "Knights of Malta" order, a Roman Catholic organization. No wonder the Book of the Revelation portrays the false prophet appearing as a lamb (representing Christ) but actually speaking for the devil![486] Many leaders of the "New Apostolic Reformation" and the associated "International Coalition of Apostolic Leadership" organization (organizations of self-proclaimed "prophets" and apostles") espouse Dominionist teaching. If the "People for the American Way" are alarmed by the Dominionists' agenda, how much more should true believers in Christ be--and guard against this error!

Seek Christ's Heavenly Kingdom

Let us *"seek those things which are above, where Christ sits on the right hand of God. Set your affection on things above, not on*

---

[485] (Latin Vicarius Christi): A title of the pope implying his supreme and universal primacy, both of honour and of jurisdiction, over the Church of Christ.-The Catholic Encyclopedia (http://www.newadvent.org/cathen/15403b.htm)
[486] Revelation 13:11

things on the earth."[487] *"For many walk...they are the enemies of the cross of Christ: Whose end is destruction...who mind earthly things.) For our conversation is in* **heaven; from whence also we look for the Savior, the Lord Jesus Christ**:"[488]

Until Jesus comes, let us *"go into all the world and preach the Gospel to every creature."* Jesus is coming soon to Rapture the true Body of Christ (those watching and waiting for Him):

> *"Let not your heart be troubled; in My Father's house (Heaven) are many mansions... I go away to prepare a place for you; and if I go away and prepare a place for you, I will come again and receive to Myself, that where I am (in Heaven) you may be also."*[489] **Amen! Come Lord Jesus!**

---

[487] Colossians 3
[488] Philippians 3
[489] John 14

In Closing...

In closing, I trust that the Biblical truths presented in this book will help you to grow in your appreciation for the great love that God has for you. The principles will establish your spiritual foundation and walk with Christ. The studies are designed to help you to recognize and withstand false teaching. Until Jesus comes, may we all be "steadfast, unmovable, always abounding in the work of the Lord, knowing that our labor is not in vain in the Lord."[490] God bless! ~Ann

PRAYER OF SALVATION:

If you have never made a personal commitment to Jesus Christ, please do so today. The Bible says, "Today is the day of salvation," and none of us are promised tomorrow. To receive the gift of eternal life through Jesus Christ, pray this prayer:

Dear Jesus, I have sinned against Your commandments. Please forgive me of my sins and cleanse me with Your precious blood. I believe that You died on the cross, and that You were raised from the dead the third day to pay for my sins. I am willing to turn away from sin, and to follow You as the Lord of my life. Please come in and make me a new person. Thank you for saving me.

Bibliography

Bible references are from the King James Version of the Holy Bible

Referenced Work:

Joyner, Rick, *The Harvest,* Morning Star Publications, Charlotte, NC, 1989

Joyner, Rick, There Were Two Trees, Morning Star Publications, Charlotte, NC, 1992

Morris, John D., *Acts & Facts,* Institute For Creation Research, El Cajon, CA, 2000-2003 (multiple referenced articles)

Strong, James, *Strong's Expanded Exhaustive Concordance of the Bible,* Thomas Nelson, Nashville, TN, 1981

Vine, W.E., *Vine's Expository Dictionary of New Testament Words,* Fleming H. Revell, Old Tappan, NJ, 1966

Online References:

http://www.newadvent.org/cathen/15403b.htm The Catholic Encyclopedia

https://en.wikipedia.org/wiki/Jehovah's_Witnesses_beliefs Jehovah's Witnesses beliefs

https://en.wikipedia.org/wiki/Preterism Preterism

http://www.rightwingwatch.org/content/martyrdom-and-dominion-jim-garlows-future-conference#sthash.0O98zguA.dpuf Martyrdom and Dominion-Jim Garlows future